THE MASTERS RETURN

The Angelic Book of Healing

by Joseph Crane

edited by GW Hardin

The Masters Return

by Joseph Crane
edited by GW Hardin

AngelGate Creations
Lakehills, Texas • 2006

This is a true story. Some names have been changed at the request of the individual or to honor another's privacy. The angel Michael asked that exact wording be used in all the teachings given to us. Brackets were used as editorial license to clarify certain concepts.

Library of Congress Cataloging-in-Publication Data
  Crane, Joseph
  Hardin, G.W.
  The Masters Return:
          The Angelic Book of Healing
  Inspiration, Spirituality, Angels, New Age, Religious Studies
          pp. 252

  ISBN 978-0-9701593-11
  1. Inspiration 2. Spirituality 3. Angels 4. New Age

Cover design: Ken Elliott and G.W. Hardin
Book design: G.W. Hardin and Gary LaCroix

Set in 11 point Times New Roman typeface
Printed in the United States of America

Contents

PART I
THE ANGELIC BOOK OF HEALING

INTRODUCTION: by GW Hardin   3

CHAPTER 1:   Michael's Return   13

CHAPTER 2:   The Seven Stones   29

CHAPTER 3:   The Death of Annie   43

CHAPTER 4:   The Gate of Grace   49

CHAPTER 5:   The Halls of Healing   55

CHAPTER 6:   The Appearance of the Shekinah   61

CHAPTER 7:   The Tree of Life   77

CHAPTER 8:   The Well of Souls   93

CHAPTER 9:   "Physician, Heal Thyself"   101

CHAPTER 10:   The Art of Healing and the Healing of Art   111

PART II
THE HEALING GIFTS OF HEAVEN

CHAPTER 11:   The Miracle of Manifesting   131

CHAPTER 12:   Gabriel's Gift   141

CHAPTER 13:   Raphael's Gift   153

CHAPTER 14:   The Oils of I Am   163

CHAPTER 15:   The Masters Oil   177

CHAPTER 16:   The Oils and Healing   185

CHAPTER 17:   Gabriel's Message   201

CHAPTER 18:   Filled Vessels   215

CHAPTER 19:   Healing Among the Sevens   220

EPILOGUE: by Joseph Crane   241

Acknowledgments

I first would like to acknowledge Diane Ballotti for her patience, understanding, and support of this book and it's completion.

G.W. Hardin for editing this book and his contributions within it. His friendship over the years has been immeasurable and his talent with words monumental. Ronnie Foster for her early support and editing, which made this book possible.

Last, but not least, my wife, Robbie, who as an RN has helped me to understand the medical side of healing, not to mention all her love and hard work.

— Joseph Crane

Part I

THE ANGELIC BOOK OF HEALING

INTRODUCTION

*W*ho would dare believe in the coming together of Heaven and Earth? Is this not mere foolishness, like some religious fanatic screaming on the street corner that the end of the world is coming? Have there been signs or wonders announcing this great event, this union of heaven and earth? Where? No blazing star has appeared in the night sky nor have angels announced the arrival of another great age. No, none of these presages have dazzled the eye nor brought wonder to the heart. Yet, it is nonetheless true: A great age is upon us.

The signal event heralding this great age began on October 22, 1999, with a single child — as do most great ages. This marvelous child is no new Messiah nor is he a great prophet come to foretell this coming together of heaven and earth. He is a Down's syndrome boy, severely simple, who had difficulty feeding himself, unable to talk in full sentences. His name is Michael. His parents lovingly call him "Buddy." Little Michael's mother, Donna, had brought him to an authors party in the suburbs of Chicago. She had heard from her sister, who hosted the party, that the co-authors of *On the Wings of Heaven* would present information from the angelic realm, which was to be given to all of humanity. Famous angel artist, Joanne Koenig-Macko, would speak there

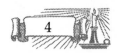

as well. Donna had read the book and heard from her sister how the angels wanted humanity to understand how the end of disease was upon us, if we so wished it. And thus she made an appointment with one of the authors, Joseph Crane, hoping he could help her Down's syndrome son, whom she loved dearly.

In a private room set apart from the crowd, Little Michael waited for Joe. The boy's mother tried to soothe him, for he had become agitated and loud. The crowded setting was not ideal for a fifteen-year-old kid with a four-year-old mind. As Joe entered the room, he peered down at Little Michael and immediately thought to himself, *This is a great soul.* Hushed sentences passed between Donna and Joe as Joe fixed his attention on the sweet child lying on the mat. "What is it you want for your son?" Joe finally asked.

Donna's voice began to crack as she formed the words. "I am wise enough not to ask for his Down's syndrome to be taken away. For I have grown to love Michael for who he is. I now know that his condition has been a great gift for so many, especially me. He has touched so many hearts and changed so many lives because of his Down's." As she gathered herself, Joe stared into her motherly eyes, recognizing the love shining forth.

"What is it that you ask for your son, then?" Joe knew the angels had made it perfectly clear that we are our own healers. He knew Little Michael could not vocalize his own desires, but could his mother ask in his stead? Her eyes told him she could. Her heart beat in oneness with Little Michael's heart.

"I just wish life could be a little easier on him. He's been suspended from school for a day because his behavior has gotten unruly. He gets that way at times, but it has become worse than before. You heard him yelling as we waited. His knees are full of pain. He complains often, of late. There doesn't seem to be anything that can be done. The doctors can find no source for the pain. He also has another condition, which is supposed to take his life. In fact, it was supposed to have taken him already. If he eats dairy, it could kill him. His body cannot handle the protein the right way. He's had so many problems. I just wish life could be a bit easier on him." Her hands stroked the boy's head as she talked. He listened silently, the way most disabled children do in a world where they often are treated as if invisible.

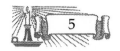

For the next hour Joe applied the techniques the angels had given. He used tuning forks on Little Michael's knees and body, and applied the sacred oils the angels had given for the good of humankind. Little Michael did not yell nor did he fuss. An amazed smile would erupt on the boy's face each time Joe would bring a ringing tuning fork to his ear before applying it to a part of the boy's body. He simply watched himself being worked on as if it were some new and wonderful game. Donna watched in complete surprise as her son quietly allowed the process to finish. The boy's agitation had already abated. Could this be for real? Was the impossible going to happen?

"What you name?" Little Michael asked during the process.

"You can call me Joe. We'll be good friends, you and me." And how right Joe would prove to be. As Little Michael exited the room, he marched over to his Aunt Tina and encircled her with his short arms, hugging her as if she were Santa Claus. For the next fifteen minutes, the joyful lad either hugged or kissed every relative at the party. Not only did it make everyone laugh it also created a buzz of conversation.

Tina sidled up to Joe and asked, "What did you do? He hasn't been this well-behaved for a while. Even if nothing else happens, this in itself is a miracle. He'll be able to go back to school." And Little Michael would continue to amaze everyone — for months afterward. Rather than take him home immediately, Donna decided to let him stay at the party, for he seemed to be enjoying himself, as well as warming to the crowd. He was actually becoming a hit with the partygoers. But even miracles have their limits. As evening approached, Little Michael tired, and Donna bid a fond farewell to Joe.

On the way home, Donna stared out at the freeway while hurried drivers sped by. Her thoughts fixated on the day's events. *What did happen at the party?* Joe had said that Buddy was responsible for his own healing. Joe had insisted that his own role was only that of an assistant. What was it that her darling son had done?

"Mommy, Joe talked to Michael." The boy's determined voice broke the silence.

His words snapped her out of her reverie. *Did he just speak in a full sentence?* she wondered. *Don't overreact*, she said to herself. *Stay calm. Act as if everything is normal.* "Uhhh, yes, dear, Joe did talk to you. Wasn't that nice of him?"

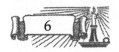

A brief pause gave way to another surprise. Rather than pleasantly agreeing with her as he tended to do, he blurted out, "No, mommy, Joe talked to *Michael*." He was insistent. His voice spoke with emotion and conviction. He was trying to get her to understand. How odd. The tables had been turned. He was speaking to her the way she usually needed to speak to him.

"Yes, yes, Michael. I was there; I was with you when Joe was talking to you. Remember? We were all in the room together? And Joe helped you?"

As if exasperated, the boy looked over at his mother and tried one more time. "No, Mommy, no. Joe talked with Michael, the angel." The shock of his words hit her like a locomotive! Her son had never been able to speak in full sentences, only short phrases at best. *What is happening?* she asked herself. The highway rumble strip snapped her attention back to her driving just before the car edged off the freeway. A chill ran right up her back and down again. Had her son seen the angel while Joe had been working on him? Joe had informed her how Michael the Archangel had appeared to him over a five-year period and given him the information found in *On the Wings of Heaven*. But how could Little Michael even come close to understanding such notions? His mind was incapable even of understanding what an angel was. Or at least she had thought so. Donna decided to say nothing more until she got home and could discuss this with her husband.

While preparing dinner, husband and wife reviewed the amazing incidents of the day. Donna was cooking hot dogs, Little Michael's favorite food, her husband preparing the rest of dinner. The two were a real team in more ways than one. Both had gone through a lot, learned a lot from their Buddy. As was usual, Donna boiled the hot dogs, later to cut them in pieces so Buddy could easily chew them. More often than not he would pick up a piece of hot dog with his fingers and pop it into his mouth, chomping on it as if were candy. Just as Donna was taking the pan off the burner to cut up the hot dogs, Little Michael blurted out, "I wanna hot dog bun with my hot dog." Both parents turned an about face like army cadets in an exercise.

"What?" both chimed together, their mouths hanging agape. Never in his life had Buddy eaten a hot dog bun. He didn't even know how to use a hot dog bun. To their knowledge, he didn't even know what a hot dog

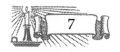

bun was for. Their startled reaction took Buddy aback. He thought he had done something wrong.

"I wanna hot dog bun, PLEASE." There. That ought to do it. The magic word had been spoken. But why did both Mommy and Daddy still look so surprised?

Shaking himself out of his stupor, Michael's dad ordered proudly, "Well, get the boy a hot dog bun." And thus began a series of vignettes where Little Michael would continue to amaze parents and teachers alike. Little Michael would never forget Joe Crane, which in and of itself is a miracle for a kid who hadn't displayed use of a long-term memory. To this day the lad calls him "Angel Joe."

Little Michael is the first in a growing number who have benefited from the teachings of the angels on healing. How did all of this happen? How did this child usher in an age when the incurable are being cured? If a Down's syndrome child can bring healing to himself, then why not us? And here is the real beauty. This child has become our teacher.

The light shining forth from this young child reminded Joe of a time five years ago when another light entered his life. At that time, Angel Joe had been Skeptic Joe. Every now and then, over a twelve-year period, he had heard his name being called out of nowhere. And for twelve years he dismissed the incidents as pranks of friends or his ears playing tricks on him. Not until attending a seminar put on by his spiritual mentor, Alexander Everett, did he finally wonder if maybe he ought to be doing something about this unexplained phenomenon. Alexander had said that all of us are called by heaven in one way or another. Some of us actually hear our name being called. It's up to us whether we answer or not. After class, his mentor had suggested to Joe that he might respond to the calling of his name the same way Samuel had in the Bible. And three years later it happened again — quite unexpectedly. Just as Joe was about to turn out the bedroom light, he heard, "Joe." The voice had called out as if coming from inside the bedroom. Suspended between fear and silliness, Joe couldn't decide whether to answer or not. Frankly, he felt ridiculous at the prospect of talking to thin air. But Joe finally sealed his fate when he echoed Samuel's words: "Speak, Lord, for your servant hears."

Seeing nothing, filled with a sense of foolishness, he leaned over to turn out the bed lamp. A strange sparkle flickered in the bedroom doorway. At first it resembled a piece of glitter caught on a black velvet

background. The more Joe stared at the intense glittering, the greater it grew. Adrenaline shot through his veins as a flood of light began filling the entire bedroom. The blueness of the light had reminded him of a scene from the Twilight Zone. Except Joe knew he wasn't in the Twilight Zone because his four beloved mastiff hounds, sleeping in the bedroom with him and his wife, were all wide awake and staring at the same thing he was staring at. A bit of calm began to balance his sense of panic as he realized he was protected by 700 pounds of dog flesh. Mastiffs are like miniature ponies in doggie costume. As the expanding light consumed the entire door, Joe could begin to see what looked like the figure of a man deep within the light. The being — whatever it was — began walking toward him, stepping from some unknown world that had opened into our world. And there standing before Joe radiated a platinum blond man, seven feet tall, wearing a white robe. A smile spread on the man's face, his shoulder length hair framing the most beautiful countenance Joe had ever seen. A loving voice announced, "Put down your books for they hold no truth for you." It was close to Christmas, and as a spiritual exercise Joe had decided to reread the Bible. Joe wondered why something so beautiful would appear as male. **"As the sands of the desert have been moved to suit the winds of time, so has the light been darkened by man's ink on these pages."** Was this being of light talking about how man had constantly translated and retranslated Scripture? *What is this being talking about?* Joe wondered.

"This you must do or you will not be called upon again. Teach this which the Lord God has charged me to give you. For it is the Last Baptism of God's children. Have those you teach in turn teach others, for they are well-meaning in their houses of God. You are not a Christ or even a prophet but a servant of God, who will put words into your mouth — and God's children will hear and understand."

This must be an angel! Joe concluded. And the angel went on to instruct Joe how to prepare himself for the teachings which would be given to him. The Last Baptism consisted of a ritual where wine was poured into a bowl, and the bowl placed outdoors on sacred ground before sunrise. At the point when the sun had reached its highest place in the sky, Joe dipped his hands into the wine and washed his feet up to his knees, and then his hands up to his elbows. Afterwards he prayed as instructed: "My loving Father, your child has come home to your counsel.

Guide me in all things I must do." Then he poured the bowl of used wine upon the earth. The angel had then instructed, **"As your Mother Earth drinks the unclean liquid, all that is unclean within you — her brothers and sisters — is absolved, just as the blood of God's Son was said to do. Go now, be at peace and take care of all I have given you. Teach only love. After you do this, we will speak again."**

Many weeks had passed before Joe, at the insistence of his wife, finally performed the Last Baptism. And shortly thereafter, the angel appeared again and instructed Joe to find seven master souls to whom Joe would give the teachings, and they, in turn, would take the teachings out to the world. It was at this time that Joe asked the angel its name. What issued forth was a magnificent weaving of musical sound, light and energy. But it was unpronounceable, leaving the angel to suggest that Joe could call the angel whatever he wished. And so the angel came to be named "Michael."

A two-year journey ensued as Joe went forth to find the seven masters. At first he questioned how he could possibly visit the likes of the Dalai Lama, or the Pope, or Sai Baba, or Deepak Chopra. But as it turned out, the seven master souls appeared cloaked in the lifestyles of everyday people. Michael had told Joe that he would find four men and three women, and out of the seven three would be gay. Joe had no idea what this meant nor the consequences of the angel's bidding. In the end, each of the seven masters he found possessed unique gifts and carried the inherent potential of awakening these seven gifts in the entirety of humankind. But what a journey it would be. Being all too human, intrigue, failure, self-discovery, and self-awareness would play major parts in the lives of these seven as they began an unpredictable journey as they gathered with Joe.

The Seven convened with Joseph Crane on August 1, 1997, in an unassuming house in Walnut Grove, California. In their midst Joe revealed two pieces of long-forgotten sacred geometry the angel had asked him to bequeath to them. Michael would tell Joe nothing more than to present the information to the masters and they would know what to do. The first geometric configuration was what came to be called the Formation of the Seven. During the gathering, the seven masters sat in meditation in the formation, with Crane sitting in the east, and the Seven sitting in the other major points of the compass. Joe sat across from the

master in the west who held the gift of wisdom. In the north sat the master who held the gift of mercy or help-bringing, across from the master in the south who held the gift of healing. To the northeast sat the master who held the gift of joy, while in the southwest sat the master who held the gift of peace-making and creation of beauty and harmony. In the northwest sat the master who held the gift of truth or natural knowing, and to the southeast sat the master who held the gift of power and leadership. Those who sat in the minor directions (northeast, northwest, southeast, southwest) sat roughly in a seven-foot square, while the masters in the major directions (with Joe sitting in the east) sat roughly in a fourteen-foot square. All experienced a strong energy or vortex envelop them as they sat in the Formation of the Seven. In the center of the formation Michael appeared to one of the Seven and told of further information to come. Shortly thereafter, another of the Seven began to shake uncontrollably as the words of the angel were announced to her, which caused the rest of the masters to move into the second formation given to them by the angel. This formation is called the Formation of Giving and Receiving. Like the first formation, this geometry came from ancient knowledge being returned to humanity. The formation is made of two triads of giving which bestow the most profound love to the one person who is the receiver of this love. Because of the power of this formation, it is only taught to those who come together in a gathering of seven masters willing to represent the seven gifts of heaven for humanity.

When the gathering was over, the seven masters returned to their respective homes, knowing that their lives would never be the same. Each of the masters was to find seven more masters and call them to a gathering where the teachings of the angel would be passed on. And in turn each of those would find seven more, and seven more. But true to their nature as human beings, the Seven had the choice, the free will, to engage in furthering the teachings of the angel called Michael, or not. Some chose not. As Michael likes to put it, "Many are chosen, but few choose."

In the months that ensued, a human drama of the greatest proportion began to unfold as Michael continued to bring to Joseph Crane teachings to give to the seven masters. As the teachings became more and more profound, it became more and more apparent that Michael was not kidding when he said that humanity not only had the capacity to return to

the Garden of Eden, but find a garden even greater than that of Adam and Eve. Michael instructed Joseph Crane to write down the teachings of what the angel called "The Book of Healing." For the time has come for humanity to suffer no more. If we choose to give up disease, we have that right, that power, that gift. And Joseph Crane did as he was invited.

What follows is Joseph Crane's journal containing the description of the angels' appearances and the teachings from the angelic realm. The teachings are meant for all of humanity. Those who have ears to hear, let them hear. For a great age has indeed come forth. All you have to do is visit one little child, one Little Michael to lose all skepticism. For even in this child rests a master's soul that will touch you like you have never been touched before. It is to him that this book is dedicated. For if he cannot teach us to see the miraculous in ourselves, to heal ourselves and one another, then no one will be able to. For Little Michael walks with peace and teaches only love.

G.W. Hardin
December 2000

MICHAEL'S RETURN

*W*hen the angel first appeared to me that late December night in 1994, I had no idea what I was getting myself into. How many times since have I been told by others that they wished they could see angels the way I do when Michael appears? If they only knew the consequences when these kinds of appearances occur. At first, the only thing the angel had asked of me was to write down his words in a manuscript called "The Book of Bricks." Strange name for a book, but I did as I was asked. The manuscript described how we can build our celestial mansions in Paradise by living life to the fullest here on earth. And we can live life to the fullest by giving blessings to one another along with gifts of the heart and spirit. To further the beauty of such efforts, the angel also explained how we bless one another by our deeds. The manuscript was powerful in its simplicity. But when I asked the angel to whom I was to give the information, he told me to find seven master souls and bequeath the teachings to them. They, in turn, would take these teachings to the world. It seemed simple at the time. But before I knew it, he asked more of me.

This is the tough part. How do you tell an angel no? Especially an angel like Michael, whose beauty would melt the hardest of hearts. When

he shows up, he stands about seven feet high with radiant platinum-blond hair surrounding his extraordinary, unblinking eyes, which constantly pour out love. His voice is gently masculine, but that face of his! It's so magnificently beautiful it always makes me wonder what he's doing in male form. So when Michael asks me to do more, I can never say no.

After finding the seven master souls, Michael made a second request for a book. This book was to be written by me and one of the masters, whom I call "Gary." We decided to combine "The Book of Bricks" and the second book — the decoding of the biblical *Book of Revelation* — under one cover, which we titled, *On the Wings of Heaven*. I thought I was finished until Michael added yet another request — to write a third book. This book. It really is hard to say no to such magnificence, such walking love.

After gathering the seven master souls in California, Michael appeared and told me I had done well. He then hinted — for reasons I would understand only later — that I would be moving to Texas. And some months later, Donna, my wife at the time, was made a job offer in San Antonio, which she accepted. We found a wonderful piece of property not far from the city where she and the four mastiffs would have lots of room to enjoy themselves. After making the move, I began to wonder why it had been so long since seeing the angel. His last appearance had been in August of 1997, and here it was February of 1998.

I was awakened by the sound of Donna's voice saying, "Here is your coffee, dear." During the week she would bring me coffee and I would do the same for her on the weekends. As I lay there trying to wake up, I could hear her going out the door on her way to work. The rain started to fall and I knew the roads would be slick. I said, "God, watch over her today and keep her safe." I do worry about her on the roads when the weather is bad. Dozing off again, hoping to catch a little catnap before starting my day, I lay in the warmth of the waterbed. Out of nowhere, an explosion split the air rattling the windows and shaking the bed away from the wall. If it had been California I would have sworn an earthquake had hit. Was this a thunderstorm? Even the dogs started barking. Annie was standing on the bed making all sorts of noise, and I knew there was no way I was going to be able to get back to sleep.

OK, I said to myself, *time for me to drag my butt out of bed.* There was a little chill in the bedroom air, raising the hair on my bare legs. I shuffled over to the dresser to retrieve my pants, which were draped over the top. In Texas, one does not drop pants on the floor. Not out of neatness, but more because of scorpions finding a place to live in during the night. Staring out the window, I could see the rain coming down really hard, and wondered if Donna had any trouble on the way to work. Yesterday had been a perfect afternoon and evening in Texas.

Heading down the hall toward my office, I wondered what e-mail I had received during the night. Halfway there the phone rang, so I hurried into the office to hear Donna's "Hello?" on the other end. My first thought was, *Oh crap. She had an accident and I need to come pick her up.* However, she reported she was OK in spite of hail breaking windshields of trucks and cars on the road. I told her I asked God to watch over her on her way to work and not let anything happen to her. She was so funny when she replied that the storm had been coming her way but suddenly changed directions and headed toward the city, away from her. She mused how I must have saved her by having the storm head in a different direction. After hanging up, I had to chuckle at the very thought of affecting weather. *Oh yeah, like I am so powerful I can affect storms. Interesting concept, but I don't think so.*

"Why do you think so little of yourself and of what you are capable?"

I knew that voice. It was Michael's. I turned, expecting to see his resplendent light intensifying before he physically appeared. There was nothing to be seen. His voice had come from no direction and yet from every direction. As I walked into the living room I spied the ball of brilliant light forming as I had seen many times before. His shape materialized into view until the fullness of his face and white robe became solid. Like some unannounced relative, he stood there calmly in the middle of the room. He stood considerably taller than I remembered. Our new home had a fifteen-foot high ceiling, and his head almost reached the crossbeam. "Did you get taller since the last time I saw you, or are you just showing off?" I asked him. He smiled down at me and began to shrink to his usual seven to eight feet.

"The space was here, so I was using it," he replied. **"Come walk with me, we have much to talk about,"** he said as he headed into the

back yard through the patio door. And I do mean right through the door. It always amazed me to watch him walk through solid objects. The rain was coming down harder, so I yelled after him, "Just a minute I need a raincoat."

"No you don't. Come."

Trust is a big thing with Michael and me. Over the years I have learned to honor whatever he asks of me, for I have always been safe with him. Opening the sliding glass door, I sauntered outside. The rain fell hard but I wasn't getting wet. "This is like dodging raindrops without moving," I said to him.

"Precisely," was his reply. A smile inched across my face as I noticed how his vocabulary had loosened up a bit. I guessed it was because I had asked him to talk more like we do rather than the more stilted, poetic way he usually conversed. The angel glided toward the chain-link fence heading in the direction of the arroyo on the south section of the property. We had put up a sturdy fence to pen in the four dogs, the heaviest being close to 230 pounds. I started to angle off toward the back gate, now wishing we had put a second gate on the side so I didn't have to walk so far to get out of the fenced area.

"This way, Joe, follow me," Michael instructed.

I did as he asked thinking, *This is pretty cool, I get to walk through a fence.* Michael went right through the chain link but when I got to it a section of it disappeared. Part of my new fence was gone! Shaking my head, I walked through the open space after Michael. Nothing surprised me anymore.

The rain poured harder as the sky darkened. Streaks of lightning flashed through the sky with the crash of thunder immediately following. *Oh this is one of those learning times, I can just feel it*, I said uneasily to myself. There had been an appearance in the past where thunder had foreshadowed one of the most dramatic teachings Michael had ever given me. And this weather reminded me of that unforgettable time. We continued out toward the back of the property where I had placed a bench with angel designs on it.

"You picked a good spot."

"Yes," I said, "It just felt right."

"So, Michael, just what are we doing out here in the rain? True, I am not getting wet, but don't you think it's a little crazy to be out here with the thunder and lightning? I don't think I would like to get struck."

The angel looked down and smiled as we walked toward the bench. I noticed the water on the ground as we walked across the grass. As I approached a puddle I started to go around it when he said, **"Don't."** I froze in my tracks.

Don't what? I thought. *Don't go around? Don't move?* I raised my arms and said, "Don't do what?"

"Do not alter your path."

"Well, OK," I said and watched him turn around and face me. He stood about ten feet in front of me and held out his hands for me to take. As I moved toward him I stepped right into the puddle. The water receded from around my foot as it touched the ground. The grass, covered by water an instant ago, felt dry to the bottom of my foot. It was as if I wore invisible galoshes. "This is way cool, Michael. But what is this all about?" A large smile came over his face, yet I felt something was wrong. A tingling sensation began to cover me as I watched the hair on my arms stand up. I had heard Lee Trevino tell about the time he was struck by lightning and just knew this was what was going on now. Michael looked skyward, spread his arms out and up, and then leaned forward toward me. I looked up to see what he was looking at when it happened. A white-hot vein of liquid light formed just above him. He was still smiling as it grew in thickness and intensity. Now, like I said, trust is a big thing with Michael and me, so I just let happen whatever was going to happen. Looking down, I checked to see if my feet were still dry while standing in the puddle of water. They were. That had to mean something, didn't it? As the white liquid started eating its way up through the sky, lighting everything above us, I stared, mesmerized. Fear was not an option at this point, and I ain't saying fear wasn't gnawing at me. Events like this in the past have taught me to let go of fear.

That's when I saw something I had never seen before. Michael began to glow differently, and started to take on mass as if he were even more solid. I watched as his shoulders began to look bigger, but then knew they weren't. As I watched what was really going on, and followed the outline of what was emerging, I gawked, amazed at what I was seeing. Exuberantly I yelled out, "Michael, you sunnuvabitch, you've got wings!" I had never seen anything so beautiful as they rose from his shoulders and arched over me. They were like feathers of light radiating from some divine being who could only have come from God. You don't

know how many times people have asked me if Michael had wings and I had said no. Witnessing this aspect of my divine friend was such an amazing experience.

I was just so caught up in it all as spirals of light as if from a prism shot out from each feather in slow motion. It was as if a starburst of rainbowed snowflakes were going out in all directions. The splendor and wonder of it all drenched me in awe! Michael brought his hands together and took hold of the liquid line of bright light, and as he did, the light took form. As quickly as a bolt of lightning is born and dies, the bolt moved from the sky into Michael's hands. This formed bolt was not some twisted branch of light scattering out like that of a tree. No, I could see clearly it was like a sword of light. But this sword left no feeling of malice or violence. No harm could or would ever come from it.

Michael stared into me with his jewel-like eyes and brought the sword between our common gaze. As I looked through the sword, I could see clearly we were connected, as are all things. I began to understand why Michael had come, and what this lesson was all about. With that thought, Michael raised the sword over his head, and as the tip moved up past his head, his wings of light began to vanish. The tip of the sword then arched back toward the ground behind him. He reminded me of a knight carrying his sword on his back rather than to his side. All of a sudden I had an odd thought: that I knew something about him I wasn't sure of before.

I looked at the angel and said, "You are him, aren't you?"

Without a pause he said, **"You speak of the Archangel; the one they call Michael the Archangel. I have served our God as such."**

"And the sword, is that the one you guard Eden with?"

His eyes turned kind and gentle. There was almost a softness to them as he replied, **"The sword was never meant as a weapon to guard, but as a light to guide. Most of you don't know where to look to see it."**

"I haven't seen it till just now, myself," I admitted, and he just smiled back at me.

"This is not why I have come, and we have many things for you to learn."

"Why do I feel like I am going to get a lesson on healing and energy?"

"There are several different kinds of energy. Most people only

understand chemical, electrical and other physical forms. Out of this understanding your kind believes that energy is what does the healing. So you have a number of people believing that if you rearrange the energy, healing has taken place. Not true. Now let me make this simple for you. People who can move energy by thoughts, actions or deeds would tend to believe that they are healers. The truth of the matter is, all they are doing is rearranging, and it won't last. The very most it will do is give one a false sense of healing. What you need to remember in any kind of healing is that energy is fluid. That means it moves, it is in motion, always in motion.

"The basis for healing takes more than just moving energy. If someone is truly going to heal, you need to have three things in place: 1) a desire to be healed, 2) a knowledge of what is incorrect, and 3) a space in which healing can occur. These are the things I am going to teach you, and in turn you will teach others. You have heard it said, 'No one has ever healed anyone' and this is true. Even Jesus said that he never healed anyone. What he did say was 'Your faith has healed you, for I have done nothing.' What he did was create a space for healing to take place. All the energy in the world cannot cause healing. So let me explain to you in simple terms how healing happens. When I told you the first thing that is needed is the desire to be healed, you must realize nothing will happen without the person wanting healing on a physical, mental, emotional and spiritual level. Otherwise, they waste your time."

"OK, Michael, I hear that, but what about this: If I see someone who is ill, and I want to help him or her, does this mean I can't do any healing without permission? Because if this is true, why even bother? According to my understanding, when it comes to healing, given we are all perfect, whole, and complete, we should be able to heal anyone at any time just given who we are. Something else is bothering me about this whole energy thing. Now you tell me that those who use energy to heal are like children playing with toys. So if it isn't energy, then what is it? How do you describe what everyone has come to know as energy, if it really isn't?"

"Joe, you are still seeing things, when you speak of energy, as though it were a force. Like so many other people, you think in terms of making healing happen — as if you had some power within you to

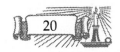

cause the healing — and this is just not true. God has given each one of you all you need to be whole. Most of you were taught over the years that if you get sick, you need something outside of yourself to make you well again. You have chosen to believe this — so nothing can be done by you to make yourself well. Once you go to doctors and they tell you what to do, you begin to feel better. What is taking place is that your mind is connecting with your heart and you have allowed healing to begin. Your kind has a word that almost touches on the healing love God has for you. The word is 'grace.' "

"OK, Michael, I think this is opening up something for me. Correct me if I'm wrong. Basically, what you're saying is that grace is the atmosphere or the space in which healing of any kind takes place. And what true healers do is access that space for those unaware of accessing it themselves."

"Blessings to you for your eyes are beginning to open. You see that grace is given to all, yet few remember that they have it. Your kind has forgotten that, so too have they forgotten how to heal themselves. What you call 'divine energy' is truly the grace of God. Many have been taught that grace comes from without, and that they must follow rules in order to receive it. God gives grace freely and abundantly to all."

"Let me see if I've got this straight. It seems to me that force is what we use in order to have something not be. Grace on the other hand, is something we allow to fill us. Once we do this, everything that should be whole within us, is. So then it is our allowing ourselves to be well rather than making ourselves be well."

"This is why I have come to you. You will lay aside things that you think you know to grow wise with that which is given to you. Should you find yourself lost on this path of wisdom, you will stop and ask for your way back to the path."

"Thanks, Michael. I would rather you teach the way that it is instead of the way I think it is. I know it isn't always the way that I think it is. Left to my own way of thinking, I am afraid I might just screw it up. So go on with what you're saying."

The angel raised his hand and the space between two trees began to radiate with what looked like the same silverlike liquid I had seen him create on my lily pond back in California. Those previous visions

reflected in the silver liquid related to the *Book of Revelation*, as described in *On the Wings of Heaven*. The trees before me now appeared as if they were two golden pillars, holding a silver screen. As I watched, I began to see what appeared to be a human form taking shape. When the shape was complete, it was the strangest darn thing I had ever seen. Granted, the form was human and had all the characteristics of a human being, however it wasn't male, nor was it female. It looked more like a generic body that could have been anybody. I could see it was breathing; the chest would expand and contract as the air went in and out. But here's the really strange part: As I looked into the eyes, I didn't see any light — you know, like the spark of life that is in all living creatures. It was almost as if it didn't have a soul. I guess this whole thing struck me as rather odd. Two factors in particular stood out: one was that it was alive, and the other (which was the weirdest) was that it looked like anybody and nobody at the same time.

"So Michael, what is this? Some kind of zombie or what?"

"Only you would say something in that way. You are great with humor. Look closer. What do you see?"

As I gazed closer, it began to look transparent. Whatever I wanted to see would come into focus. If I wanted to look at the heart, it would become the most prominent anatomy in the body. But not just a front view, or a side view, or a back view, or bottom or top. It was as though I could see the whole heart at once. It was the same thing with the lungs, kidneys, liver, stomach, the bladder or any other organ I looked at. Even the veins, nerves, muscles or bones would show up that way. Yet, even with everything working, the human form did not seem to be alive.

"What do you see, Joe?"

"Well, Michael, it looks like a perfectly healthy body. However, there is no life in it."

"Can you see how this figure before you is perfect?"

"Yes I can," I replied, still a little amazed at what I was viewing.

"This is the state of all humans; it stands in perfect physical health. This is how you can compare the health of all others. Now look again, for I have given this body an illness. Find it."

I looked to see if I could find what Michael was talking about. I looked the body up and down examining every part but I couldn't see anything. So I closed my eyes and raised my hand in front of me. I

looked, with what we call the third eye, through the back of my hand at the body standing there. I learned this technique early on, and Michael had asked me to teach the Seven how to scan this way as well. However, some of them had their own techniques, which they still like to use.

Moving my hand slowly down the body I stopped at a spot about halfway down the right side, just to the right of the solar plexus. There I could see a red dot. The dot was about the size of a pencil eraser, and that's when it hit me. This body had no color. When I scan anyone this way, whomever I scan has a colorful glow. Pretty much like the colors of the rainbow, each person radiates a different color. This one did not. So I went on scanning the rest of the body. No. There were no other dots. Dropping my hand, I opened my eyes and turned to Michael.

"OK, Michael, I'm done," I said. "The only thing that I can find is a red dot. Do you want me to fix it?" figuring there had to be a reason for going through this exercise.

"Yes. Only look at this which I show you."

I looked at the body again, only this time I saw what appeared to be seven balls of light. Each one was about the size of a softball of seven different colors. "They look like openings to the seven chakras," I told him. Traditional Eastern thought teaches there are seven gateways to the body, which are like energy wheels. These are located on different parts of the body: the top of the head, the forehead, throat, heart, solar plexus, lower back and tailbone.

As I gazed at the seven spheres, I started to see other balls of light appearing. This was all new to me. It looked like there were two more chakras above the head and two more below the hips, one hovering at mid-thigh and the other between the knees and ankles. The last one went around the whole body. Now this is where it starts to get strange. There was a pattern that the seven masters were to sit in, called the Formation of the Sevens, when I called them to gather together in California. Each master was to sit according to the gift with which he or she had been blessed, and each of the masters radiated a different color of light from his or her spiritual body. In *On the Wings of Heaven*, Michael had said that these seven gifts had once been given to the seven churches spoken of in the *Book of Revelation*. Instead of the seven churches sharing these gifts with humanity, as they were supposed to, they kept the seven gifts to acquire power and influence. In the process, the churches lost the seven

gifts, which were now being returned to humanity through the seven masters. When the seven masters sit in the Formation of the Sevens along with a servant, it causes a flow of energy that opens what the angel calls a gateway or opening to the realm of angels.

To look at the formation from above you might describe it as two squares. The larger, outer square is diamond-shaped with its points facing north, south, east and west, twenty-one feet from north to south. The inner seven-foot square is rotated forty-five degrees with its points facing the minor directions (NE, NW, SE, SW). The masters gave a name to this pattern, calling it the "Matrix."[1]

As I continued to watch, this same pattern of different-colored dots started appearing at the feet of the human model, only much smaller than the pattern the masters sit in. Matrix after matrix of colored dots rose in helix fashion like a strand of DNA, and the pattern continued to repeat itself up the body, hooking up with the chakras as it went. When the helix

---

[1] Diagram 1 — the Formation of the Sevens

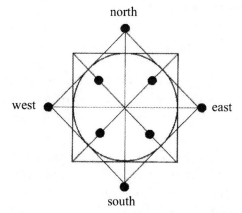

The servant (in this case, Joseph) sits in the east. The master who holds the gift of the church of Philadelphia sits in the west, emitting the spiritual color blue. In the south sits the master who holds the gift of the church of Sardis, emitting the color green. In the north sits the master who holds the gift of the church of Laodicea, emitting the color violet. In the minor directions sit the four masters who hold the following: the gift of the church of Pergamum in northwest, emitting the color yellow; the gift of the church of Ephesus in the northeast, emitting the color orange; the gift of the church of Smyrna in the southeast, emitting the color red; and the gift of the church of Thyatira in the southwest, emitting the color indigo or purple.

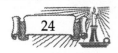

made of matrix-patterned dots rose above the head, it connected to the two new chakras the angel had shown me. So it looked like a beautiful multi-colored web of small dots throughout the body. As it reached the very top chakra, that ball of light there lit up like the liquid light I had seen in the lightning, and then it was gone. When the light turned dim the body came back into a clear focus, and I could see it as I had before with all of its working parts.

"Wow! Michael, this is something new to me, and to see the matrix pattern run throughout the whole body like a DNA spiral is telling me I do have a lot to learn."

"You do have much to learn."

"You keep showing me things which I have no idea of what they mean or what they do. So what's this thing with the matrices and the chakras anyhow?"

"That is for another time. Finish what you were going to do."

I remembered that I was about to do some work on the body. So I started to walk toward the image.

"Stop. Do it from where you are standing."

"OK, if you say so. It's not the way I usually do it. Most of the time I need to put my hands on the people ... or at least I think I do. Why? Am I doing something wrong?"

"No, Joe you're not doing anything wrong. Most people feel they must be touched for healing to take place. What you need to develop is your ability to heal without touching. For I tell you, this is one that you cannot touch."

"I'll take your word for it," I said. Not really knowing what I was doing, I closed my eyes and focused on the red dot I had seen. After taking three deep breaths, I could feel myself filling with what I guessed to be what Michael had called grace. I then allowed this grace to flow from my heart to the dot. There appeared to be what looked like a light halo or aura around the dot. The red dot then began to lose its color, assuming a white glow, which was absorbed throughout the body, and then it was gone. Amazing!

"Did I do that, Michael?"

"No. You didn't do it. You allowed it to happen. There are many like you who can do these things. Did you not teach your seven and will not your seven teach others? There will come a time when

everyone will have access to the grace God gives freely. This time has not yet come. So you and others like you will give this to your brothers and sisters."

"You know, Michael, this whole thing started out with you coming to me by calling my name. But don't you think this has gotten just a little bit out of hand? Every time I turn around, you have something else for me to do."

"You speak as though I am presenting you with things to do. I have not come to give you more to do. I have come to show you what you can do."

"OK, Michael, this is what I think I found out. The red dot is physical, the orange dot is emotional, that yellow dot is mental and the green dot is spiritual. Now what I've been doing when I scan someone is the following: I scan four times, first looking for the red dot, then the orange, yellow and green, because we all are fourfold in nature. The red shows the problem as physical, the orange as emotional, the yellow as mental, and the green as spiritual. On some people I find no red dots, although I may find a dot of a different color. So what I'm beginning to believe about all of this is that it's not the illness itself that's the problem. The illness is only a symptom of what is really going on when someone is sick. If whatever it is that's happening with people is only a symptom, it's kind of crazy to treat it. When I sit down and talk to people, I don't ask them what is wrong with them, nor do I ask where it hurts. I'll sit and ask them, 'What is your average day like?' and I will listen. The next thing that I notice happening is we begin to build a relationship of trust. And I just let people talk. You would be surprised at some of the things I hear. Well, maybe you wouldn't. After we've talked, I feel a kind of connection between the two of us. Then I will scan them and see which of the seven gifts they are meant to hold — you know, like what archetypal church they are connected to. This has even gotten to be pretty easy for me to do now."

"These are all the things that you know and are aware of. Yet in the times to come, you will find that you know things you have only dreamed of."

"Well that is just what I need to hear. Knowing who you are, I don't think you are going to tell me all about it now. Another thing I think I know about the dots is that just because there's a dot there, it doesn't mean that's where the illness or the sickness is. See if you can follow me and correct me if I get off track."

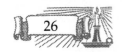

"Speak what you will and I will guide you should you get lost."

"OK, that's cool. Now by my understanding, different parts of the body relate to other areas of the body where functions are going on, given that every cell in the body has a complete blueprint for a whole body. If the dot shows up, for instance, in the liver, that doesn't necessarily mean the liver is damaged. However, if a liver is damaged, that dot will very probably show up somewhere else. Now, what this is saying to me is that something is out of whack or disconnected. And how it shows up in the body is as a disease of the liver or wherever else. So then when this blockage is removed, or the connection is re-made, it allows the grace to flow and healing begins. Now, Michael, what I think my job is going to be is to teach others to do this kind of healing."

"There is so much you have to learn and each learning will take you to another level. I will answer your next question before you ask. Yes, when the instant healing does take place and brings the body back to perfect health, this is what is called by your kind, a miracle. Long ago everybody could do this individually. If they found themselves with an ailment, they would simply heal it. The healings would be in the blink of an eye. Yet through time and the loss of awareness, the ability is lost."

"So Michael, what you're telling me is that instant healing can and does take place all the time? But how can this be if we, for the most part, have lost the awareness of how to do it?"

"It's really very simple, Joe. When you have a healer that opens a channel of grace with a person that knows and has faith that it can be done, one is healed. No miracle, nothing extraordinary, yet it does happen now."

"I'd like to see that sometime."

"This you will see and many others will see it, too."

As I looked back up at the screen where the perfect body was I could see it all start to fade away. As the body vanished so did the screen of liquid silver. The bark on the trees were now brown and cracked like before. I figured that this session with Michael was about done and I looked over at him expecting to see him vanish, but he didn't.

"Walk with me."

I watched as he walked away, giving him only a few paces before I started to follow. *This is crazy*, I thought, *and here I am walking around my*

backyard in my bare feet. I no longer worried about stepping into doggy land mines like I did in California. For the dogs had their own area on this new property. Here, we had something far more dangerous to the bare feet than doggy-do: This danger was called cactus. I have seen Michael many times and I've always been safe with him. However, this was the first chat in a yard that grew cactus. I just didn't know what his powers would be like here.

"Joe, walk beside me. Let us see what this new land holds. You have chosen wisely. The ground is high and will not flood. You have gardens to grow food, you have trees to bear fruit and nuts."

We walked a little bit further, around the workshop shed, across the far end of the property, and headed back up toward the house. "Are we going back inside?" I asked. He just shook his head no. We made our way up the side of the house along the fence line until we reached the front of the house. We stopped at an area where Michael pointed to the ground.

"This will be where you will place your pond. It will give water to God's creatures and help cool you in the summer. Come let me show you where you will place the Sign of the Seven."

I had no idea what he was talking about. Now, I know there are seven masters in a group. Each master carries a special gift and each has a color, a sound, a stone, and a day of the week[2] that corresponds to each of the seven. I figured what the angel wanted me to do was to set up a Matrix that would be the symbol of my first seven who had gathered in California. So I asked, "Michael, why don't I just set this Matrix up so that the house is in the center?" His reply was quick in coming.

"Joe, it is not fitting for your house to be in the center. That space in the center is for me and those like me. Whenever someone is open to hearing what they need, they have but to stand in their place [in the Matrix], and they will receive."

"So you mean if someone comes to visit, they can come in this spot and be in contact with the angelic realm?"

"Yes Joe, that is what I mean."

---

[2] The days of the week corresponding to each church:
        Sunday — Smyrna
        Monday — Ephesus
        Tuesday — Pergamum
        Wednesday — Sardis
        Thursday — Philadelphia
        Friday — Thyatira
        Saturday — Laodicea

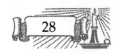

Michael walked from one spot to another, pointing to the ground where each place of the Seven would be. As he pointed, he would say the name of the corresponding church — Philadelphia, Pergamum, Ephesus, etc. He continued in this manner until all seven churches had their places marked. When he finished, he stepped into the center and began to glow brilliantly.

Looking at me with those kind and gentle eyes, he started to speak, **"Our time is over for now. When you have done these things I will return. Be about the healing work that is before you. You will know how to put the teachings together so that others will hear."**

"Are you sure I can do this right? What if I make a mistake, how will I know?"

"I will be with you. And that which you think you are discovering, I am teaching."

Michael started to fade into the light as he had done so many times. Moments later he was gone. It is nice to know I have an angel guiding me in the things I am to teach. It's even better to know that he will correct me if I get off track. And then again, the last thing I heard him say was, **"Teach only love."**

The days following Michael's appearance, I mulled over all I had seen and been taught. Little did I know that this was just the beginning. In the months and years to come, the miraculous would become the everyday, the unexplainable would become a testimonial to the heart. Day after day I would walk out to the place where Michael had pointed out spots for the Sign of the Seven. Something inside of me said I needed to build a Matrix there. But how? And out of what? The answer that came to me would take me where I never dreamed I'd be. Not only where I'd be but also where many of you will be. For the angel Michael stated clearly that the information that follows is not for me, but for you.

THE SEVEN STONES

*O*ne of the truly great realizations about the gifts of the seven masters is that the seven gifts teach us that we are not alone in our efforts. We are not isolated islands but a blended bridge of colors that touch both the earth and the heavens like a human rainbow. Oftentimes this becomes quite evident when I have to take the teachings Michael has given me and explain them to another. And once again, a simple conversation with Gary over the phone led to an event neither of us expected.

"Joe, you mean Michael actually said he was giving us a gateway into the angelic realm? What kind of instructions did he give you?"

"Basically, he pointed to eight spots on the ground and gave the name of one of the seven churches for each spot, plus the position of the servant. I noticed right away that the eight spots were the same formation we had sat in during the gathering of the seven masters in California. He was forming the Matrix. As Michael would point out each spot, I'd dig a dimple with the heel of my foot and run and get a brick to mark the spot. Afterwards, he reminded me that the seven churches of the seven masters also had a corresponding stone or crystal. If the seven kinds of stones are placed on the spots Michael pointed out, it will allow the angelic realm to come through."

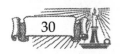

"But they are here anyhow. How would this be any different? They don't really need a gateway do they?"

"Not if you see it that way. But with this gateway, they will be able to better work with us when it comes to healing and guidance. The environment is purer, more powerful for the interactions to take place. Michael said I'd understand better as we learned more about this matrix of stones. My sense is that it assists us in raising our own vibrations so that we can detect them more easily, and so they can more easily work with us."

"Well, I've got to see this for myself. At the gathering, all of the masters saw a vortex of spinning energy in the center, and all of us at one point or another, during the gathering, connected with the angels. But the idea of using the stones to open a gateway to the angelic realm sounds mind-blowing. Have you set up the stones yet?"

"Not yet. I'm still looking for all of them. Not many places around here that have these kinds of stones."

"OK. Remind me what stones you need for the eight spots. Let's see, you said the servant's position uses the same stone as does the position of Philadelphia?"

"Yes, blue goes in both the east and the west. Well, let's see. In the north I need either lavender jade or violet calcite. In the south, I need green kyanite. In the east and the west, I need either azurite or blue sapphire. In the northwest I need either yellow topaz or yellow calcite. In the northeast, I need either orange calcite or orange sapphire. In the southeast, I need ruby; and in the southwest, amethyst or benitoite."

"Seven stones for the seven rays of the rainbow. Well, I'd like to come down there. How about I stop in Tucson and get the stones you need? I hear it's the crystal capital of the U.S. Can you put me up?"

"Hey, come on down. I could use some help, and we could talk about this book Michael wants the two of us to put together."

"Great," Gary said, "I'll start making arrangements for the trip right away."

After repeated phone calls, Gary had a list of stones and places to shop for them in Arizona. However, he found that violet calcite and lavender jade were almost impossible to buy. They were either not available or were far too expensive to acquire. So it was decided he would bring a couple of substitutes to try out for the church of Laodicea, which

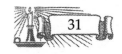

is the northern position in the Matrix, or what Michael had called the Sign of the Seven.

In a matter of a few weeks Gary arrived in San Antonio with a bag of crystals and stones in hand. That evening we sat down to review what stones went where. He had brought two beautiful blue azurite stones, which were indigenous to Arizona. One piece of azurite was for the church of Philadelphia and the other for the servant, or the positions of east and west. The next color was yellow for the church of Pergamum. In his hand, Gary held both yellow topaz and yellow calcite. However, it was difficult to tell the yellow calcite from the orange calcite. We found out later that this is a common problem even for rock hounds. There are differing opinions on what is yellow and what is orange. Much later I found out that yellow calcite is oftentimes called honey calcite. We decided to use the yellow topaz in the construction of the Matrix, where the stone is placed in the northwest. For the church of Ephesus, orange is the corresponding color, and with it orange calcite or carnelian. We went with orange calcite since Gary had decided not to buy carnelian while in Tucson. The calcite would go in the northeast. For the church of Thyatira, he had brought a beautiful dark piece of purple amethyst. We would place it in the southwest. In the southeast, the ruby would be placed for the church of Smyrna. The stone was big enough to choke a horse. I had never seen a rough ruby, which is quite different from the gem quality, and much more affordable. Green kyanite would be placed in the south for the church of Sardis. We knew emerald would work, but Gary found a nice piece of kyanite for a good price. That left the church of Laodicea. A friend of mine had mailed me a small bead of lavender jade. We would use that to compare with the charoite and the purpurite Gary had brought, hoping one of those stones would work as a substitute. Otherwise, how would we ever be able to afford more than one Matrix? Already, some of the other masters were considering putting up a Matrix in their area once they got the details from me. With Gary here, we could work out all the mathematics and make sure we had everything geometrically correct.

The next morning I took Gary to where Michael had pointed out the seven places for the seven churches, plus the place for the servant. "Joe, this gives me chills just being here and looking at the geometry. At the gathering in California we sat in this formation, but we were a bit lax about our placement. These bricks you have on the ground, showing

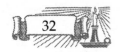

where Michael pointed, are much more symmetrical, more mathematical." I smiled as I listened to him go on. Gary drools over mathematics the way most men would over a football game or a beautiful woman. As we talked, we decided the bricks should be replaced with wood so that the seven kinds of stones would not be affected by the crystalline components of the brick. The bricks I used had a vibration created when they were fired in a kiln. "Are you sure the formation is oriented toward true north?" Gary asked.

"I can't say," I said, "I just put them where Michael told me."

"Well, I can check tonight when the North Star is out. I didn't bring a compass with me. And even if I did, I don't know the angle of declination for this part of the country to calculate true north. I just like to check these things out to make sure we got our information correctly." Perhaps it's the mathematician in him, but Gary always likes to check and crosscheck any of the information we get from Michael. Perhaps part of the reason stems from the fact that we'd be writing the next book together, and he likes his books to be as accurate as possible. It was time to set the stones up. As Gary went back to the house to retrieve the stones he'd brought, I ambled over to the workshop to get some pieces of wood. They were all different sizes and shapes, but they were wood. After replacing the bricks with wood blocks, I looked up to see Gary arriving cradling the stones in his arms like I do a newborn mastiff puppy.

"It ain't the prettiest setting you ever did see. Kinda looks like some carpenter finished a project without cleaning up." We both laughed, given that I was a carpenter when all this angel stuff started. Gary opened up his package and showed me the azurite stones he had brought. "Beautiful," I cooed. "Never have I seen something that blue with such rich color. Michael's eyes are close to that same color, except the stone doesn't come close to the love his eyes hold." Gary nodded with understanding. He, too, had experienced an angelic presence, and knew of this love.

Once all seven kinds of the stones were in the eight places, the two of us stood outside the Matrix to see if anything happened. Would angels appear? Would voices from the heavens speak? What we did notice was an electrical kind of feeling filling the air. Neither of us knew what we were supposed to do from here. I decided to get my meditation stool and sit in the middle where Michael said was the place for his kind. As I sat there, I could feel a growing energy swirling around me. Just as I was

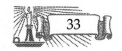

about to ask Gary if he felt the same thing, he commented, "Wow, I can now see the same vortex of light swirling around as I saw at the gathering of the seven masters. It's getting increasingly stronger."

"OK," I said, "I can see it as well from in here. Let's try to substitute a few of the stones you brought to see if it makes any difference." We exchanged the lavender jade bead with the charoite, and it seemed to work just as well. In fact, if I were to describe it, the energy seemed even a bit more intense or pure. Gary picked up the same sensation. Then we tried the chunk of purpurite he had brought. In short order, the swirl of energy in the vortex turned lopsided. Everything seemed out of balance. We both decided the purpurite was out and the charoite was in. Later on we discovered that green fluorite would work as a substitute for the green kyanite. We had all the stones we needed to keep the angelic opening permanently in place. "Gary, why don't you sit here in the middle and see what kind of sensations you get." A silly grin crossed his face as he removed his shoes and socks.

"I feel like Dr. Who stepping into his phone booth," he said sheepishly as he eased himself onto the stool. At first he stared at the ground like a man looking for scorpions. But then his eyes froze and he seemed to get real calm. It was then that I noticed the light starting to build around him.

"Do you see what I see?" I asked him. "You are completely wrapped in energy."

"I can't say that I see it, but I sure can feel it. This is really weird. You are starting to fade in and out, like something out of Star Trek."

"I'm seeing the same thing with you. Ya know, this same thing happened at the gathering. But I was the only one who saw it. I'm glad you can see it, too. What do you think it means?"

"I've been taught about gateways by an African shaman-priest named Malidoma Somé. He told me these kinds of openings existed in very special locations in nature. I remember his talking about how objects would disappear from view in them. You're not totally disappearing, but it's like bands of you disappear and then fade back into view."

Both of us just stood there like school kids on the first day of school. Gary turned 180 degrees to see if facing another direction would change anything. Wanting to see the expressions on his face I walked around to where he was facing.

"Holy cow! I can feel hands on me! I mean I can actually feel the fingers. Joe, are you seeing anything?" All I could see was a kind of miragelike shimmering of light. "Damn. My liver is aching like crazy. I mean really hurting." As Gary held his right side, he started to bend over in pain. "Do you see anything?" Once again, all I could see was a wavy miragelike green color in the area of his liver. I wasn't sure exactly what was going on with him. "Ohhhh," he groaned again. "This is *really* weird. I can feel the hands on my liver right now. Look. My liver is moving around." He lifted his shirt to expose his right side. Undulations rolled across his side. "What is going on here? I can feel fingers massaging my liver. Do you think something is wrong with my liver?"

"Hell, I don't know. All I can see is colored light in that area. Maybe the center of the Matrix is the place where healing occurs. Have you had any liver problems?"

"Not that I know of. I used to drink a lot — to the point where I came down with colitis. That's when I decided it was time to quit." Gary kept staring at the movement on his right side. I figured there probably was some liver damage he may not have been aware of. After a few minutes I could see the green light fading. And as soon as it disappeared, Gary looked at me. "It's stopped," he said. "The aching is gone, as are the hands I was feeling. Too weird." After staring at one another wondering what to expect next, Gary asked, "What do you think we should do now?"

"Well, Michael said there were two places we could stand. One place was in the middle and the other was in the place of our church."

"That sounds good to me. Why don't you go stand in the east, which is your position of the servant, and I'll stand in the west, the place of my church, Philadelphia. We'll both be standing over the azurite stones."

As soon as we had taken our places, my eyes nearly popped out of my head. "Hey, I can now see angels at every position in the Matrix." They didn't look solid like Michael does, but I could still see them. "Do you see any of them?" I asked Gary.

"Can't say as I do. I can feel their presence, though. This whole place is alive with energy. I'm surprised my hair isn't standing straight out." He was right. Both of us could feel a buzz in our bodies as if we'd stuck our fingers into low-voltage electric sockets. It was then that I saw Gary look around, and immediately I saw why. There stood another

angel quietly behind him as well. His whole body was being surrounded by light.

"Gar, I see an angel behind you, and there's this glowing light around you."

"I was just going to tell you that I felt Bahram's presence. He's right behind me." Bahram is the same angel Gary had seen after he had done the Last Baptism given to us by Michael. In the book, *On the Wings of Heaven*, Gary tells about how he first came to see Bahram and how Michael later told me to tell him that Bahram stayed with him as his protecting angel. "Sure will be your footing," Michael had said in a message I was to pass on to Gary, "for you have seen the angel that protects you. Your path will be lighted and your steps will be guided. Humble yourself not in his greatness but rise up to the greatness that is yours." Gary had called Bahram "The Laughing Angel" because that was how he first appeared to him. Well, Bahram wasn't laughing now. He seemed quite intent but pleased.

"Damn, Joe. This gateway really works! This is incredible. What a time to be alive." The two of us just stood there for the longest time trying to soak it all in. Then Gary's eyes got round as cactus buttons. I was just about to ask him what he was seeing when he started talking in almost whispered tones. "Joe, I'm seeing a magnificent sight, almost like a vision where the vortex or ball of light is. I'm being shown a cloth of energy weaving across the Earth. People from all parts will create these seven-stone matrices like this one. They will all connect to one another starting with this one here in San Antonio and spreading across the country, and eventually around the globe." As I listened to him, I nodded my head in affirmation. I felt the truth of his words. Sometimes Gary sees these things ahead of time, and little did he know what Michael would say later regarding this exact phenomenon. Gary continued, "What I am seeing tells me that this will cause a shift in energy around the globe. This is how we will set up the coming together of heaven and earth." A shiver rippled across him as he stared at the vision in the center of the Matrix. Activity ceased after that, except for the continuing charge of electricity in the air. We stood silently for a while and then decided to call it a day. And what a day it had been.

Bright and early the next morning the two of us stood silently next to the Matrix. We couldn't get enough of the swirling energy in the center.

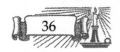

"We should do something about protecting some of these stones," Gary half mumbled. "It gets pretty hot here with the direct sunlight overhead. Some of these crystals like the the calcite will fade in sunlight." And with those few words we began another adventure like two prospectors looking for more gold.

"What would happen if we elevated the stones?" I proposed.

"You mean all the same height but off the ground? How would we raise them? We should use something that has no crystalline structure in it, like wood. I don't think bricks or rock should be used."

"What if we didn't make them all the same height? Remember from the gathering that each church has a tone? And remember how Ben said that these tones of the seven masters were like stepping stones of sound?" Ben was the master who knew the most about music and sound, holding a degree in music. "Why not make wooden posts like the tones, only use physical height to represent the tonal increase?" Gary thought about that a bit with his mathematical mind running like a hamster on an exercise wheel.

"OK. OK. There's one problem though. The servant's position in the east has the same tone as my position in the west. In the Matrix you and I have the same tone, which is "do," or the tone of C. We could make each increment in height seven inches, but which of our positions is the starting position? Would the post for the servant's position be seven inches and my position forty-nine inches, or vice versa?" The two us haggled over whose post should be the lowest. We both argued for having the lowest post, but in the end I won out. The servant's post would be the seven-inch high post. It was settled. While I ran off to the lumberyard for four-by-four posts, Gary grabbed the post-hole digger and made an attempt at starting a hole in the rock laden ground. By the time I got back, he was sitting on the ground with the digger beside him staring up at the sky with a small dent in the ground next to him.

"You didn't get very far," I teased as I started unloading the posts. Ignoring my comment, Gary took off on another topic, as he is prone to do.

"While you were gone, I realized that we can't use seven-inch increments at each position. There are two places where the tones only go up half a step. So there are two places where the posts are only three-and-half inches higher than the previous post." How he thinks of things like this is beyond me. As I stared down at him, I was tempted to tell him that

a deeper hole was more important. But then I did remember Ben spending a lot of time telling us about the half steps and the geometry of triads or chords formed by the four triangles, which made up the Matrix.

"So, do you remember where the half steps are?"

"I've been sitting here trying to remember."

"Maybe driving the post-hole digger into the ground might have cleared your mind better," I kidded as I picked up the digger and continued with the hole.

"I think I'd better call Ben in Missouri. OK to use your phone?"

"Sure," I said smiling at him. Anything to avoid manual labor. "Why not get the portable phone so we can both talk to him out here. I'll just keep digging as you fetch the phone." Gary smiled at me with that grin of his that says, *It's OK if you want to be a smart ass.* As he turned to walk toward the house, his middle finger began scratching the side of his head in an obvious manner. Friendship is a wonderful thing.

Ben reminded us that the first half step occurs between "mi" and "fa," the second half step between "ti" and "do." By this time I had three holes already dug, working up quite a sweat in the process. For a man who works out in the gym, Gary sure loved exerting himself — not. He absorbed himself in the math, marking the lines with exactness on the posts where the chainsaw would be used. Assuming each hole would be twelve inches deep, he managed to arrange lengths so the eight heights would work with just the four posts I had purchased. As I chain-sawed the first post, Gary drew on a piece of paper the positions and post lengths so we could tell the other sevens how to create their own Matrix.

Just as the sun was about to set, we finished the last of holes and the placing of the four-by-four posts. The stones were placed on top and the two of us went in the house for showers and dinner. After a fine meal, the two of us discussed how to present the angelic material in the upcoming book when Gary got the funniest look on his face. He kept staring at the piece of paper with the diagram of the Matrix on it. "Joe, I can't believe this. I gave you the wrong directions for the Matrix. I got north and south backwards, which means that east and west are flipped as well. The posts need to be repositioned." All I could think of was all the work I'd put into digging postholes. I would have strangled Gary but he had the sorriest look on his face, which reminded me of one of the mastiffs when they know they've done something wrong.

"Well, I guess we start over in the morning," I said. As I got ready for bed I could hear the patter of rain on the roof. At least we'd have a cooler day tomorrow. The next morning I woke at the crack of dawn. All I could think about was how the Matrix had been screwed up. After swallowing several cups of coffee, I slipped out into the cool morning air and found my way to the debacle. Standing there with my hands crammed into my jeans pockets, I examined how I might fix this fiasco without doing any more work than necessary. The best option seemed to be pulling out a post and redigging a hole. But after rocking the first post back and forth and pulling it out, I realized the night rain had moistened the soil enough so that none of the dirt fell back into the hole. *Great!* I thought to myself. *If I'm careful enough, I can slip the correct post back in and just pack it down.* By the grace of Mother Nature, I was able to re-arrange all the posts except one without doing any redigging. By the time Gary got up, with his head hanging between his legs, I was sitting on the couch looking like the cat that ate the canary.

Gary didn't want to eat breakfast. He made a beeline for the Matrix and was relieved to see the posts in the correct positions. "How'd you do this? You must've gotten up before the crack of dawn. Was it tough work getting it all fixed?" he asked almost apologetically.

"Back breaking," I said in my most convincing imitation of exhaustion. He began to smile at me.

"OK. How'd you do it? Did Michael show up and replace everything?"

"I wish," I said, then confessing to the blessing from Mother Nature.

As we both checked out the energy, we both concluded it was more pure and intense than without the posts. Using our sensitivity at reading energy, we determined the range of influence from the Matrix extended fifteen feet past the stones. Impressive, we both thought. Little did we know how all this would change in the coming months when the sevens would begin a process that would affect not only us but also our planet.

Gary left early the next morning to return to the Northwest. That day, I kept revisiting the Matrix and beholding the beauty of its geometry. How nice it was for my friend to come and help out like this. The whole place seemed wonderfully different.

That night, as I was sitting in the office answering some e-mail from some of the sevens, an unexpected light began filling the room. *Michael,* I said to myself. It was late and I was just contemplating crashing in bed.

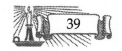

What in the world could he want now? Staring at the growing circle of light, I waited to speak until the image of Michael grew fully clear. "Well, Michael, this must be important to have you come so late," I said. "I do wish this could have waited till morning, because I am tired and was thinking of going to bed." Then, as I yawned, I felt something strange happening to me. My limbs that were heavy and the eyelids that were ready to slam shut a moment before felt like they had rested all night. I felt wide-awake and ready for anything. "OK, Big Guy, what do you want from me this time?"

"You and Gary are as children with what you do."

Now that was an opening line I hadn't heard before. I started to think about all the things Gary and I had done the past three days, so I could get some idea of what the angel might be after. "Can you tell me what you are talking about?" I asked in all seriousness.

"Come with me," was all he said.

As I followed Michael's light down the hall, I saw him perform one of his typical exits right through the closed patio door. Having learned my lesson, I slid the door open to let myself through. Never bored by the altering of reality, I watched as he passed through the fence, dematerializing a section of it so I could cross through as well. I knew where he was headed, and followed him to the where Gary and I had set up the Matrix with the stones and posts. Michael's light pushed back the darkness of the night, and I could see everything around the Matrix as if some giant spotlight had been turned on. However, there were no shadows cast by the trees, or anything else for that matter. This made me wonder what kind of light the angel emitted — a sun that casts no shadows? As we approached the Matrix, I could see the stones start to glow with their prospective seven colors. Each stone glowed like — this may sound strange — but each glowed like the liquid lightning I had seen last time Michael had appeared. And each was giving off sound, too. They were all connecting to one another, looking like laser beams going from one post to the other post linking each stone to the next. The beams appeared to form two pyramid-shaped objects, one inverted into and intersecting the other. These, too, were made of light, and the two pyramids seemed to correspond to the shape of the Matrix and the eight positions where the seven masters and the servant sat at the gathering. The whole thing was quite beautiful, and I could feel a vibration coming from it. "How did we do?" I asked Michael.

"**Enter to the center,**" was all he said. And as I did, I could feel the lines of light pass through me as I crossed them. I could feel the energy and the gifts of each color — or church would be a better way to put it. How strange to have your senses detect inanimate gifts, to appreciate the forces at play in this laserlike light. To me, light was something you watched, not felt. The awe of all this lingered in me as I wondered what was about to be shown me.

"**If you are going to set these stones in this way, you must set them as they should be.**"

It looked to me as if we had done it right; but I wasn't about to use that word with Michael. I'd only get another lecture in "there is no right, there is no wrong," and I didn't care to suffer the embarrassment again. "Is something out of place?" I asked, not wanting to use the "r" or "w" word.

"**You should trust yourself. That which you told one of the Seven is the way of setting them. They have power now, yet not as they could. What is it you feel in the center?**"

"I feel like a humming vibration is happening and moving through me. Something is happening inside of me but I don't know what it is. I feel a little numb in my head and off balance all in the same."

"**As it should be. You knew this when setting them.**"

I was trying to understand what he was talking about when he raised his hand. The azurite stone that was in Gary's place in the west lifted off the post and floated in the air. It still had light coming from it as it rose high into the air. And then the post started to rise up out of the ground as well. I watched as the post floated in midair and turned horizontal. This was really cool, like a levitation trick of some kind. I started to wonder if I had understood where Michael wanted me to place the stones, thinking I had done it as he had instructed. He moved his hand down, and a piece of the post fell off as if sawed by an invisible blade. The sawed-off section fell toward the hole that the long post had come from. As it did, I wondered if the angel would have as much trouble as I had getting it back in the hole without the dirt caving in. Of course he didn't — he was an angel, and things go the way they want them to. The short post eased right in. The part that was now sticking out was the same height as the post standing in my part of the Matrix, seven inches out of the ground. Our argument about which post was supposed to be forty-nine inches had been a waste of time. Neither post was to be forty-nine inches high.

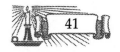

"The stones will be all set the same [level] or they will be set like this."

I watched as the azurite stone, still suspended in the air, started lowering down to the post once again. As it got closer to its place, I wondered what all the fuss was about. The energy didn't seem that much different to me. I felt the same; and the vibrations were the same, and so were the light beams the same. Just as I saw the stone touch the post, I heard an explosion of music. Loud and just this side of noisy. A flash of light erupted from the azurite stone that had just settled into place, followed by flashes from the other stones as well. The erupting light flared like a ball all around me filling the space above and below me. It got brighter and brighter until it was so white I couldn't see anymore. My knees grew weak until I could no longer feel them and my head started to spin. In the brilliance of the light, seven more angels appeared around me just as I passed out.

I don't know how long I was unconscious, but I remember hearing Michael say, **"Teach only love."** When I heard this, I started to think again, and was able to start focusing my eyes. Something cool pressed against my legs and butt. Somehow, I had been moved to the stone bench about fifteen feet from the Matrix, and I found myself sitting on it. How I got there I don't know. As soon as I was able to get it together enough to walk, I wobbled into the house. On the coffee table was Gary's sketch of the Matrix and the information about the stones we had placed. After scrounging for a pencil I sat down to make the correction Michael had been so kind to show me.

CHURCH	HEIGHT	TONES		STONES	PLACEMENT
Philadelphia	7 in.	do	C	azurite (blue)	west
				blue aventurine	
				blue sapphire	
Pergamum	14 in.	re	D	yellow topaz	northwest
				yellow calcite	
				yellow sapphire	
Ephesus	21 in.	mi	E	orange calcite	northeast
				carnelian	
				orange sapphire	
Thyatira	24.5 in.	fa	F	amethyst (purple)	southwest
				benitoite	

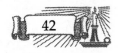

Smyrna	31.5 in.	so	G	ruby (red)	southeast
Sardis	38.5 in.	la	A	green kyanite green fluorite emerald	south
Laodicea	45.5 in.	ti	B	charoite (violet) violet calcite lavender jade	north
The Servant	7 in.	do	C	(same stone as Philadelphia)	east

Thus the Matrix now looked like so:

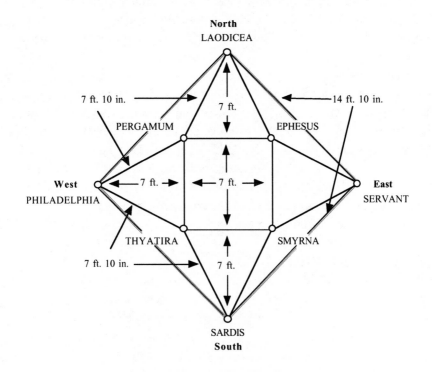

THE DEATH OF ANNIE

*T*wenty-four hours had passed since taking Annie to the vet. Spaying is a simple procedure for a six-year-old dog in good health who has never been sick. I had dropped her off on the way while taking my wife to the airport. We talked about Annie's neutering being the best thing for her since we never intended to breed her again. After finishing some shopping, I got home around one o'clock and called the vet to see if Annie had been operated on yet. The vet's wife told me Annie was coming out of the anesthesia and was waking up just fine. That Annie might be able to come home early. Someone in the office would call me as soon as "the patient" was ready to come home.

After hanging up, I decided to check my e-mail. Halfway through reading my messages the phone rang. "Joe, this is Kenny," the vet's voice said on the other end of the line. Gladness spread through me at the thought of picking Annie up so soon. "I'm sorry," he stuttered. Terror immediately scattered any joy. My mind would not allow me to conceive of what he was he was trying to say.

"Oh no, Kenny, don't tell me ..."

"I'm sorry," he said again. "She's gone." For a second I stood there in shock.

"I'll be right over," I said as I unconsciously dropped the receiver into the cradle. In a flash I was out the door, mumbling over and over to myself, *This can't be happening.* Jumping into my wife's jeep, I barreled down the driveway. As I approached the security gate, I noticed the gas gauge was leaning on empty. Hitting the breaks, I instinctively screamed, "Michael, dammit, you'd better do something!" I had always counted on my angelic friend in times of crisis. Panic filled me as I backed the jeep up next to my truck. The sun beat down on me as I mindlessly fumbled for the correct key. Like a man trapped in the desert, everything around me blurred as if life itself were a mirage. All that was happening to me had to be a mirage. Almost blindly I raced down the driveway clicking the remote repeatedly for the gate to open. An eternity passed as I waited for the sound of the squeaking hinges to stop. *Get a hold of yourself*, I thought. *You're no good to anyone this way. Plus you could kill someone on the highway. Get a grip.*

It was all I could do to stay close to the speed limit. As the miles buzzed by I tried to think of what I could possibly say to Donna. Annie was our delight, our favorite of the dogs. Donna would want to know exactly what happened and why. Her success as a corporate executive stemmed from her insistent attention to details. I had to get the facts as to what had happened so that sense could be made out of this travesty. The vet's office loomed into view, shaking me from my stupor.

As calmly as possible, I asked Kenny what had happened. Annie had done fine with the surgery and had done fine coming out of the anesthesia. But when he went to check all the animals before leaving for house calls, he found her lying in her cage not breathing. He had tried to bring her back, but with no luck.

"Can I see her?" I asked quietly. Kenny and his assistant led me to the back. Annie's body lay on the floor with a blanket draped over her from her shoulder down. She looked as if she were sleeping. God how I wished she were sleeping. "My poor little girl," I whispered to her as I knelt at her side. Pointing with his thumb, Kenny motioned to the assistant to join him as they left me alone with my beloved Annie. "I'm so sorry, I just thought it was the best thing for you." Like a grieving father I tried to tell her all the reasons or excuses for this happening to her. Whether it was more for her or for me, I couldn't tell you; I just felt like I owed it to her. How I wished I could take it all back as if it never

happened. "Please, Annie," I pleaded, "Come back to me! I love you so much." Her body still felt warm to my touch. *Maybe she can still come to life again*, I thought. *If Jesus could raise a dead man, maybe I can raise a dog. That's not asking for too much, is it? I would just say she came to, that she wasn't really dead after all. I won't tell anyone. If I could just have her back.* Using the healing techniques Michael had taught me, I began moving grace into her body. With all that was in me I tried to move as much grace as was humanly possible. But nothing happened. Again I tried and nothing happened. Tears flooded my eyes as choking filled my throat. Like a father weeping for a lost child, I wept with heaving sobs. My eyes could not see through the well of tears. Laying my head on Annie's shoulder, rubbing her soft fur with my face and hands, I wailed for my loss.

It's hard to tell how long I lay there, or all I said, but I could now feel the coldness of death creeping through her. I knew it was all over. She was gone. Saying good-bye to her, I made a promise. When it came my time to go home, I would have a Viking's funeral, with her as the dog at my feet. It was my way of honoring her. As I left the vet's office that day, I realized life as I knew it was over.

Last night I tried to sleep again with no luck. I woke up over and over thinking about Annie. *Enough is enough*, I said to myself. Getting up, I got dressed and headed out toward the back of the property where Michael had me set up the Matrix. Anger swelled in me. Annie was gone and I wanted some answers. All I could think about was how could this happen? Planting myself on my meditation stool resting in the middle of the geometric formation, I buried my face in my hands and started to cry again. "Annie, Annie," I said over and over again. "How could this have happened? I'm so sorry you are gone, and I miss you so much." Then I started to speak to Michael or God or whoever was in charge of this whole mess. Tears streamed down my face, and mucus flowed from my nose as I bawled like a baby again. Only this time I was pissed as I screamed through the tears, "Why would you let this happen? Didn't I do everything you asked of me? Didn't I let my work suffer to get done what you wanted? I don't ask for much, and haven't for years. If anything, you damn well owe me."

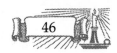

Like I said, I was mad about losing her, and someone needed to make it right. Then the sobbing erupted again, trying to wash away the pain. A hand touched my shoulder and a kind of peace filled me. I knew it was Michael. Jerking my shoulder away, I told him "This really sucks, you know. I thought you were on my side and would protect Donna and the dogs. No wonder you have so much trouble having someone want to throw in with you. Do this, do that, and give very little in return." I could feel Michael move from behind me to somewhere in front of me. I didn't want to look into those eyes of his unless he had an answer for me.

"Joe, what do you know of this?" were the first words out of his mouth. I looked up to see the beautiful angel I had seen so many times in the past standing there.

"Well, I know one thing for sure: It really hurts." He looked at me the way he always does — without blinking, with only compassion on his face. "Michael, I know that when it is time to come home, it is time. I know whatever we are doing or wherever we are, all that is around us will support us in going home when it is time. That's just the way it is; and I guess it was Annie's time to go home?"

"It was her time." I knew it was, and there was nothing I could have done to change it.

"But you should have told me. What good is having an angel if you can't help me out in times like this? You know. Prepare me."

"Joe, no one can know their time or that of others."

"Well, tell me one thing then. Would she have lived if we hadn't taken her to have her spayed?"

"Her time to come home was set. She came without a whimper as I folded her into my wings and brought her home.

"You came for her Michael?"

"As I will for you someday, and all of your family."

"I would have liked to have been with her when she left."

"She lives now in spirit. For as I have told you, she has a soul."

"Well, that's nice to know and all, but I would rather have had her here with me."

"Annie's time with you is done for now, and her time with me begins."

I watched as Michael stepped to the side and raised his hand in the light that usually foretells his coming. In the distance I could see

something moving toward us. No, it couldn't be ... but, yes, it was — trotting as she came into view. It was my Annie. Tears flooded my eyes again. She stopped at Michael's side and looked at me, turning her head as if trying to see why I was crying.

"She will be with me whenever I come to you, that you will know of God's love for you."

As he said that, she walked over in front of me and placed her chin on my knee as she always did. She looked up at me with those beautiful eyes I have stared into so many times — once again to see the love she held for me. Reaching down to pet her head, I could feel the smoothness of her fur again. Annie was the same loving dog I had always known but she seemed to be more majestic, more regal. "Michael how could you take her from me and Donna? It feels like we are being punished for something we did wrong."

"You have done nothing wrong, either of you. You know God does not cause pain to punish. Can you see the love God has for you in having her come with me? I was sent to bring her home, and she walks with me now. In the times to come, whenever I visit you, so will she. Many claim to see and speak with me, but only those that see Annie at my side are true in what they say. Here at my side she will be until it is time for her to return to you. Yet I tell you, when she returns it will be for a while, and you will feel the sting of her leaving again to come home."

"When she comes back? Do you mean to tell me she will be coming back to us as a puppy? That she will be alive again as a mastiff? How is this possible?"

"Yes Joe. Your Annie will be returned to you and Donna. She will walk with me till she does, for this is all of God's plan."

"Did you hear that Annie? You are going to come back to us," I said as I bent down to kiss her. She raised up her head and licked my face as if to tell me she knew this. "When Michael? When will I have her back?"

"You will know the time is close when you see her no more with me. She has been with you before and will be again as have the other 'children' you care for. Blessed are you that you are to have so many to love and be loved by. I tell you truly, when one of the 'children' come home they will return to you quickly. Each person is given a chance to care for 'children' such as these, yet many hold not the love for them as you and Donna."

"Michael. Donna wants to know why Annie died — like, what was the cause? Was it a heart attack, stroke or an aneurysm? She needs to know so she can make some sense out of it, just so she will know and can accept it."

"Joe, tell her there was nothing that caused it but for her time. She felt no pain. She saw me and came, leaving her body behind as you would leave a car to greet a friend. What you write down of this will help others to see of God's love for all things. Nothing is taken from you that does not come back in love. Animals have souls, too, that return to help your kind learn to love on the highest level. You will be getting more than Annie to care for. Tell Donna that Little Bob is even now on her way to you. Look for her coming. It will be soon and you will know her."

"Is she to be a mastiff too, or something else?"

"Mastiff. Come, Annie, our time is done for now."

Her tail wagged as she stood up to leave, grabbing my arm to pull me with her the way she did when she wanted me to go someplace. I could feel her teeth on my skin, just firm enough to hold but never hurt.

"No, Annie, he will not be coming with us now. We will be back in seven days to see him again."

"Michael," I said. "Thank you for letting me see her again. Can you have Donna see her too?"

"Not yet. She will see that Annie has come to visit her by the leaving of signs."

"I guess that will have to do."

With that, Annie walked to Michael, tail wagging, her head turning back to me. "Bye, Daddy," I heard her say, and then she was gone. *Holy shit!* I said to myself. She can talk.

THE GATE OF GRACE

*J*ust as Michael had promised, he returned once again with Annie by his side. After the two of them fully materialized, Michael raised his arm as if to say it was OK for Annie to come to me. While watching her approach me, Michael began to speak. **"I have work for you to do."**

"Well, I kind of figured you did. Thanks for bringing Annie with you."

"It is time for you to set God's Gate throughout the lands. This will make way for the sevens."

By now the number of gatherings of what I called "sevens" had increased by three. That meant, including the very first gathering, there were now twenty-eight souls who had come together in embracing their giftedness and the teachings from the angel. "OK. And just what might God's gate be?"

"You were given a way of setting stones that a gate of grace may be opened for healing and understanding."

"Oh, I see. You are talking about what we have been calling the 'Matrix,' made of stones."

"This is of what I speak."

It was a little hard for me to pay attention to Michael and be with Annie too. Even though I do honor Michael and the messages he brings,

my love for Annie and the heartbreak it caused me is still with me. I guess it was the real reason I was looking forward to seeing Michael again, and not to listen to anything new he may have to say. Like a butterfly, my attention went back and forth from one to the other. Annie's head rested on my knee as she lay on the ground next to me, looking up with those loving eyes.

"Joe. Hear what I am saying to you, for it is important that you do these things."

"OK. Tell me what you want me to do," I said trying not to get absorbed with Annie.

"God's Gate, which you call the stone Matrix, is to be set across the land."

"I heard you say that but just what do you mean by it? What good is it going to do to set these things up all over? Not like I won't do it. I am just asking."

"You do, as we speak, know the reason for this."

"OK. I see. I get to tell you what I think I know, and you tell me if it is so. Well, let me guess. I know the Matrix is for creating a stable ball of grace, so to speak, for healing and to open lines of communication with angels for guidance." Whenever Michael would show up in the Matrix, the colored beams of light from stone to stone would create two rotating pyramids of light, one upside down intersecting the other. These pyramids rotated, one clockwise, the other counterclockwise. As they rotated, a ball of light, roughly ten feet in diameter, would appear in the middle. This ball of light I call the "ball of grace," for I can feel the essence of God's love, or grace, emanating from it. "Now let me tell you what I have noticed in my matrix. Every time others have set one up, I can feel an ever so slight shift in the energy field. Not like stronger, but purer would be the best way to describe it."

"It would."

"What I think you are getting at is that by setting up more of these gates that bring through grace, there will be a shift on a greater scale with the whole field. As more and more of these Gates of Grace are set up, they will somehow link together to create some kind of unified field between them that will allow something to happen."

"Again you know that which I have not told you."

"I want you to know I don't mind doing what you ask, but I don't know how I would go about it."

"You will find a way."

"Oh, I am sure I will. Back to what you are saying about opening the way for the sevens. I get that it means once enough of these gates are set up, it will be easier for groups of seven to come together?"

"You see why you are the right man for the job now?"

"Yeah. I guess so. I just keep coming up with the answers before you tell me. Oh lucky me. Now I have people set up the stone Gates of Grace and it will make it easier to gather the masters for the soul matrix?"

"This is so, yet you call it by what it is not"

"OK. So what is it then? If it is not a matrix of souls what should I call it?"

"The Well of Souls."

"Wow. Now that's cool. The 'Well of Souls.' Has a nice ring to it, don't you think?"

"Not that you would hear with your ears."

"Hear with my ears huh? I ain't even going to start to touch that one, for I think I know where this would go if I did."

"Yes, you know this and more."

"So tell me, why is it called the Well of Souls? It sounds like something deep and dark that you fall into. Has a little bit of a scary sound to it."

"Is a well scary to those that thirst? Does it not hold the water of life in it? Does it not refresh the body to drink of it?"

"OK. OK. You've made your point. Now let me tell you what it means to me. First thing that comes to mind with me is the well part. There is a structure made around the source of the water to draw from. That would be the seven masters of each church forming the pattern you gave me for that. Once they are set in place, each may drink from the well and receive what they thirst for. Once they have been filled, they in turn go out and build another well for others."

"You say it as it is. The Gate is needed to bring about the gathering of masters quicker. That which was lost must be returned, that humankind will know the love of God."

"Well, I am doing the best I can."

"As are others. Is there more you would know?"

"I don't think so. Besides, you probably wouldn't tell me if there was. You like for me to learn for myself. You want me to get Gates set up all

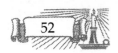

over, using the stones of each church. But there is just one thing you didn't mention. The stones cost money, and everybody doesn't have the funds or a place to get the stones close by. So just how do I do this?"

"You will find a way."

"That's just fine. But I will tell you one thing. It ain't coming out of my pocket."

"It was not asked of you, nor should it."

"Well then, I will come up with something so people can get the things they need. Why do I get the feeling you are saving something? OK, Michael, drop the big one. What else do you have under your robe that you haven't told me?" I really didn't want to ask because I just knew he was going to give me something really hard to do along with the building of more Gates. Michael looked at me as if knowing what I was going to say. He had that look he gets when he knows I am going ballistic. I braced myself for the worst.

"You are to build a hall for healing and learning."

"A hall? You mean like a center don't you? I thought you told me this wasn't about building temples. Sounds that way to me."

"It is not. It is for all of God's children, and matters not what religion they serve. This is to serve God's children, not to be served by them."

"I hope you don't want it yesterday. I have no idea how I will do this or where the money will come from, but this ain't coming out of my pocket either. You know what Michael? This is beginning to sound like the 'gimmie gang' all over again. Didn't the religions do something like this before?"

"Not like this. In the past it was taken from God's children, yet this time it will be given freely. Before, it came from those that belonged to a religion for that religion. This time it is to be for all."

"Well it will be interesting to see how you pull this off."

"Our time is done for now. We will speak again."

Annie stood up, so I knew it was time to say good-bye to them. She walked back to Michael after giving me a kiss with her wet tongue, the way she used to. I didn't feel so bad about her leaving this time nor was I saddened by it.

"Joe, you need sleep. You need to rest your mind. So, you will not remember this for four days. Teach only love."

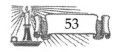

With that they faded back into the light and were gone. The office was as it was before.

THE HALLS OF HEALING

W hat strikes me as amazing is how seemingly unrelated events end up connecting ordinary reality with the emerging angelic messages. More than once has an appearance by Michael tied into what was going on in my personal life or what was about to happen in my personal life. I was out working on the Gate of Grace to clean up what the lawn mower had blown in. Not so much because it would effect the Gate but because it just looked bad. After setting the rake down with the other tools, I walked away until I heard my name being called. Turning around, I saw Michael and of course my Annie. As I headed back toward them, Annie leapt out from the center and ran to greet me. Her tail was wagging with happiness. I knelt down to gather her up in my arms as I used to do so many times before. Her soft fur covering her powerful frame gave me a sense of safety as I hugged her, her lick-kisses washing my face like a wet hand towel. She was always a playful dog, wiggling and nudging me to let me know she wanted to play. Annie had one habit she kept even when she went with Michael. She would grab my arm in her mouth and take me where she wanted me to go. Like a kid tugging a parent to a candy store window, she pulled me toward the Gate where Michael was standing. As I looked up at Michael he raised his hand for me to stop.

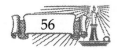

"Enter not," was all he said.

The angel then glided toward me, and the brilliant light of the ball of grace began to grow at the center of what he had called the Gate of Grace. He stood next to me and I could feel the peace and love emanating from him. He pointed to the ball, and as it started to take shape I could see it changing into a globe. On it I could see the outline of what I knew to be North America, and thought this is going to be interesting. Land masses appeared on the glowing globe, displaying the clear relief of mountains and plains.

"This is where the halls of healing and enlightenment will be," he said.

"Halls? Halls? I thought you said I was to build one. Halls mean more than one to me, Michael."

"It does mean that."

"Why did I think you would let me get by with one?" Looking back to the globe, I noticed what looked like dots of light beginning to shine at different spots across the land. The one in the place where Texas was I knew to be San Antonio, and that was no surprise. Then I started to look and saw places I kind of knew the location of. Coming from Missouri, I saw what looked like one of the halls in St. Louis. "Is one to be in St. Louis, Michael?"

"Yes, this is so. One will be in what you call Tennessee, Minnesota, Colorado, New Mexico, and Montana."

I looked down and said, "See, Annie, what happens to someone when they answer an angel calling their name?" I should tell you that when Gary heard about the halls of healing and the seven different locations, he started asking me a lot of questions as to where the other cities within each state might be. Because I could remember where the shining lights had been located within the outline of each state, Gary peppered me for visual references. For instance, was the city in Montana near the area of the state that looks like a nose on a face? And with the answers I provided, he was able to determine that the other cities were the following: In Montana, it was the Missoula/Hamilton area; in Colorado, the Boulder/Denver area; in New Mexico, the Santa Fe area; in Minnesota, the Minneapolis/St. Paul area; and in Tennessee the Knoxville area.

"This is not beyond you and the things that are asked. Yet you are not the one to who will do this work. Others will come to do the

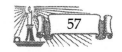

work that is not done yet. Some of the halls are standing now waiting for the Gatekeepers."

I had heard Gary use the word "gatekeeper" before. But that had to do with African shamanism. I wondered why the angelic realm would be using such a word. "Seems to me a gatekeeper is someone that only lets in those who are invited. They bar the way of everyone else."

"The keepers of these Gates are there to have them open to all. They stand as a beacon of hope for those that have none."

"I see now what you are saying. The Gatekeepers are there to make sure none are turned away. That the halls are for everyone, and no one will be denied entry to God's grace."

"You speak truth. Give what I have shown you to your sevens and they to theirs. Those who are called to be the Gatekeepers will know."

"So you are telling me I don't need to do all this myself?"

"Joe, you would like to think you are the only one that is up to the task. Yet you are only the starting place for those that would do the work. I give to you, and you give to others and they to others."

"Well, Michael, this is some good news to me because I don't see how I could get it all done. I have a lot on my plate, so to speak, and am doing the best I can."

"This is why you were called. You are to take another direction for the teaching you do, and have little time for the halls. I will be giving you what you will write in the *Book of Healing* you will bring to the world. This is not new to you, for you have started to know and to teach this even now."

"Well bless my heart," I said jokingly.

"And a brick is made," was Michael's reply.

"I have something to ask you, Michael, about the stones we use." There had been some discussion among the sevens about what exact stones could and could not be used. He looked at me as he does just before I answer him with the answer I seek. "OK I get it. You want me to tell you what I know, and then you will tell me if I speak the truth of it. One of my seven said if you didn't have a stone, you could rub it on a clear crystal and it would pick up the energy and you could use that one in place of the stones I gave them to use. Is this true?"

"No. What you were given to use as the stones for the seven, are what you will use. When a stone other than the one that is to be used

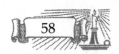

is substituted, it, too, will give off energy. All stones do this. Yet it is not of the seven, and will not open the Gate of Grace. As the false truth of God's love was given by religion, so will this stone give you false energy. You may well indeed feel that you are in the Gate of Grace, yet you are not."

"I see it is important that we use the correct stones then. Can I tell you what I say are the correct stones, and you tell me if I am correct?"

"Yes," he said in a no-nonsense kind of way.

"OK. Here goes. For the church of Smyrna, it is a ruby — jewel or crystal — and red aventurine."

"Not red aventurine."

"I thought you said we could use aventurine?"

"I said blue aventurine for the church of Philadelphia."

"Blue sapphire, I thought you said. Not red aventurine. OK. So I will change it. Ruby is the only one then—jewel or crystal—that is OK then?" I knew the tendencies of the sevens to experiment with the information we were given. And, in all fairness, Michael had encouraged all of us to use our intuition when taking the information forward into the world. And at the same time, the angel was always careful to let me or the sevens know when we had taken a wrong turn.

"Yes."

"Next, the church of Ephesus works with orange calcite or sapphire. Is that correct?"

"Yes, and you were told one other."

"OK, refresh my memory."

"Carnelian is what your kind call it."

"Yeah. Now I remember it. Then for Pergamum: yellow sapphire or yellow topaz or yellow calcite. (He said nothing so I guessed it was correct.) For Sardis there is emerald, green kyanite or green fluorite." And again no comment from him. "Then comes the blue stones for Philadelphia. What I have is blue sapphire or azurite."

"And blue aventurine."

That was what he added, so I guessed this is the one I mixed up with red. "Then comes the purple stones for the church of Thyatira, which is amethyst or benitoite." Again, no answer, so I went on to Laodicea, which is lavender jade, violet calcite or charoite. "That's what I have for each church."

"You have the stones to open the Gate."

It was not lost on me how my physically cleaning up the lawn clippings in the Gate seemed related to the cleaning up of the information on how to correctly open the Gate. Looking back at the globe I could see what looked like all the seven stones at each of the places Michael had said to place the Halls. I could see others starting to form in other places all over the globe and asked, "Michael, what are all the others that I see? Do I need to set up halls there?"

"No, Joe. They will come to pass. You will not be the one to do this."

"Cool. I like that someone else will be doing it other than me. Oh, yes, one more thing. Donna said that I shouldn't sell the stones but tell people how to get them and let them do it."

"As the gift, one seventh is yours. Those who would sell the stones will return it to you."

"Oh, wow. You mean I get to make some money in this?"

"You will be told what to do with the seventh you are given."

"It figures. I knew it was too good to be true that I could make some bucks."

"Our time is at an end for now. Yet when we speak again, we will start the *Book of Healing*."

Annie got up from my side, where she was sitting, and headed back to the Gate with Michael. I called after him, "Hey Michael what about the book with Gary? What about it?" Gary and I had been having a terrible time getting a publisher to take a look at *On the Wings of Heaven*. We both had been wondering if there was something wrong with the writing or the make-up of the book for there to be so much difficulty.

"It is done," he said as he and Annie faded into the light that had brought them and the globe, too. I could still see the ball of grace even after they left. In fact its light is there all the time now.

THE APPEARANCE
OF THE SHEKINAH

*T*he phenomenon of the sevens not only shows those involved the best they possess, it also allows them to see even their darkest shadows. Part of the reason for that is so we will eventually be able to give up judging ourselves, and in turn others. Then we can see that we are beings of the Divine, here to have experiences. What is most important is that we learn from those experiences. It's why Michael taught the sevens early on that we are perfect, whole, and complete just the way we are. Unfortunately, I am no exception to being human. There are times when I feel I've screwed up, or gotten away from the path that brought me this far. And this was one of those times. Some stupid choices were made that caused me and several of the sevens to be tested more than ever before. My nights were filled with self-doubt, and I feared I might have cast doubt upon the teachings because of my own actions.

My heart was so troubled one day that I grabbed my meditation stool and headed for the center of the Gateway. As I sat there, the breeze quieted immediately and the air cooled. I hoped this meant what I thought it meant. The smell of roses surrounded me as I heard the familiar voice of Michael. Turning in the direction of the voice, I saw my angel companion standing there as big as life. Like a penitent child, I poured my

heart out to him over all that troubled me. He stood there oozing patience while I rambled.

When I finally ceased, he asked, **"What is it that you do?"**

"Michael, what are you talking about? What are you trying to say? Are all the sevens out of line, or is it the book that's the problem, or is it me?"

"Joe, all of you are in your traps. Only one of your seven has gathered his seven. Like your seven, they lay sleeping, though awake. They all think that what they are to do will be done when the time is right. They hide in all they are not, like needy children waiting for you, Gary, me, or an act of God to save them from themselves. Traps within traps. Yet none of you sees that you are the ones setting them. After the Seven entered the pattern I had you set them in — that of the church they are — they wanted to go back to that which they already knew to do their work. Which is the first trap they set. And when their old ways failed them, they fell into the traps that each church is."

When Michael had told me to give messages to the Seven at the gathering, he presented me with information about the gifts and traps each carried. These gifts and these traps were the same gifts and the same traps the original seven churches of Asia Minor possessed. Each of the Seven had the choice of living in their gifts or living in their traps. There was no judgment either way. We all have that choice. In *On the Wings of Heaven* and *Teaching the Masters*, the gifts and traps of each archetypal church are listed.

"So what you are telling us is that me and the sevens are all lost in the 'how-to,' so to speak?"

"No, they are blind to the work. All they need is to be the gifts they are."

"And I myself am in a trap because I have done nothing to help them out of their traps."

"Your fear comes from not wanting to push them or seem like you are telling them what to do. Your fear comes from thinking you would rule them. Yet this is not of you."

"You may have a point there, and I can see what you are saying to me. I want them to know how great each of them is by finding the way that works for them. If I start telling them what to do, I am no better than what has always been throughout religious history. I become some kind of leader or guru, and they answer to me for what they do or do not do."

"It is in that where your trap holds you. You are not to tell but to show the way for them."

Michael then showed me the Matrix the way it is with the people in it rather than the stones. One of my seven took the place of a stone and then one of Gary's did, fading in and out of each other. Each one became the other seven, and one at a time they took their place in the Formation of Giving and Receiving. I watched as each was changed somehow as they took turns standing in the middle of the pattern. I could see how each had a strand of spiritual light turned on within their bodies. The strand spiraled up their bodies like a helix made up of tiny matrices, allowing each person to become more than they were when they first arrived. I saw the way the sevens were all linked together like one big matrix. Then I saw all of the first seven gathering their own sevens, and each walked away from the Matrix. But each became like a walking Matrix, a living Gate of Grace. Then Gary's seven did the same and my second seven did it too. As each group became complete at a gathering of seven, every one became a living Matrix, each with a ball of light around them. I saw as they walked past people, their mere presence changing the people around them. I saw sevens adding to sevens and then to other sevens, and as they grew I could see something new. The Earth had a kind of fog all over it. Then, as the groups gathered more upon more, the fog was replaced with light, and all was clean and clear. I could see the energy of the Earth and her people shift with each completion of a new group. I could see the love that is God made clear so all knew of this love.

Michael did not speak. He just let me see this, and then it stopped. Everything in the back yard was as it was before this vision.

"Do you see the greatness of all?" Which I certainly did. **"It is time to say to the sevens that the time is at hand. Go forth and be the gifts that you are. Gather your sevens and teach only love. Blessed are you in the sight of God, and in doing these things, blessed you will be in the sight of man. Follow what is given in the 'Book of Bricks' and teach it, and you will become tillers of souls. Give what I have given you to the sevens so they may grow. Teach only love."**

With that he was gone.

I stood there for quite a while pondering, over all I had witnessed and had been told. My personal troubles paled in the light of what I had seen. But how could I show the sevens the way out of their traps when I was

having problems with my own? And what really made me pause was the good-news/bad-news thing. The good news is that we have all come far on our path. The bad news is that we have come too far to ever go back. It was obvious that many of the sevens wanted their lives to return to the mundane and the ordinary. But you cannot put the genie (or the angel) back in the bottle. How could I tell the sevens this? Maybe the only way was for me to get out of my own traps. Show them.

The days turned into weeks as I worked on all this. Many conversations sizzled back and forth over the Internet. I had just finished chatting online and was on my way to bed. Walking out of the office, I headed through the living room to turn off the lights in the kitchen. While peering out the patio door, as I often did, I saw the light from the pump house reflecting off the water tank and trees around it. Or was it? I don't know why I always look in that direction. Perhaps it's because that's where the Gate of Grace sits. I guess I'm half hoping to see Michael out there. Five months had passed since the last time he appeared, and to be honest, it was starting to worry me that he'd been gone for so long. Was it because of my actions? Was I still in my traps?

This time as I gazed through the glass, I could see a light beyond the pump house and my heart skipped a beat. Could it be that he was back, or was it just the moon? I had felt like something was going to happen for the last few days. Taking a second look, I saw a ball of light coming from the center of the Gate. *OK, Joe, it looks like it's show time,* I said to myself. Grabbing a jacket, I headed out the door and walked toward the light with anticipation.

The night air nipped at me, the temperature hanging somewhere in the low twenties. I was glad I had brought my jacket, and decided to put it on. The closer I got to the Gate, the brighter the ball of light became. I walked through the herb garden Donna had planted over the summer, half-looking at the stone path I was on. As I approached the Gate from the north side, I still couldn't see anyone in or around the ball of light. "Michael," I whispered as I looked for the angel I had seen so many times before. Stopping at the charoite stone that represented Laodicea, I just stood there staring into the light. *Where the hell is he and, what does he want?* I asked myself. The warmth emanating from the center of the Gate of Grace was palpable as its light poured forth. *Well, if it's warm in there, then that's where I should be,* I reasoned. Walking into the center, I

noticed it was actually as warm as springtime there. Coming to a halt, I paused, then retreated a few steps just to check if it was as cold outside the Gate as it was before. Yep, it was still in the twenties. I walked back into the center and waited with growing excitement to see what was going to occur next.

Quite a length of time passed without anything happening. "Michael?" I called out again. My attention was drawn to the south end of the Gate. Staring at the emerald stone, I noticed it started to glow with the most wonderful greenish light. A wave of peacefulness washed over me just like when Michael was present. The emerald shone like a small sun, getting brighter by the second. *Wow. Something new has been added to the coming of Michael.* Unfolding from the light was a figure dressed in white. "Well, Michael, you have sure taken your time ..." I cut my words short, for this was not Michael at all. This was someone else! The eyes were as green as the sea and as sparkling as a jewel. Soft and loving were those eyes, and they seemed to know something I could only begin to understand. Looking at the beautiful face, I saw luminous red shoulder-length hair. Past experience taught me not to be fooled by what you think you see, when it comes to an angel. Just because it looked female didn't mean it was. Michael was just as beautiful, but was male. I studied the features of this new angel. They were so much softer than Michael's. *Something's wrong with this picture,* I thought to myself.

"Joseph." The voice was definitely female. I wasn't sure if it was the shock of hearing a woman's voice or the beauty of the sound it made, but I stood there stunned.

"Wait a minute, you are a female angel aren't you? You are even built like one." It was obvious that this angel was feminine by the way the robe covered her body. Yet make no mistake; the soft female body under the cloth was one of great power. I felt she could snap the oak tree behind her like a twig if she was so inclined.

"Yes. To your way of thinking, I am." The sound of her words caressed my soul as if being told the girl of my dreams loved me. Soft and gentle, the tone of her voice was full of love. I was even surprised to hear her talk like a regular person. Not at all like Michael did when he first came to me.

"So, to what do I owe this honor?" I addressed her respectfully.

"I, like Michael, have come to teach you of the things you must know and remember. It is time for you to know of the healing of your kind."

Oh, I knew what was coming. "I thought Michael was the one to do that with me."

"No, he was to bring you to a place of understanding. You have grown much since he first came to you."

"Well, thanks. It hasn't been easy or fun these past years."

"Yet, you have done well." It felt good to hear that all the crap I have been through wasn't a waste.

"So, where are we going to go with all this?" was my next question.

"You have learned much and have remembered more. Yet there is much more to learn."

"I guess that's where you come in, isn't it?"

"For some things I will teach you, and for other things you have two women to help you."

"Well, that's all I need, two more women in my life! Given I have a wife and most of the sevens are women, don't you think you guys could have picked a man here to help me out?" Then she did something I have never seen Michael do. She smiled. Not a big smile, like something was funny, but more like the kind of a smile a mother gives a child. It was the smile of understanding and compassion that warmed the heart.

"Joseph, the ones that are to help you with what you are to know have chosen to be here for this. It has nothing to do with male or female."

"OK, OK. Go on with what's next," I requested apologetically.

"I will visit you in the days to come and you will learn many things to help your kind, yet there are women who will carry these to the world."

"Well I know a few men who won't be too happy with this. Aren't there any males around that can do whatever it is you are giving me to teach?"

"Yes, there are and they will come and learn from you and others."

"Cool. Before we get into this I have a few things to ask you." I thought that since I had a captive audience, I'd try to get some more needed answers. "What about the book Gary and I are trying to get out?

We haven't had too much luck with it as of yet. As a matter of fact there has been one failure after another, if you know what I mean."

"You haven't even gotten it ready for the world. Your work must be done first with it, and then your book will do well."

"Gary is going to love to hear that."

"The work you two have labored over is close to finished and it has happened in a blink of the eye of time."

"That may be, but I can blink faster than that. What's taking so long?"

"You have learned to speak in a way that people hear your words. You have lost the need to make someone listen to you. You now teach with the love to open minds to the love that God is."

"Well good for me."

"Yes Joseph, it is."

"That's another thing. Why do you call me Joseph when Michael calls me Joe? Oh, it just occurred to me, you know my name, but I don't know yours. I know I can't pronounce it, but give it a shot will you?"

"I call you Joseph because that's who you are. However, if you wish, I will call you as you wish. My name is ___." And she spoke that wondrous collection of sounds mixed with colors and feelings just like Michael did when he first appeared. Her name was unpronounceable yet as beautiful as his.

"Is this the part where I call you whatever I want? I called Michael 'Michael,' and that started a bunch of stuff till later down the road when we got it straightened out that that's who he was. So, it would be helpful if you had a name that you could be known to us by."

"Shekinah is what I am called by your kind. You will know it when you see it. My name can be found in your books of angels. Yet as Michael has told you before, do you think Gabriel is really the name he is? Now you must rest and we will speak again."

"One more thing before you go." I needed some more information. "These two women that are to help me with this, when will I meet them?"

"You know them. Teach only Love."

"Hang on a minute," was all I managed to get out as she folded back into the light. I hate it when they do that. Leave before I get the answer to my question. *Well, here we go again, only this time I have two angels talking to me!* Heading back to the house, my mind was running a

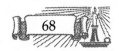

hundred miles an hour. I knew I needed to write down what had just happened. *Donna is going to love this,* I thought. She'll have all kinds of questions and I have no idea what to tell her. Passing through the herb garden, I glanced over my shoulder to see the ball of light in the Gate fade. As I walked back to the house I could feel the cold start to close in on me.

As the days passed, the e-mail across the Internet continued to grow more and more troublesome. Though I had wanted to hide the messes I had created after last talking to Michael about the gifts and traps, there is no way of keeping secrets from the sevens. They are like a living community of souls. Some are psychic, some are intuitive beyond measure, and still others have ways of getting information that would make the CIA jealous. Before I knew it, a veritable war of words had exploded. One night, while chatting online with one of the sevens I noticed a light coming from within the house. Immediately I signed off. As I walked out of my office and down the hall, I could see the brightness growing in the living room.

"Joe." That was all I heard.

"Michael, is that really you?" It was the sound of his voice, and, frankly, I could have used some comfort about then.

"Come," was all Michael said as he headed toward the back patio and right through the glass door. Once again he had dematerialized part of the fence for me to pass through. I followed him toward the Gate of Grace, watching how his light lit up the area.

There was excitement in my heart on two counts. One, because I needed to talk to the Big Guy, and two, because I couldn't escape the feeling that I had screwed up, and wanted to see what was going to happen because of it. I crossed the driveway following toward the Gate of Grace lying next to the trees. Like a child I went trotting behind the angel to find out if I was to be sentenced for something. He stopped in the middle of the Gate and waited for me to come in. His face hadn't changed since the last time I saw him — still the same grandeur in his appearance and the love and peace in his eyes. I felt for the first time in a long time that I was at home with a friend.

"Boy, do I need to talk to you," I said. "I would like to tell you all about the things that have gone on but you already know that. I am just at a loss as to what to do about all of this."

"It is so, that you would be. Much has happened in the time we have not spoken. I have work for you."

"Excuse me. You have work for me? What about all that has happened? Don't you want to talk about it?"

"No," was the only word he said.

"No? What do you mean, 'No'? I am in a lot of trouble here. I just pissed everyone off at me, and the ones I didn't, I hurt. Now you tell me, 'No'? I have some of the Seven telling me that I shouldn't be doing any of the work because I am out of integrity. I need to heal myself before I can move on. It was my ego that got in the way of all this."

"Joe, you are not lost to the work I have given you. You have sums to work, as do all the Seven. Did you think you would be free of this?"

"Well, I did think you would come and help me out when I needed it, if I got away from the path I said I would take."

"No one has stayed on the path. Yet you are angry with yourself for this. Did you have anger for those that did not follow the path?"

"No. Why should I?"

"You should not, for them nor yourself."

"But Michael, do you know all that I have done?"

"Yes, and other things you did not do."

"Yeah. Like doing the work."

"No. The things you did not do would have taken you out of the work."

"Just what are you talking about? The things I didn't do?"

"You lost faith in you and became ensnared in your traps. You think you have lost your covenant with us and you have become unworthy to serve? This is one of the traps you fall into. You listen to the lies that others tell."

"Well, I did do some rather bad things."

"Your kind will not be done with this talk of good and bad, right and wrong. Have you forgotten of this when we spoke of it before?"

"I guess maybe I have."

"Has no one read the words from the book I gave you? Has all been given for not? Do you use it to judge one another and yourself after I told you to do this not?"

"I think I get your point, Michael. Sometimes I forget but I need to

know what I should do to make things right." He gazed at me as a father would look at his child who hadn't heard a word of what was said. It was almost comical the way he looked at me but I didn't think I should laugh, even if it was partly at myself. "I know I said the 'right' word again."

"It is as it is. What is done is done. I have not come to play the games your kind does. I tell you this truly: If you or the seven masters wish not to do this work we can find others who will be about what we have given. You knew something was about to come to pass. You spoke of it and were visited by one that would teach you. In the time to come, you will be given things you must do and teach."

"Well, I am on shaky ground with some people, and I don't know what they will say about this."

"Some will hear and some will choose to not hear. This is the year — as you measure time — for the work to grow. Your kind is ready to reach another level and some will come now and some later. Some will not for many years."

His words pricked my ears, for 1999 had already started out in memorable fashion. "So Michael, what do I do? Do I step back from this till I am healed?"

"Joe, the only illness you have is that of working your sums. I have given you work to do and things to teach. This you must do. If you wish to stop, it is you who will decide. Our time is done. I will return with the other and teach you of things soon. Remember: Teach only love."

He stepped into his own light and was gone. I walked back to the house and found the fence was as it was before. At least Michael could have left it open till I got back inside. I felt emotionally exhausted. The only thing I could think of was going to bed.

As the next couple of weeks progressed, all, including me, continued to work out their sums, as Michael likes to put it. It was one of the most difficult times of my life. I suppose I ought to say a few words about "sums." Even in the first book, "sums" was a word used often when it came to the sevens. Some people might use the word "karma," or others "shoveling our shit." Whether using profane or sublime words, it all means we have to face the consequences of our actions if we are not able to forgive ourselves and one another. Even though Michael insisted that all of us are "perfect, whole, and complete" just the way we are, our consciousness, our illusions, want us to believe otherwise. Life is a

school, or life is a stage; whichever way you want to look at it, we choose to have experiences. But why? Why would we bring such misery upon ourselves? There can only be one answer: ego. We choose to see ourselves as islands or individuals incapable of understanding or being understood by life around us. To this day, I struggle with the limitations I impose upon myself. And to this day, I speak with hope that all of us will eventually give up these figments of struggle, allowing ourselves to see the love we truly are, allowing ourselves to see the love that surrounds us.

Though I feel this way now, in the days that followed Michael's last appearance, there was trouble in Paradise. My friends, my wife, the sevens, all entered into their "sums." And only now can I recognize that this is the same stuff wars are made of.

During one of those sleepless nights, came one of the more profound lessons of my life. As I sat in the office staring at the ceiling, the circle of light started its process of blazing. I wasn't sure whether I was glad Michael was appearing or not. **"Time for you to come with me."** Michael moved out through the office door and down the hall. I got up from my chair and followed him into the living room. Through the patio door he went again. Opening the door, I followed with slight trepidation. *What does he have in store for me this time?* The last time we talked, Michael had said he would come with another to teach me. I hate to admit it, but I do worry when he has something new to give me. When he showed me *Revelations*, I saw more than I really wanted to see. Keeping pace with Michael, we walked to the Gate. I could see the ball of grace shining brightly. It looked almost like a solid sphere of liquid. Moving to the east corner of the Gate, the place of the servant's stone, Michael stopped. I followed and stood by his side. Taking a deep breath I waited, wondering what was to come next.

"You have grown in wisdom and in love. You have learned to heal though you wanted it not. You have kept what I have given you, though in doubt. You have been judged and have judged not. You have stumbled and have fallen not. You have been tempted by greatness and have remained humble. You have kept in balance the humanness and the divine in you. You have kept faith when all seemed lost."

I was starting to feel like someone being honored for something they didn't do. Compliments are something I don't take too well and never

have. A simple "Good job" would have done me just fine. This was getting embarrassing. Looking at Michael, I blurted out, "Enough is enough already. Besides, if I was all that good at this, more should have been done with the work that you gave me to do."

He turned to look at me and simply said, **"Take off your shoes for you will stand on holy ground."** *Oh great, here we go again,* was what I thought as my stomach started to churn. **"Behold,"** was all Michael uttered as he raised his hand and pointed into the Gate. Turning my head, I fixed my gaze at the center. All the stones began to glow with a wondrous light. Each stone shimmered as if it was water but remained solid. Something started to take shape in the middle of the ball of grace. As the light grew, a form started to appear. It was the same angel I had seen before, rising out of the light. This was the one called Shekinah. Not knowing much about her, I stood there wondering what was going to happen. For an angel, there wasn't much about Shekinah in any of the books I researched. All I could find on her was that Shekinah was the female part of creation. There was something about her that meant "indwelling," but all in all, it was rather ambiguous. As I focused on the ball of grace, I could see Shekinah begin to rise, and I looked up to see her face complete with those beautiful green eyes. Her head had risen to just below the branch of the tree that hangs over the Gate. It occurred to me that she was almost twice as tall as Michael. My eyes started to wander downwards, and I realized she was off the ground. The light from the other stones shone as big and bright as the ball of grace itself — like balls within balls, connected but not connected. Michael was actually swallowed up by the ball he was standing by. Every sphere was about ten feet high and I could see a figure in each one. All of a sudden, the balls just disappeared and an angel stood fully materialized where each ball had been.

What do nine angels have to do with all of this? I was thinking. I began to take notice of the angels one by one. Knowing that the one called Shekinah came from the green stone last time, my attention went there first. I saw a male angel standing there now, and wondered how many angels could come from that stone or place in the Gate. As I studied his features, I could see that he looked like an Indian or Pakistani. Very masculine, but with the same beauty as Michael and Shekinah. They all looked alike but profoundly different. Each had a glow of light, the color

of the stones they were standing by. I saw other male-looking angels and female ones, too. At the place of Smyrna (red), Ephesus (orange) and Laodicea (violet), the feminine angels stood. The other angels were male in appearance. Each angel's countenance reflected another nationality — just like the ones I saw when Michael took me through the visions of *Revelations. Is there some connection here?* I wondered. *There must be.* My sight went back to the angel in the center, and as I looked at her I said to Michael, "How come she didn't come from the green stone's place?"

"Shekinah comes from all."

"Oh. Maybe it just had to do with where I was standing last time. Come to think of it all of the stones did start to glow this time. So where do we go from here?" I asked, but not really wanting to know. As I stood there, I could see something beginning to happen, like vibrations emanating from each, resembling sound waves or even heat waves. Very slowly each angel started to move to the center toward Shekinah. An involuntary sense of fear crept into me as I wondered what was going to happen. All of the colors were coming together. Michael stayed a little behind the rest as they moved into the center. I could see them blend together and start to become one. The light from each began blending into one color now — a whitish or clear light. Their combined essences shimmered like silver fire, filling me with awe.

"Stand where I stand," were Michael's words to me. With my shoes off, I could feel the softness of the ground under my feet. I wondered if I should have taken off my socks and come in barefoot. Stepping into the outer edge of the Matrix, I watched Michael move toward the angel or angels that were now Shekinah. Michael's voice interrupted my thoughts with a warning: **"Cover your eyes."** The last thing I saw before doing so was Michael's stepping into the one called Shekinah. I could see the light flare more intensely and start to turn a yellowish-gold. Bringing my left hand up to my face, I turned to my right, looking down and away to shield myself. I could see the group disappear in the brilliance of light emanating from the center of the Gate. *Is this what a nuclear blast is like?* I thought. *Am I about to be blown away?*

I started to feel a cold yet warm radiance against my skin, the palm of my hand, forearm, and the parts of my face, which were not covered. It didn't hurt; it just felt funny, like strange. It felt like I was being pushed back a little, too, though I know I didn't move from where I stood. After a

while, the ground came back into view and I could see the blades of grass. They wore a gold tint that seemed to be on everything. The intensity of the light began to fade. Since I determined it was all right to look around, I dropped my hand and turned slowly. Raising my head, I closed my eyes, not knowing if I should stare at the source of the light. Then I heard Michael's voice, yet it wasn't his voice. I could hear the love in it as I always did. I could feel it in the vibrations as it moved through my body.

"Behold the love we are. Behold the love I am." I did as I was told. My eyes opened to see the greatest love and peace of all times. Its immensity swept over me, through me, into my heart and brain, and touched my very soul. Such a love I have never known, and such a peace I have never found. So much was my awe that I felt I could never humble myself enough in the presence of this magnificent composite being. My mind raced to do the right thing, and I could feel my knees buckle a little. Frankly, I didn't even know if I could stand, feeling as weak as I did. I found myself starting to drop and ended on one knee. As I did, I heard the voice call me again. **"This you must not do. Nor shall any of your kind to us. You have been told this before. Do it no more."**

Quickly I got to my feet and stood at attention as a soldier would for his commanding officer. I did this out of respect for whatever I stood in front of. "I am yours to command in all things," I said.

"I am not come to command you. I am come to give you gifts and to give gifts to others."

"OK," I said, not knowing what he/she or they were talking about.

"The gifts are to heal your kind and the world in which you live. Your kind has suffered for too long. You will be given gifts to bring you all into the light of love. Wholeness will be with all. We will be with you and others to bring this to pass."

"What do you want me to do? Receive that which is given and give it out? I will do as you ask. How do I give it out? I mean give it to the sevens, and they to others?"

"Joe, you teach that which you have been given. Others will be visited and shown what they will teach. I am come to you to show you that which you do is blessed. Be the gifts you are and listen not to the lies of others. They truly know not what they speak."

"I understand what you are saying. I will live out my giftedness as best I can. However, don't forget I am only human, and I can make mistakes."

"Yes, you are free to do that. In the time that is to come, you will be visited by each of us and all. Others of your sevens will be visited from the church they are. Our time is done for now. We will visit you again. Tell them to make ready our coming. I am to come to make things new."

"As you ask I will do," I said.

"Teach only love."

That was the last thing she/he/they had to say. The angels then split like a covey of quail, each speeding back to the stone they had come from. The golden light was gone as quickly as it had come. The only thing that was left was Shekinah and Michael. Michael stepped toward me, and as he did the one called Shekinah folded in on herself and vanished. I looked to Michael and said, "All I was supposed to do was write a book." For the first time, I saw Michael do something he never had done before. He smiled. Such warmth fell over me, I got a little misty and could feel my eyes start to water. A tear ran down my cheek.

I watched him as he began to fade into his light. **"Our time is done. We will speak soon. Teach only love. One more thing, Joe."**

"Yes, Michael," I said.

"Put some butter on it."

Put some butter on it? Now that is the strangest thing I ever heard him say. *What in the world is he talking about?* I turned to go back to the house to write down everything I had seen. *Put some butter on it? Was he trying to be funny?*

THE TREE OF LIFE

*I*t just keeps getting stranger and stranger. As I was driving home from town one day, a ball of light started to form on the passenger's side of my truck. This indicated to me that Michael was probably appearing for a chat of some sort. I kind of think it's a little funny when he shows up in the truck. He isn't as tall as he is outside, more about my size. As the rest of his body began to materialize, I said, "Well, Michael, I have been wondering when you were coming back." I looked at him sitting there without a seat belt on, thinking of the ticket I got a week or two earlier. What a hoot it would be if the same cop stopped us and tried to give out another ticket for no seat belt. "Why do I get the feeling that we are going for another ride?"

"Go north. I will tell you where to turn."

"OK. You got it." As we approached the turn-off to the house, I hit the turn signal and half hoped we were going home. The handle for the signal flipped back, stopping the blinking lights.

"Go straight."

"Guess we are not going home," I muttered.

"No," was all he replied. We drove to a highway where he instructed me to turn left, which I did. After another left further on, we drove for

quite some time. It was getting dark. As I pulled over onto the shoulder, I told my angelic hitch-hiker, "Michael, I need to call Donna on the cell phone and let her know I'm with you, and that there's no telling when I'll be getting back home." Of course, the humor of such a call wasn't lost on me, thinking what any other wife might think if her husband called up with a tale, "Honey, I'm gonna be late cuz I'm busy with this angel." But Donna had gotten used to my life being interrupted by angelic business.

After the call, I headed back down the road but with Michael no longer in the truck. He had disappeared. I gave up long ago trying to figure him out. After a bit, I saw him waiting on the side of the road pointing which way he wanted me to turn. It seemed it was taking a long time to get wherever we were going. But each time I needed to make a turn, Michael would show up at the intersection, pointing the way. Finally, he stood in the middle of the road holding out his hand for me to stop. I pulled over to the side, parked the truck and got out. I had no idea where we were or how I would get back. Here I was in the middle of nowhere, at night, with the only light in miles coming off of Michael. It's a good thing I trust him.

As I walked what seemed to be uphill, the angel floated along by my side. It wasn't all that long before he said, "**Stop.**" As I looked around for any evidence as to why I was here, he said, "**Behold what you are given.**" I peered out in front of me to see what looked like the Gate of Grace about three or four times the size of the one in the back yard. Only this one was about twenty feet out from us and suspended in mid air. I could see we were standing on a cliff with what could have been a valley below. The placement of the stones was made up of small balls of light set at the proper heights for the size of this huge thing.

Looking over at Michael, I asked, "Is this going to be another Shekinah thing?"

"**No. This is that which you will know.**" A shiver ran up my spine thinking of the *Revelation* visions I had a few years ago. I wondered what lay in store for me this time. "**Joe. You are to learn of our kind and the ties to the seven masters.**"

"Oh good. It is about time, because Gary has asked me some questions about this, and I didn't know what to tell him. So do I ask, or do you just tell me?"

"**Speak what you know. I will tell you if it is true.**"

"Well, let me start with the nine angels that were at the Gate last time. Gary and I figured out that the angels that make up the body of Shekinah are you, Ratziel, Gabriel, Tzaphqiel, Haniel, Khamael, Raphael and Tzadqiel."

"You have done well to see this."

"Given what we have checked up on, we think they should be Tzadqiel for Mercy, which is Laodicea. Raphael of Healing for Sardis. Smyrna would have to be Haniel or Khamael. However, Gary thinks Haniel has to do with him. That would have to do with Philadelphia. Pergamum in turn would be Ratziel or Tzaphqiel, and since you were standing by me, you would have to be what the kabbalists call Beauty. We figured out you would help us with the ones we didn't know. So how did we do so far?"

"Joe, do you not listen to that which is given? Is your way of thinking so limited?"

"OK. So we didn't do too well, given the way you are talking. But how many did we get?"

"One."

"Well, are we even close in thinking the seven angels that poured out the bowls in *Revelation* are the same angels?"

"Yes, and yet there is more. Each of us is as the church you are. You would see us in the places you stand. Yet there is another place for us to stand with your kind."

"So, Michael, does this mean we not only have the names mixed up but the placement of each of you as well?"

"I will show you what you seek."

Michael then lifted his hand up and out over the edge of knoll we stood on. I could see the lights of each church grow a little brighter. The colors of the Matrix of stones were just the same as in the back yard. As I looked up at them, I saw what looked like Orion in the sky. However, something was wrong with its placement. I knew by looking at the stars, Orion shouldn't be in that part of the sky. Then I noticed it was a pattern that only kind of looked like Orion. As the heavenly pattern got closer, I could see it was the same pattern as in the Formation of Giving and Receiving, just like the one we used at the original gathering. I could now see there were seven angels that made up the configuration as it floated down to the Gate. One angel descended to just above the red stone. It was

the angel with the red hair, the first angel to pour out its bowl, which I had seen in the visions concerning *Revelation*.

"Behold the first angel, for she is the color of Strength."

When she took her place above the red stone I knew she had something to do with the church of Smyrna. She stood as tall as Michael, and her red hair was the color of flames. There was a certainty in her emerald green eyes. The sculptured features of her face gave her a somewhat mannequin-like quality. Under the soft tissue that covered her face and neck, I could almost see the muscle and sinew. The women that I have seen in bodybuilding competitions would have appeared to be sickly weaklings in comparison to her. "Michael," I asked, "what is the name of this one?"

"You would call this one Khamael in your tongue."

"So she stands at my stone or church position and is the angel that works with Smyrna?"

"She is likened unto your church, yet stands not there. Look to her true place."

In square-dance fashion, the red angel floated over to the place of the violet stone, or the position of Laodicea. When she got just above the stone, the color of the light of each blended to one color. It looked like a mixture of the two with a very powerful glow to it. I thought, *This doesn't make sense yet, but I will see where this is going as more is given.* This Irish Colleen was one powerful looking angel, and the mixture with the violet made her more so.

Next came the one that looked Polynesian. Her dark skin reminded me somewhat of those who live on the islands. However, there was a radiance coming forth from the dark tan covering her features. Her long black hair fell to her shoulders. The only thing missing would have been the crown of flowers woven through her dark hair and the lei around her neck. Her physical demeanor was not quite as powerful as the first angel, but make no mistake, this was a powerful being of light that for some reason had a feminine pleasantry about her — joy. Joy was present in her rhythmic movements as she descended to her place and stood over the orange stone, or the church of Ephesus. She did not move. Her light just mixed with that church and became a stronger radiance. I looked to Michael to see why she didn't move to another color like the first one did.

"This one is known as Tzaphqiel to your kind, and is that of Understanding."

"Hang on a minute, Michael. What does this one have to do with understanding? That place is for the emotions, not the mind."

"Joe, think about what you are asking, and you will see the truth in what you ask."

I pondered it for a minute or so and answered the only thing that came to mind. "Oh. I get it, Michael. This is the part about the understanding heart, like Solomon."

"Blessed are you in wisdom, for you see and know. You have another word for understanding, which is awareness."

"Is this like knowing what you are feeling in your heart?"

"Yes."

"OK, I am beginning to see a pattern here, I think. The next angel should be the church of Pergamum or the yellow stone."

"Blessed are you, again."

"Not so fast. I still don't know who he is or where he goes."

"This one is known as Gabriel, the Foundation."

This angel of the yellow position, who looked like an Arab, moved over to the green stone of Sardis. As in the Arabian tales, this one stood as a Suleyman or a Sinbad, not at all appearing like a scholar. His dark eyes appeared to be black with a light that shone of a knowing of all things. The only thing missing from this distinguished looking Arab was a scimitar. He looked perfectly at home in his white robe. *Hang on again,* I thought. "Sardis was the one of Healing. What does Gabriel have to do with foundation? No, don't tell me. Let me guess. Mohammed did unite the tribes of the Arab people with Islam and gave them a foundation, which stopped the fighting between them? I guess this was a healing of sorts."

"Blessings on blessings, for you see."

"Don't go crazy over my intellect yet, Michael," I said with a smile. "There are still five more to go." I turned to see the next angel descend to the church of Sardis and this one looked Indian or Pakistani. He, too, had dark skin and black hair. I could see he possessed a great deal of power. He appeared as what could have been mistaken for an Indian ascetic or holy man. A Deepak Chopra, he was not. His knowledge of the healing arts would have surpassed anything medical science could have to offer us. There was softness to his hands, which looked as though the mere touch from any of his fingers could relieve the greatest pain. He just about

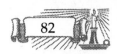

came to rest above the other angel, at the green stone, then drifted over to the place of the yellow stone.

"This one is Raphael and is of Healing."

The next angel to come down took the position of the church of Philadelphia or the blue stone. He looked African. In my mind's eye I saw this one on the ranges of Africa as a Zulu warrior. He was physically magnificent and mentally alert. The white robe that flowed over his dark, strong body gave him the appearance of a chieftain or a holy man. I didn't know who this one was but I did know where he was going. "This one, Michael, will be going to the church of Thyatira or the purple stone."

"This is true. His name is Ratziel for he is of Wisdom."

After moving down to the place of the blue stone, he then floated over to the position of the church of Thyatira or the purple stone, and the light changed there, too. Next came an angel who looked Asian, or from the Orient. The light tint of his skin gave him almost a sterile appearance, as if nothing had ever touched him. His dark hair and eyes were so black they had almost a purple shine to them. This would truly be a khan of khans, for had he ruled the Mongolian hordes, Christendom would be no more. He then did the same as the last two. He moved almost to the place of Thyatira and then over to the place of Philadelphia.

"Haniel is his name and he is of Victory."

The last angel appeared as Native American, resembling a princess. Because of her great beauty, there was a softness, tenderness, in her warm, loving expression. Compassion flowed forth from her eyes. She appeared as a mother speaking to her child, stating that the child was accepted for who the child was without reservations or forethought. She descended to the place of Laodicea, or the violet stone, and then moved to the red stone's place. "I knew that was going to happen, Michael, but the last one is?"

"Tzadqiel, the one that is known for Mercy.

"OK, let me see if I have this right — so to speak." I knew I shouldn't us the "r" word with Michael around. This is how I listed them: Khamael who is Strength (red), Zaphqiel who is Understanding (orange), Gabriel who is Foundation (yellow), Raphael who is Healing (green), Ratziel who is Wisdom (blue), Haniel who is Victory (purple), and Tzadqiel who is Mercy (violet). The seven angels filled the air with their beauty and strength. I couldn't take my eyes off them.

"This is the place they stand with the first seven."

I took a quick look around at all the angels to see where they were, and the arrangement did seem to fit. But there was still something out of place. "So, Michael, as I look at the angels and what each is about, I am a little confused at this. The gifts each angel carries doesn't fit with the church positions as well as I would have put them."

"You would have them not so?"

"Well, I would have thought that Wisdom would be with Philadelphia and Healing would be with Sardis. But the main thing, with me being of the church of Smyrna, I kind of think Khamael would have been with me."

"Joe. Would you give to that which [already] is? These are not to give you more of what you are. They come to the place they stand to bring you what you have little of."

"I still don't understand how it all fits."

"Look to the seven angels of *Revelation* and you will see why they stand where they do. When you bind the gifts of the churches with those of the angels, you will see the glory of God's plan."

"Let me see if I can remember how it works. If I take the gift of Smyrna and mix it with the angel of ... I just don't understand, Michael. This is so confusing to me." I was getting a little frustrated.

"Joe. Do not make it hard to understand. Look to the first angel of *Revelation*."

"OK. Let me think. As I remember it, the first angel poured out a bowl upon the earth. That angel went to the spot of Laodicea and their light mixed. Sooooooo ... what?"

"Think. Can you not truly see why?"

"Look, are you here to help me learn, or is this Twenty Questions? You could give me a hint couldn't you?"

"I ask you this. What is the first angel doing?"

"OK, let me think. The first angel is pouring out a bowl upon the earth. So. It is an earthly act or thing she is doing. Right?"

"True. Your church is?"

"My church is Smyrna, the leader; and it is female; and it is physical in nature."

"Now do you see?"

"Let me run over this out loud with you." I started to run over in my mind just what the church and the angel had in common.

Angel Reference	Church	Gift	Race	Helper to	How the Angel Helps the Human Counterpart
Khamael (red)	Smyrna	Strength	Irish	Laodicea (violet)	Khamael is the physical giving to the spiritual church of Laodicea.[1]
Tzaphqiel (orange)	Ephesus	Under-standing	Polynesian	Ephesus (orange)	Tzaphqiel is the emotional giving to itself, allowing awareness of the emotions.[2]
Gabriel (yellow)	Pergamum	Foundation	Arab	Sardis (green)	Gabriel gives wisdom and a clearing of the mind to Sardis so they are open to higher concepts, and can see the abstract, not just black or white.[3]
Raphael (green)	Sardis	Healing	Indian/ Pakistani	Pergamum (yellow)	Raphael gives groundedness to Pergamum so they are able to put their concepts into reality.[4]
Ratziel (blue)	Philadelphia	Wisdom	African	Thyatira (purple)	Ratziel adds spiritual wisdom to the spiritual emotions of Thyatira.[5]
Haniel (purple)	Thyatira	Victory	Asian	Philadelphia (blue)	Haniel gives spiritual love to Philadelphia so they can be loving in the work they do.[6]
Tzadqiel (violet)	Laodicea	Mercy	Native American	Smyrna (red)	Tzadqiel brings spirit to the physical, giving unconditional mercy and love to Smyrna.[7]

Revelation references:

[1] "The first angel poured his bowl onto the earth and the physical began to heal itself."
[2] "The second angel poured his bowl into the sea, and emotion healed itself."
[3] "The third angel poured his bowl into the rivers, and the mind became healed."
[4] "The fourth angel poured his bowl on the sun, and the spirit came forth."
[5] "The fifth angel poured his bowl on the throne of knowledge and changed it into divine knowing."
[6] "The sixth angel poured his bowl on the great river of spiritual teachings, and they were seen to be untrue."
[7] "The seventh angel poured his bowl into the air. 'It is done,' said a voice coming from the temple of the golden tent."

The changing of positions of the angels wasn't all that clear to me. Using what I knew about the churches and the angels of *Revelation* I said, "This is where I want to go with this. My church (red) and the first angel (red) deal with the physical. Given that the angel came to the place of my church and then moved to the church of Laodicea (violet), there is a connection there. As I look, I can also see that the angel of Laodicea moved and rested on my church's place. The angel at the red stone went to the violet stone, while the angel at the violet stone moved to the red stone. Now then, as I think of what the angel brings to the church and what they are in Revelation it has to be like this. The first angel is Physical and moves to the church that is Spiritual in nature, and vice versa. So from this it has to be the Physical is given to the Spiritual and the Spiritual is given to the Physical. Ohhhhh. Now I see what is happening here. The seventh angel is really bringing the Spiritual to the Physical. In the Spiritual there is given unconditional mercy and love. In the Physical's giving to the Spiritual, it opens up a place to manifest that which isn't — and in simple terms, it's allowed to become."

"Yes. And as you do, so will others. There is more for you to discover. Go to the next church and the angel."

"This is going to be easy after the first and the last are done. The first will be last and the last will be first. Hmm. Where have I heard that before? On to the next one. The next one is the church of Ephesus, and that angel of *Revelation* deals with the emotions. Stop. I get it. That church and that angel both are of the emotions, and you said it mixes with what it doesn't have. But right here it does. So. What's the deal here?"

"Look to them both and you will see."

"OK, so I know that it deals with emotions. Emotions such as anger, sorrow, and hate, are dried up in the light. To me this is saying that once one knows what they are feeling, they can choose how they feel rather than just react to it — if this makes sense to you."

"Yes. You are saying it for others of your kind to hear. What do you see with the others?"

"Next I would go to the places of Pergamum and Sardis. This one leads me to think it is an exchange of healing for Pergamum and a clearing of the mind for Sardis. Pergamum is given a groundedness to be able to put things into reality and Sardis is able to open to higher concepts with the angel that comes to it. With this, those of the church archetype

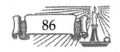
of Sardis, those who carry the gift of Sardis, can see the abstract and not just in black or white. How does that sound to you, Michael?"

"You see how easily you come to know that which is unknown to you?"

"Tell me something will you? Do I really know these things or am I learning them?" Michael looked at me and smiled, and I guess that was the answer for me, but I got it.

"The last two. Tell me of them."

"Well, as Joe sees it, this is the hardest of them all because it isn't very clear. These last two are at a very conceptual level. To me, this is because they deal with the spiritual mind and spiritual emotions. If you look at Philadelphia as the mind, it is so advanced and able to know but it can't feel the love in it. On the other hand, on a spiritual level, Thyatira possesses a spiritual love for the work they do. That is what is missing in Philadelphia. Those carrying the archetype of the church of Thyatira have no sense of thinking in what they do. They create things without rhyme or reason as they work. When they mix with the angelic counterparts missing in them, or disconnected from them, they are able to create things they only dreamed of."

"This is why I come to you. You say things such that others will hear and know."

"Michael, I think the only reason I can figure it out is that you do help me. But you have to remember that not everyone has an angel come to him to help. I hope I can serve to open the minds and hearts of those who don't."

"You will to those that are ready to hear. Look you again to the angels and the places of the seven churches. See the greatness of God's love for all of you."

I turned to observe the seven angels in their places, and wondered why and what was to come now. From the earth come more lights that were of all the colors of the seven churches, and they began to attach themselves to the seven different lights already in place. And as they did, I could see the first seven lights, along with their angelic counterpart, move down to the valley floor and come to rest there. Each new gathering of seven different-colored balls of light moved into the geometry of the Formation of the Sevens, or Gate of Grace, and connected to a light already in place, creating a growing structure. The colored balls of light

came from all over the hills and flowed down into the valley. I wondered where they were all coming from. Each set of seven lights flowed over the valley floor to the base, made of the seven angels and seven church archetypes, rising up the structure to take a place in this growing fractal of Gates of Grace. As each new group of seven came into place, the structure grew taller and began to build a tree of the DNA-like strand I had been shown before. The geometric structure grew and grew until it produced a canopy of giant proportions over Michael and me. If the sun had been out, the treelike canopy would have given shade. This is where it became clear to me for the first time what this was all about.

As I stood looking up, I saw lights falling to the earth like shooting stars. The closer they got, the more I could see they were in the geometric form of the Formation of Giving and Receiving. These were not just lights or stars, but angels. Just as the first seven angels had come to the first seven churches, represented by the balls of light, so did the new groups of angels come to the other colored lights of the earth. This was getting pretty intricate the way the groups of angels attached themselves with each set of the seven churches simultaneously. What's really hard to explain is how they attached themselves. It was as though an angel, in a group of angels, would first settle in a church position, and then move to the corresponding church they blended with. The color of light from that church would then change.

Now this is why it is hard to explain. Given that there are seven masters representing each of the seven churches, and there is only one person who stands as the servant, which makes the eighth place, each master, as they gather their seven, shall stand in the servant's place for these new seven. As the servant does this, the angel of their church leaves him or her and joins with the new master of the servant's color or church. So, for instance, Gary is of the church of Philadelphia, represented by the blue stone. When he had his gathering, he became the servant for that gathering. And Gary's angelic counterpart (Haniel, the purple angel) moved to the master at Gary's gathering who also was of the church of Philadelphia, or blue. At the gathering, the other angelic counterparts first arrived in the place of the same church, or color, and then moved to their helping position, or their counterpart. In other words, the yellow angel first came to the position of the yellow stone, or the church of Pergamum, and then moved to the master who was of the church of Sardis, or green.

But after the gathering, Gary was both master and servant, once again aligning with his church archetype, Philadelphia.

This same type of exchange was occurring before me as the angelic hosts continued to fall like shooting stars and join their earthly counterparts. Energy flowed from one angel to another angel as did energy from the masters of the churches, but not for the servant. Thousands upon thousands gathered together, and as they did a light began to fill the valley. "OK, Michael, you need to tell me why the angels are attaching themselves to the churches and not to the servant or other angels? Even you are attached to me and stand at the place of the servant."

"I will show you my true place."

With those words Michael moved down into the valley and took his place amongst the angels and the masters. When he came to rest in his new place, so did the other angels from the places of the servant in each group. I asked what this meant because we were now alone in the spots we held as the servant. "I also notice that there is something out of place now, Michael."

"There is." What looked like it would make sense is now looking scattered and out of whack. **"What is it you see that is missing?"**

I looked to the Tree of Life, or the geometric DNA-like strand, whichever you want to call it, and started my search. From high on the tree I followed it down to the base to see if I could come up with the answer. All I could see was that there seemed to be two holes in each set of the connecting churches and angels. I told him it looked like there was an empty spot where I was standing and it was the same for the others that stood also in that place.

"Your eyes see yet you do not know the sums of that which gives it splendor."

"The only thing I can think of is, as the servant, they stand with you. And you, upon completion of a gathering, move to the center spot of the tree of life. At this point the servant stands alone binding the new seven and their angels to the Tree of Life." My attention was drawn to the base of this magnificent tree made of angels and souls. I looked to see what was a lush valley — almost like a tropical garden — filled with what I guessed was everything that could grow. I wondered where in Texas this really was. On the other hand, was I really in Texas? Granted I did drive

to it, or at least within walking distance, but one never knows when it comes to angels where you truly are. One never truly knows how you got there, and for that matter does one truly know anything — truly? "Michael, how far does this valley go?"

"It runs all the way to the feet of God."

My heart skipped a beat when he said that. It was the most beautiful place I had ever seen. "I can't wait to tell others about this place," I said. "Tell, my eye; I can't wait to bring others here."

"You have been doing that since the day you told us to speak, for you would hear."

I was just overwhelmed to hear that. "You mean this is what I am doing with all of this, bringing people to this place?"

"Yes. Yet the road will be as long or as short as your kind will make it. The sevens will shorten it if they want to or they will make it as long as they can. This has been the way of your kind. Remember I told you something wonderful is going to happen and there is nothing you can do about it?"

"Yeah, I remember it. And this is it?"

"It is."

"So what do I do now? Just start bringing the sevens here? If I can find my way back."

"Joe, you are welcome here whenever you wish. However, the others will need to find their own way here."

"Hold on, this isn't one of those places where you have to die to get here is it?"

"No, those places are saved for cults and religions."

"Very funny, Michael, I didn't think you had it in you. Really, can I bring someone with me?"

"No. Yet you may meet them here."

"How do they find their way here?"

"Many are close, yet they have stopped before they have come to the valley."

"OK. I get it. You are not going to tell me."

"They will find their way."

"Great. Everyone is going to move to Texas now."

"They need not, for it is just down the path from the house in which they live."

"Gee, just like in the *Wizard of Oz*. Is this the Garden of Eden that was spoken of in the Bible?"

"No. It is grander than that for your kind. In that book, it tells of a garden you were cast out of for sinning. Your kind chose to leave, for God does not throw God's children out for any reason."

"So, Michael, are you telling me there was such a place, and we chose to leave?"

"What I am telling you is that your kind has the power to create it this way again. Joe, this is a garden that is coming to your kind."

"Michael, ol' buddy, you got me all mixed up again. You say I can come here whenever I wish but I can't bring anyone with me. You also say I will meet others here and this isn't the Garden of Eden we were thrown out of. You say we chose to leave, and still this is a place I have never seen."

"Do you remember being told that when enough sevens have gathered that there will be a change in all that is? And also that the debt has been paid and the rewards of the Father will be visited upon all of the children?"

"Of course I do. So what does this have to do with anything?"

"When the empty places that you have seen have been filled, then will this valley begin to cover the earth."

"So what you're telling me is, when I figure out what is missing in the Tree of Life and put it there, it will come to us?"

"No, what I tell you is when you and the others fill the empty places it will be yours."

"OK, I do have another thing to ask you. So, Michael, am I pretty much done with this stuff? I mean do I go on teaching, healing and promoting the book?"

"You have more books to write. You have other times to be with the other angels and learn. You have time yet to be with Shekinah in the changing of your heart."

"Just what is that supposed to mean? The changing of my heart?"

"As you were told, you will be changed, and others will see and know you for the gifts you bring."

"This has me worried — as to if anyone will know me after that."

"Joe. You will be the same, yet you will look other than you do now. The others will know you have had union with Shekinah and have been blessed."

"So when will this happen? Because if your 'soon' has been anything like in the past, I won't hold my breath."

"You will not have to. Our time is done for now. Return to your home and write this down. Send it to your sevens and then we will speak again. Go in grace and teach only love."

As he said this I could see the dawn break and the light begin to get brighter. The tree became like it was in a fog and I couldn't see it too clearly anymore. I turned to walk back to the truck, and felt a peace about me. Wow! What a night this has been. The air on the way back to the truck was filled with a mist almost like a light rain. Climbing in, I started the engine but just sat there for a while. This seemed like a moment for celebration, so I reached over and pulled out a cigar and lit it. The smoke rose to the cab roof, and I opened the window. I put on my seat belt, then put the truck into gear and started down the road. The haze was all around me as I drove — and I thought, *Well, I am back in Kansas again.* Down the road I went, just barely able to see through the haze and fog. *How in the world will I ever get back here again?* It seemed like it took forever to get to the spot where Michael first had given me directions from the road, but the next thing I knew I was traveling down the street to my house. I remember thinking to myself, *Ain't that the way it always is? It takes forever to get to Paradise but only a moment to leave it or loose it.* I pulled into the driveway and parked the truck, easing my way out. Slowly I walked to the front door and checked the doorknob — as if to see if it were real — and then ambled in. Donna was standing by the kitchen staring at me. I just held up my hand as if to say Don't touch me. She completely understood what I was asking, and honored my request. She told me she had never seen me so at peace.

It just keeps getting stranger and stranger.

THE WELL OF SOULS

The vision of the Tree of Life stayed with me for weeks. This was the "something wonderful" Michael had spoken of, and now I knew what he meant. This was the new heaven and new earth prophesied for millennia. This Tree of Life was the de facto Age of Wonders other traditions had spoken of. Even the Vedics speak of the turning from the ages of darkness to the ages of light at this time. What was shown me, and I now tell you, is that the coming together of the angelic realm with the realm of humans is to create a new kind of world — better than Eden. Often I tried to imagine what this might mean. Little did I know what actually was in store for me or, for that matter, you.

As I closed my eyes for a good night's rest, I wondered why Michael hadn't shown up for six months. When he stays away this long, it gets me to wondering if there's something I haven't done. Waiting for him hadn't gotten any easier, especially with sevens often asking if he'd shown up yet. It kind of makes me feel responsible for what the angels do and when they do it. Questions from friends, as to what I saw and what I was told, serve as constant reminders as to the role I play in this divine unfolding. If other sevens receive some communication that is different from what I got or if an angel shows up differently from what I saw, I get asked why.

Questions, questions, always questions. One thing for sure; I was going to ask everything I could think of to get everything answered next time Michael showed. If and when Michael showed, and if it suited him.

"Open your eyes and see the wonders laid before you."

Michael. My eyes opened, I saw where I was and knew it was not earthly nor of my world. The previous night I had dreamt a dream unlike any dream I'd had before. In the dream I saw what looked like the stems of water lilies pushing up their pads to the surface. They were in clusters about thirty yards apart as far as the eye could see. The stalks were as big around as a car wheel and maybe fifteen feet tall. The ground was white, as was everything else, except the stalks. These were different colors but not hard colors or deep rich colors. They were pastel reds, blues, yellows, oranges — all the colors of the rainbow. I remember thinking in this dream what a strange place — beautiful, but strange. In the dream I also felt this had something to do with Michael. I didn't know why but I got the feeling it did.

"I remember this place," I said to Michael. "This looks like the place I saw in the dream I had last night."

"It is. I showed it to you to make you ready for this, that you would not be in awe of it. What do you see here?"

"I see the same stalks I saw in the dream. Each is a beautiful pastel color and set in a circle or pattern of some kind."

"Look closely at them."

I did as he said and noticed there were eight stalks to a bunch or grouping. Each had the seven colors of the rainbow, and some groupings had the same color twice. "OK, Michael, so why do I get this feeling this is about the things that have been going on?"

"Not feeling. Knowing."

"Does this have to do with the gal that set up a Gate and saw angels in it?" I was referring to one of appearances that showed up differently from what I had seen with Michael. Lots of questions about that one.

"Yes and more."

"It's the 'more' thing I am interested in. You have gotten me into a position of being the answerer of questions for everybody. If something doesn't seem to be the same from someone as what I have said or seen, I am the one who has to clean it up. Since when am I the one to have to answer all this? I thought all I was to do was tell what I saw and what you

told me, and that was it. Now angels are showing up in the Gates of others, plus they are seen in different positions, different nationalities, and different colors. This is beginning to make us look like we are not consistent in what we are getting from one person to another. Gary says this kind of stuff will come back to bite us in the ass if it keeps up without clearing it up."

"You are looking for proof that what I give you is said the same way to others receiving it? If they do not say it the same way, they must not be getting messages from us?"

"No, I didn't say that. It is just you guys need to be more consistent in what you say."

"We are."

"So how then is it that some things you guys say comes out differently, depending on who you say it to?"

"You have your answer. The message is the same. Yet, the telling of it comes from all of you."

"You mean you say what you do and our interpretation of what we heard makes it different. Is that correct?"

"It is. Is what you say the only way of saying something? If you take this path in thinking, it would lead you to everyone must think as you do. It would lead you to 'right and wrong.' [What is happening,] also, is that we speak to you [each individual] so you will understand."

"So, you do say it differently to others?"

"No."

"OK, let's you and I clear something up while I have you here and willing to explain things to me. This thing about others channeling angels is getting out of hand for me. I am getting some flack, in the way I see it."

"You speak of your seeing me and talking to me as a person?"

"Well, more physical, rather than a voice or an impression of some heavenly being giving a message. Oh yeah — what is all the 'Dear One' stuff people say you guys use to start a message? You never call me that. You know my name and use it."

"Angels use a person's name when we speak to them. Yet your kind hears what they want to hear. As you were told, an angel will come to someone in whatever form that person will understand and listen from, so that the person will hear."

"Hmm. OK, I can live with that. What you are telling me then, is when an angel talks to someone, they call them by name."

"This is true for all we give a message to."

"Hang on. Are you now saying that when you tell me to get something out to the sevens or the world, you are using everyone's name?"

"Yes."

"Wow. You say everyone's name and I only hear 'the sevens' or 'the world'? That is pretty cool, and must save a bunch of time."

"Joe. You speak as one who thinks time has something to do with what is given."

"I just thought if you said everybody's name, it would take a long time to get through them all."

"When I have come to you and told you that which I have, do you think it took hours of your time?"

"Well Michael, it seemed like it to me."

"All that is at the same time. When I do what you call 'come to you,' I am really already there."

"Which brings up another thing, before I forget it. If you are already here and don't come from the other side ..."

"Other side? You speak as if I come from some other place."

"I was talking to some people and they said people who channel information get it from the other side, and what I am getting is from there."

"Joe there is no other side."

"Well, what about all the dimensions there are? Where are they? They can't be in the same place at the same time."

"Look to your feet and see."

I looked down and saw I was standing on this white stuff that was everywhere. "Yeah. It looks like everything else around here — all white," I told Michael.

"Look closer, look deeper, and tell me what you see."

I did as he said. I peered into the white ground. It then became like a film that I could see through. It was all cloudy at first, like milk. The harder I looked the clearer it became — like adding clear water to milk. The more water you add, the clearer the milk gets. I could see I was really standing on carpet.

"Now look deeper."

As I began to look deep into the carpet, I could see it doing the same thing the white floor did. I saw what seemed to be liquid sky with a sun of some kind, and I started to drift into it because it was so beautiful.

"Joe. You may not enter there."

With those words, I was back to standing on the white floor again.

"The 'other side' is what your kind has come to call it when someone has died. It is said by you that the ones that have gone home are on the 'other side.' "

"That sounds fair to me. Since we can't see and talk to them, they must be someplace else."

"This is what I speak of. Your kind has a thinking it must be here and now for it to be. If it is not seen, it must be someplace else. Was not Jesus here after his death?"

"That's the part where he arose from the dead and appeared to the women and the twelve?"

"Joe. Jesus was not on the other side. He was here as he is now. Some choose to see and others do not. Your kind has some who can go from one dimension to the next at will. Gary knows of this well."

"So what you are telling me is that there is no other side to get to?"

"All that is, is God's love. All that is to be is now as in God."

"This is getting a little deep for me. God is everything that is, and God is love."

"Yes."

"Then that means there is no other realm, so to speak. There is not a place that you angels hang out until you are needed to do something. Is that right?"

"This is true. We are with you always, as is God. There is no separation as you think there is, Joe. People, such as you, see angels because they know they can or don't know they can't. Those that see us not are not aware they can."

"The woman that saw angels in her Gate just found out she could. But Michael, she saw the angels in different spots in the Gate than the ones I saw. She said some of the nationalities were different than the way I saw them. Can you explain how this is possible?"

"The angels you saw were of your soul group, and each has the names you were given. As you go from one soul group to another they will change. As each group is added to the Tree, an angel comes to that spot yet they are not the same angel as the ones in yours. They have, as you say, the same attributes as the one you have. Yet each may look different."

"When you say soul group, you are talking about each group of seven? The Gate, then, is only a representation of where the people stand — given that we have souls, and the stones don't? So we stand as a well of souls giving us a soul group. So what you are telling me is that there is more than one angel for each spot? The first angels that are in the first group are as I saw them. The next group has other angels that take on the attributes of the first group but are not them?"

"If they look different, it is because they are not the same angels in your Matrix."

"I get what you are saying. Tell me if I am correct on this one. I see the angel that looks like it is of Irish nationality or African or Chinese but someone may see them reversed. That is because the angels someone sees in their soul group do not show up the same. Not too hard to understand, because there are as many angels as people, and we don't each look alike."

"True."

"So. How come the places of Smyrna and Laodicea are changed? I also know that the angels change places with others in the same soul group. You showed me that."

"Do you not know?"

"My only guess would be that there have been more gatherings of these two churches than another of the sevens."

"This is so."

"Is this because they are just different angels in a spot randomly? Or has the number of gatherings opened up a place for more angels to come in, which means there are chances of other nationalities showing up in a different spot? But I know that the races of the ones in my first group mean something, and I think it has to do with the gifts each of the seven are in relationship to the world."

"You are wise in thinking so."

"OK. So tell me what it means."

"There are two that have not gathered. When it is done you will know."

"Why did I know you were going to tell me something like that, I wonder?

"Look to this place I have brought you. What do you see?"

"Back to the stalks again, huh? Well, I see these different colors of stalks, and each is tall. Some have the same color twice, and there are

eight in a bunch. I do see that whatever they are, there are eight, and a closer look brings me to see they are in a Matrix of sorts. The one thing I see is that they are not as spread out like the Well of Souls are, nor the Gates."

"**Come,**" was all Michael said, and we started to move but I couldn't feel any motion. It was more like the ground — if you could call it that — was moving under us, and we were standing still. The bunches of stalks were moving past us. As one of the bunches of stalks came toward us, looking like it would run right into us, it swung to the right side of us. It was at this time I noticed it was not the only group of stalks that did this. It was the whole landscape of stalks that swung around to let us pass through. As they whizzed by, I noticed we were picking up speed.

I could also see, way off ahead of us, that there were some groups of stalks which looked different from the ones going by us. The closer I got to wherever we were going, the clearer I could make out what it was that was different. Some of the groups had one stalk that was different from what I would have expected. Instead of the full spectrum of seven colors, one or two colors would be missing. And as we got to the center there were more groups that had a different stalk in it. The center set of stalks had all but two changed. Why was I not surprised to see they were orange and yellow? That's when I knew this was the angels' Matrix, just like the human sevens. The instant I realized this, I saw angels in the stalks, as if they had been released from some kind of tubular casing. But then again it wasn't a casing. What I thought was casing turned out to be folded wings of light. The wings were holding the angels as if they were encased in sugar or a crystal bowl. As the wings spread out, the true colors of their robes and hair could be seen. I saw the angels of the center like the ones I had seen in my Gate. The only one missing from the set was Michael, and he was with me. We stopped short of this group of angels, and Michael began to talk to me again.

"**Look to the other groups and see what is there. See the ones you have opened up to join with your ring and see the ones other of the sevens have made way for.**"

"I see them, Michael, and I can almost feel which group goes to whom. So what is this all about? Why have you brought me here for this?

"**It is time for you to receive from each. You will be visited by them with gifts.**"

I had no idea what he was talking about. But I knew I would be seeing each of the seven angels very soon. I could see gold light coming off of them like a glow. Each was holding something that looked like a gold box covered with jewels. "You mean I get these boxes?"

"You get what is in them."

"Cool. Do I get to keep what they give me? Or is this like the gold at the pond? When you were gone, so was the gold and silver.

"This you will keep."

"Even better," I said. As I looked to the side I could see the other angels in their groups holding boxes. "Are those mine, too?" I asked.

"Not those. They are for the others of the sevens."

"Well, I know there will be some happy campers to hear that."

"Come, for our time is done."

I could feel motion again as we moved away from the center — if that was what it was. We moved toward something that looked like a bench. As we approached it, Michael told me to be seated. I did as he said and looked to see what was going to happen next.

"Say to Donna, what she has done will bear fruit. She is close to the key. She has not worked in vain."

"OK. But she is going to have a lot of questions I know."

"That which she feels she needs to decide will work out yet. Be not hasty to have it done. Be at peace and teach only love."

As his words left his lips the white light that filled everything was gone, like turning off a switch. I was left sitting in my truck wondering how I got there. Hadn't I just been in my bed?

"Physician, Heal Thyself"

*I*t had been awhile since I had changed a tire on my truck. The muscles in my back were starting to tighten up from the wrestling match I'd had with the spare. *Hope this doesn't aggravate the muscles I pulled in tae kwon do,* I said to myself. Last night had been an exercise in tossing and turning, trying to calm the pain. The last thing I wanted was to have the pulled muscles flare up again. My mind was everywhere except where it should have been — on the road. However, I was paying enough attention to slow down as I coasted into the tiny little town ahead. The thirty-mile-per-hour sign stood like a sentry guarding the town as I rounded the curve. Usually, the local police car scouted this section of the road. But not this time. No officer of the law lurked in the shadows trying to protect his burg from hurrying city folk. As I passed through to the far edge of town, I began to push the pedal to the metal. The hum of the engine announced the changing speed: thirty-five, forty-five, fifty-five, sixty-five, as the white lines in the road began to blur past me.

"**Slow down,**" I heard from somewhere in the car. Or was it in my head? *Hey, I know that voice.* As I looked to my right, a light unmistakably was coalescing on the passenger's side. Michael was coming. Within moments, he was sitting next to me. "**Slow down,**" he

101

said again. Too captivated by his appearance, I just kept staring at him. **"Too late,"** he stated calmly, staring straight ahead. Quickly I scanned the road in all directions, looking for some impending danger. Was it one of the creatures of the night, like a deer or raccoon about to cross the road?

Behind me, out of nowhere, appeared the lights of a car. They were closing in at a rather high speed. *This is really no problem,* I thought to myself. *I'll just let them pass.* Was this what Michael was fussing about? All of a sudden, as if out of thin air, exploded a light show straight out of *Close Encounters of the Third Kind.* Pretty red, white, and blue lights flashed like a super K-Mart special. Then I realized what Michael had meant by "too late."

"Oh give me a break," I groaned, "I wasn't going all that fast. Damn! This is all I need." Then came the agonizing wait. You know what I am talking about. You just sit in your car and think about how you are going to get out of the ticket. I looked over at Michael to see if he would offer some help. He sat there like a statue made of light. How many times had Gary and I made jokes about Michael's appearing in my car? And how many times had we laughed ourselves silly about how funny it would be if a cop drove by one of those times while Michael was sitting on the passenger's side. Well, for some reason, it wasn't quite so funny at the moment. The staccato of footsteps echoed across the gravel as the owner of the extra-terrestrial lights approached my car window. There was no mistaking the authority in his voice as he asked, "May I see your license, registration and proof of insurance, sir?"

Fumbling for my wallet, I half-mumbled to Michael, "He can't see you, can he?" Michael just sat there. What a time for an angel to turn to stone.

"Excuse me?" the officer responded.

"Uh, nothing," I muttered as I rifled through my wallet.

"The reason I stopped you, is that the speed limit at night here is sixty-five, and you were going seventy-five."

"Yes sir," I said. If I could see my insurance card by the light of Michael's glow, it just seemed fair that the cop should be able to. My mind drifted back to the last time Michael had appeared. He had tried to teach me about dimensions and how some of us can cross them. Obviously, Michael was sitting in a dimension privy only to the two us. I still wondered how the angel was able to do that.

"Wait in your car, sir. I will be right back."

The officer's heels crunched across the gravel once again. "So, Michael, this means I'm getting a speeding ticket, right?"

Michael turned his head and looked at me with those loving blue gemstone eyes. **"If that is what you will,"** he said matter-of-factly. Scenario after scenario rolled over in my mind. What could he be talking about?

Looking straight ahead, I heaved a deep sigh. "Michael ..." I said, and then it hit me. "Well, bless his heart. This police officer is just doing his job. He holds no malice for me, so why should I be holding any for him?"

As I sat thinking about how this officer puts his life on the line every day to protect us, a sense of peace came over me. Once again I said, "Bless his heart." The crunch of footsteps returned to my window. The officer started giving the speech that all police officers give when they are about to give you a ticket: "Signing this ticket is not an admission of guilt; it only means that you have received it," yada, yada yada. "I am giving you a warning ticket," he said. My ears pricked up. "This is not a speeding ticket. However, your inspection sticker has expired, and you will need to go before the judge and show him the receipt for having it updated."

"Well bless your heart," were the words that came out of my mouth. I signed the ticket, and as he started to walk away, I told him, "I know you guys don't hear this often enough, but thanks for protecting us."

"You're welcome," he said, the authority no longer hanging in his voice. "And please slow it down." As I sat putting my license and registration away, I watched as he pulled around me, taillights fading into the distance. Putting my car into gear, I pulled out onto the highway. Only this time I paid close attention to the speed limit.

"You know, Michael, I guess I'd forgotten how powerful a 'Bless your heart' can be."

"Yes," was all that he said in return.

"I had a feeling you would be showing up about now, given it has been awhile since I saw you last. There just seems to be so much going on now. There is a lunar eclipse, a Grand Cross, and a solar eclipse. People are kind of getting crazy, if you know what I mean. Not to mention there is a lot of fear going on. People are worried about solar flares and the end of the world. People are coming up with all kinds of warnings for

other people. Hell, Michael, some people are even seeing angels coming to them with a warning of what will happen if they do or don't do something. What are you guys up to?"

"If someone hears a message from any of us and it is not of love, it is not us, or the message was misunderstood. Would I have told you to teach only love if our kind would do otherwise? Is the 'Book of Bricks' that I gave you filled with don't-do-this-and-thats?"

"Now that you mention it, Michael, it isn't. So why all the uncertainty lately? You know, for a long time I have felt off-balance and sometimes confused. At times, I even feel nauseous and dizzy. I was talking with Donna, and she was telling me how crazy things are at her work. She has really been worried about whether she is going to keep her job or quit. She said she didn't know if they were going to fire her or not. Things just keep falling apart."

"I have told you before, she worries for nothing. Donna is not alone in this. A great many people are feeling the same. That which you would call energy is changing. The consciousness of this world is changing. It is leaving what has always been and becoming what could be and what is to be: the love that God is. This love is beginning to enter every fiber and cell in the body. It moves down to the very structure of DNA. All things are changing.

"Take the next road to the right, stop the car, and walk with me."

Slowing the car down, I turned to the right, up what looked like a side road.

"You may stop any time."

Ahead lay a patch of asphalt for turning around. Pulling up onto it, I stopped the car. After walking around to the side where Michael stood, the two of us ambled off into the sparse grass, the Texas soil giving way easily under my feet. In case you're wondering, Michael didn't leave footprints. We stopped at a spot where a tree had fallen.

"Sit and rest yourself as we speak. Nothing will harm you."

Michael must have read my mind, knowing the concern I had for what might have taken up residence in the hollow of the dead tree. He must have seen me looking at the tree to see if there were spiders or scorpions crawling on it. As I sat down on the trunk, I noticed how it was just the right height to allow my feet to rest gently on the ground. "Well, since you have me sitting down, you must have something important to say."

"I do. Too long have you been from writing. Too busy have you been with worldly things."

"Of course I have a need to make a living. I know you're not going to give me the winning numbers for Lotto."

"No. I will not. Yet, this is in part my reason for being with you tonight. The work that you do is too important for you to be spending time on how to make a living." Easy for him to say. If it hadn't been for one of the sevens setting up a workshop for me in Chicago, I'd be broke.

"Oh really. If it wasn't for Joanne and the class she set up, I would more than likely be living in my truck right now. The money that I made from that is going fast. The woman that was supposed to be setting up a class for me in Florida has not gotten the help that she needed. Therefore, that's not going to happen. The next thing I have coming up is at the end of September. I spent more than half of what I made in Chicago to rebuild my inventory. In addition, with the bills and money I owe, I'll be broke again in no time. At least Gary has an agent working for him, finding him things to do."

Joe, you have someone at your beck and call willing to do this for you. Yet, you have not used her. She would do this out of love for the work you do. You need but to ask her.

"You're talking about Robbie, aren't you?" Robbie was one of the sevens in Texas not far from where I lived. It was more than interesting that Michael should point out her willingness to help after telling me earlier, in private, that the two of us were from the same soul group, and therefore did not have that much to teach one another. I think he had used the phrase, "What good does it do to mix water with water?" And yet, now he was telling how she could help out. This is the kind of stuff that can get me confused.

"Yes. Others that you would hire would only do it for the money."

"She did do the work for the last engagement, didn't she?"

"She would again if you give her the opportunity to serve."

"So, does this mean Joanne would have to go through her to set up the next class in Chicago?"

"No, Joe, it doesn't. What I say is she will find new places for you to teach your class."

"Makes sense to me."

"That which you and Joanne have put together in Chicago has opened a door that was closed there before. Those who truly heard your teachings in your last class will make your next class even greater."

"Well, Michael, if this is your counsel, I will go for it."

"There are so many people wanting to help you, and all you need do is let them." Little did I know this was the central theme of everything happening to me this night. It would not be easy for me to discern the difference of making things happen and letting them happen.

"OK, Michael, I get your message. Sometimes I just don't know how I am going to get everything done that you have given me."

"Joe, look at the things you have already done. Do you not have two books that carry the words I gave you? Have you not found a way for those who wish to set up a Gate of Grace to gather what is needed without being robbed? Even now, you're waiting for your tapes to be finished that teach people to meditate and to balance their energy."

"I know that. There seems to be so much more to do that I haven't done yet. I don't know how I will ever get it all done."

"There will come a time when you will look back at this time and wish you had it again."

"So, what you're telling me is I'm going to be a very busy boy."

"Once again you know without my telling you things that are true."

"Before I forget. There is something I have to ask you about. I've noticed there seems to be some kind of thing going on with certain people coming up with illnesses. I've noticed it among the sevens and people who have been attending my classes. It's as if some of these people are having illnesses crop up because of their effort toward finding enlightenment. When some people accept the gift they are, it's as if God is saying you got the idea. Now that you know it, you can come home or stay. You can check out or learn more. When this happens, a disease of some kind shows up. It looks to me like God is giving them or us a ticket home. We can choose to overcome our illness, if that is what we really want to do, or leave."

"Joe, for some, their traps are their illness. As you would say, they manifest themselves in that way. Yet, look deeply, for not all

become ill; some become frustrated in life. Others may go to resentment or anger, or blame others for the things they do or do not."

"I can see what you are trying to say in this. If I point the finger at somebody else, making him or her responsible for the way things are in my life, I don't have to do anything, and I can just live in my trap. Is that kind of what you're saying?"

"Yes, Joe. There are those who will create chaos and bad feelings for others around them. In this chaos, whether it be a real physical ailment for themselves or the imaginary action of the others, both will keep them from the work they do."

"Well, Michael, since you brought it up. I have pulled my lower back muscles doing leg lifts. Can you give a guy a hand here and fix my back muscles for me so they don't hurt so much?"

"Physician, heal thyself."

So why was I not surprised he said that? I know I'm the one who let my body go, not exercising the way I should. If I strained a muscle, I am the one who needs to work with it. It isn't as if I have some major disease and it's going to kill me. I have just used muscles I have not used in a long time. And like they say in New York, "Forget about it."

"Our time is short. I will show you again two things you have forgotten. You have begun to remember one yet not the other. I will show you these, and you will remember. You will teach them in the healing class you teach; yet you will not speak of them until you teach them in the class."

Michael took his time going over what he had shown me before, and I remembered his telling me people would not be ready for this yet, given that my "Introduction to Healing" class was just that: an introduction. When he was finished showing me again, I told him I would have loved to do this in Chicago when I was there. But Joanne had already been talking about having me back for another weekend of classes in October. Perhaps that would be the best time to bring this information forward.

"Not many would have understood the power of these two things. The people that came to your class, you have opened to an understanding or consciousness that will allow them to see the truth in this. Those people in turn will bring others after telling them what they have learned, and they will be able to see this also."

"I get it Michael. The ones I taught in the last class know things now that they may not have realized before. Now that they know these things, they will share them with others, and, in turn, the others will be open to understanding it."

"This is so. It is time for you to begin the *Book of Healing*. Yet in order for you to do this so that people will understand, you must first make clear to them a way for them to know the gifts and the traps they are."

"Well, I wrote up this whole thing on how to tell what church you are. I mean, it's self-explanatory. I don't know how much easier I can make it."

"Joe, for you it is easy. I have been with you for over five years teaching you. I have sent others to teach you, and you have learned much. Not everyone has been as fortunate as you to have the teachers that you have had. As you have learned, you have discovered things that I have not taught you. You have put them in usable form that others might learn. The key that unlocks the door to the wisdom of the universe lies in your own gifts and traps. This is true for all learning with the knowledge that you have of all the churches with their gifts and traps. You would do well to write the *Book of Gifts and Traps*."

"Hang on a minute, Michael. Now, you told me I would be writing a couple more books. Are you telling me I need to write another one? Or is this some kind of a pamphlet or mini-book?"

"Joe, this of which I speak to now, you would write in the *Book of Healing*. But this would take far too long for people to receive it. This is why you must do it now."

"All right, Michael, let's see if I have this straight. I am to write a small companion-type book containing the information on the seven churches, the archetypes. Only in this one, it should be more detailed so that people may more easily understand what is written there, and how it applies to them."

"You said you were not the man for this job. See how easily you know things without being told?"

"OK. I'll come up with a small book to make it easier for people to find out what their gifts and their traps are. Anything else you need or want me to do?"

"There is much to be done. Our time is over for now. We will speak again within ten of your days."

We walked back to the car with his light illuminating the way and beginning to fade. This was a sign to me that he was leaving, but before he left, he said one more thing.

"The time that I spoke of to you? It is near. Teach only love."

He stepped into the light as it folded in on him and was gone. As I got back to my car and started reflecting on what his last words were, I knew he was talking about what was going to happen to me.

The days following this appearance left me with a lot of personal questions. So much has not happened that was supposed to happen. And when events or situations don't occur, it's easy to try and blame myself, or wonder why Michael's words didn't bear fruit. Timing is certainly a key factor, especially since time doesn't exist for Michael. But I shouldn't have to endure wondering where the next meal is going to come from. Gary had spoken to me about poverty consciousness. Was that it? Was I not seeing the wealth available to me? Michael was obviously trying to teach me about manifestation while sitting in my car like an ornament while the police officer was giving me a ticket. Did the angel not say that the ticket was up to me? Why not the police officer? Why was the ticket up to me? Was my pressing financial state also up to me? Michael implied that when I asked him to heal my back. "Physician, heal thyself," he had said to me. Too often I look outside myself for my problems and for my answers.

Many of us look outside of ourselves so as not to see that we are the authors of our own "sums." That argument could certainly be made by some of the sevens who were upset with me for the "sums" I now needed to work out. Part of me felt frustrated by the fact that angels will just sit by and let us learn our lessons. Sometimes that doesn't seem like guardianship to me. I know they will not interfere in our lives, but I also know they assist as much as we will let them. Perhaps that is the real key to manifestation. Letting it happen rather than trying to make it happen. Indeed, one of the key components in healing is "allowing" the healing to occur by setting up healing space. Maybe that's what I needed to do — create space that would allow the abundance of life to come to me. Perhaps this was part of the sums I had to work out.

THE ART OF HEALING AND
THE HEALING OF ART

*L*et me tell you how useless it is to try and outguess an angel. No word, no movement, not the most insignificant detail is wasted when angels appear. It's as if they count every hair on your head making sure it is in accord with their divine mathematics, a myriad of simultaneous equations which determine the consequences of their daring to walk into the realm of humans. Michael had told me to gather seven masters. That I did. He had told me to write a book. That I did, thinking my purpose here had been fulfilled. But what angels cannot figure in is the randomness of human will and intent. Including my own. So you can guess what my reaction had been some months ago when Michael appeared telling me how well my efforts had gone, acknowledging my good work: the move to Texas, the writing of the new book, and the spreading of the teachings. I should have been suspicious right then and there.

"It is time for you to gather again," he had said after finishing the back-scratching.

"OK," I had responded without complaining. "I can see how another gathering would balance things out. Since Gary has gathered, my doing another gathering would geometrically balance out his west with my east, in the growing of the Tree of Life."

"No. You will gather six more times," Michael had countered. That's when I lost it. To say that I had protested would be like calling a cafeteria food fight a tossed salad. In spite of throwing a fit, I did decide to gather seven more masters once again.

It was during the process of trying to find seven masters for a third gathering when I received a phone call from the Chicago area. Little did I know at the time what that phone call would mean. Joanne Koenig-Macko and I had conversed over the past year. Her renown as an angel artist had connected us via one of her admirers who had also read *Blessings, Gifts, and Deeds.* Joanne could paint almost as well with words as she could with pigments. We talked for over an hour on the phone when it finally hit me that she had to be a part of this next gathering. But finding people to gather is not like the army's trying to recruit soldiers. Quite the opposite, it is like the teachings on healing: A space needs to be created for people to invite themselves. And that's exactly what Joanne did. Like many others, Joanne wanted to know what she was getting herself into. What happened at gatherings? What did people do? Why have them? And as I had explained to the first seven masters, I explained to those who followed that a gathering represented both an initiation process, where we fully acknowledge our remembrance of being master souls, and a de facto coming together of the realms of angels and humans. To someone like Joanne, a gathering opened possibilities of not only taking her art to the next level but also her spiritual journey. Like others, she wanted to make sure she wasn't involved in the beginning of a new religion or some kind of cult phenomenon. Before I knew it, a date had been set for the third group of sevens to gather.

Follow-up phone conversations with Joanne (who prefers to be called "Joann-ee") brought up a growing number of questions. Thus, she decided to fly down to Texas the week before the gathering so she could explore the Gate of Grace and work with her angelic helpers on her own. She wished to pursue all the options available to her on a personal level before the gathering began. And, as an artist, she believed no substitute existed for talking face-to-face.

Before I knew it, the week of the gathering was tapping on my shoulder, and the day arrived for picking up Joannee. The crowd at the San Antonio airport caught me by surprise. Besides being late, trying to find Joannee was like trying to spot a buttercup in a meadow of

wildflowers. Thankfully, she spied me as she was marching down the concourse. "Joe! I'm over here," she waved with one hand while dragging her carry-on luggage with the other.

"Welcome to Texas," I said back. " Can I take your bags?" It was non-stop talk from that point on. We had to get away from the airport if we were ever to hear one another without yelling. In short order, we found a nice restaurant and parked ourselves in a booth. While lunch almost turned into dinner, Joannee begged for every detail as to how Michael's appearances had started, what happened after the end of the book, why now, and where from here? I talked so much, my food turned cold before I got halfway through the meal. If I had drunk any more coffee, I'd have become the Starbucks poster boy. Finally, it was my turn to find out about her.

"What got you started in painting?" Maybe I could get some food eaten, for a change, while listening to her.

"Are you kidding? I've been painting since I was five years old. Even at that young age I knew I would be painting. The first day in kindergarten I made a beeline right to the easel. The teacher tried to get me to play with the other kids, with dolls, with toys. But no, it was the easel and nothing else. Every day, the easel. From that day on, teachers were concerned about whether I'd develop any social skills. You can't believe how shy I was, always hiding behind my mother's apron strings if anyone came into the room — painfully shy. As I grew up, different teachers worked with me a lot. Several would put me in charge of art direction or emceeing for Christmas plays. Gradually, I became more outgoing, but always had an eye for art."

Watching Joanne unfold her life story was like watching a gifted weaver creating a tapestry you couldn't take your eyes off of. Her face was alive with joy, as if she herself were a reflection of the angel paintings she was so famous for. As she sipped her tea and dabbled in her dessert, she divulged how life had made her become more practical, taking various art-related positions after graduating from college. Her laugh was genuine when she described how one of her early jobs had her working for the Federal Reserve Bank, in the research department. Research meant doing whatever was needed, including being borrowed for odd jobs by the money-destruction team. "I literally burned money for a living," she chortled. "Old money; millions at a time." Her next job

found her working for an advertising firm. It taught her many facets of the business world that she would later use in fostering her own fame: marketing, advertising, and people skills. She certainly displayed people skills. Just listening to her convinced me she could sell doorknobs at a tepee.

After starting her own company with an associate from the firm, Joannee successfully created a series of hardbound books on Ohio restaurants, their inns, their chefs, and their not-so-secret recipes. When she found out her husband had accepted a job in Connecticut, and that they were going to move, she almost divorced him. Her business partner practically had a heart attack at the news. In retrospect, she could see how all this was divine planning, which led up to her current work.

"We moved to Connecticut in 1984, and I absolutely fell in love with New England. Something within told me to pick up my paintbrushes again and paint these magnificent town square scenes. They were like tableaus out of the 1800s. I painted almost in miniature. I'd go to these town squares and get caught up in the atmosphere. Literally, I'd start seeing horse-drawn buggies and hear the clopping of horse's hooves. Women in long dresses would appear with their parasols. I really got into the ambiance. And before I knew it, the paintings and lithographs became quite popular. My name became well known throughout New England. I did that for twelve years."

It was hard to believe a person would paint tiny pictures for a living. It must have been backbreaking to sit for so long with brushes smaller than eyeliner and strain your eyes laying acrylic down on canvas. But I soon discovered that Joannee balanced her sedentary life with strenuous exercise. What a dynamo she turned out to be as she confessed how her hobby for tennis also lifted her to prominence. She had joined a women's amateur team, part of the United States Tennis Association. They took the state championship and were going on to the play-offs for the New England championship. She had a promising future as a pro. But then the unforeseen struck from nowhere.

"I was working at home on a large order, one day, for a gallery that had been a client for twelve years. I carried on business out of my home. Right in the middle of framing my 'Milford Connecticut' prints for this order, I heard a voice. I looked around, even though I heard the voice more in my head than in my ears. The voice said, 'The order you are

working on is not important.' And I am thinking, 'Oh, Joannee, you didn't get enough sleep.' So, I dismissed it and continued framing my prints. But then I heard it again. It was a feminine voice, very sweet, bell-like in quality, and quite beautiful. 'The order you are working on is not important.' The hell it wasn't. Once again I stopped the framing and looked around. 'I have to be imagining this,' I thought. And again I dismissed it. After the third time, I was about to ask who was there when the phone rang. It was the owner of the shop who had placed this large order.

" 'Joannee, gosh, I feel terrible, but I have to cancel this order on you.' And she had never canceled an order in twelve years with me. 'We just lost the lease on the store,' she informed me. After I hung up, in shock, I heard the voice once again. It said, 'You are to take a blank canvas and your paints and go outside.' I sat there, still stunned. What was happening to me? I could feel this energy, this force, as if it were pushing me to go outside. So, I retrieved a 28x36 stretched canvas out of the basement, along with my paints and my tiny brushes, and headed outdoors. The view from my house was magical, a one-acre lot flanked by sixty acres of undeveloped land out in the sticks. Feeling a bit silly, I set the easel up and was about to apply paint when the voice said, 'Put your brushes down. You are to paint an angel with your bare hands.' Now I knew I'd cracked up. Like some loony, I began talking back to thin air.

" 'What do you mean, put my brushes down? Who is this? I don't paint angels. What's going on here?' And I begin to hear this sweet laughter. I'm really getting annoyed. Here I am wondering if I was having a nervous breakdown. And I start yelling again, 'I paint town greens. That's what I'm known for. I wouldn't know how to paint an angel if you paid me a million bucks.'

"The voice said back to me, 'Trust us.' *Us?* I thought. *Who's us?* And why should I be trusting? But something inside of me felt I should go along with this bizarre scene. Throwing my paintbrushes into my paint box, I picked up a tube of paint and began smearing it on my fingers. Like some kid in kindergarten, I spread a film of paint onto the canvas. After a few more colors, a form began to take shape upon my canvas. The voice then said to me, 'This will be healing art to reach the world.' At this point, I was too into the painting to object to such outrageousness. Shivers covered my body as I continued bringing the angel to life on the canvas.

A great feeling of peace began to surround me as the angelic figure began to take shape. After about four hours, I stopped and said, 'I can't paint with my hands. How am I supposed to get detail?' The voice answered, 'For detail, you can use whatever nature provides.' So I am like, 'Oh wow, what can I use?' After searching around the nearby willow tree, I started picking up twigs off the ground, and then a dried day lily stem from my garden. Using these implements, I added to the painting and felt filled with awe over what started transforming on the canvas. It just blew my mind. It was the most gorgeous angel. She was in this horizontal position, blond, with long flowing hair. The awe began to frighten me because I didn't think I was capable of this. It had to be something guiding me. So I stopped and demanded, 'Look, I need a sign. I need to make sure that this is Christ energy and nothing lower. I want to make sure this isn't some ghost walking around in the woods or something.' And right before my eyes flew this incredible iridescent blue dragonfly, inches from my face. I just froze watching this gorgeous creature dance on air before me. Then it landed right on the upper left-hand corner of the painting and stared at me. Now, keep in mind I knew that I'd never seen this kind of dragonfly, ever, in this area — only the pale brown or black kind. I was just dumbstruck. There was truly a knowing, at this point, that this iridescent creature had been divinely guided. Spontaneously, I started crying, and said, 'Thank you, God. If this is what you want me to do, if this is you showing me my calling, then I open myself to this work.' And with that, I continued."

The waitress started clearing some of the dishes. She asked me if I was done with my food, and I said to go ahead and take it away. I wasn't going to get any eating done while listening to such a beautiful story. Joanne's hearing the voice call to her reminded me of how I felt when I started hearing my name called. After a while, you start questioning your sanity. And instead of an angel appearing in her bedroom, like with me, she sees this angel appearing on her canvas, knowing it is divinely guided. I realized that across from me sat a kindred soul — someone who truly understood what I, myself, had gone through. I had to clear my throat before asking her, "What happened when you were done with the painting?"

"When I was done? It was, 'Oh my God, who did this? It couldn't have been me! This isn't the kind of work I do.' It was so night-and-day

different from my town-green paintings. The town-green paintings required tight detail and tiny brushstrokes. What sat before me flowed with sweeping movements and free form. One of my miniature paintings took a minimum of six months to finish, while I had created this masterpiece in one sitting. Like some pirate with a stolen treasure, I carried the painting into the house and hung it on the kitchen wall, and put a light on it. I remember walking back and forth in an arc, mesmerized by the mystery of it all. As I moved from left to right, the hair color changed from a beautiful golden-blond to this rich burnt-sienna brown. It was changing right in front of me. The eeriness of it blew my socks off. I decided someone else had to see this. So I called a friend of mine. I knew I couldn't show this to my husband."

"How come?" I asked, trying to understand how her experience differed from mine. In my own case, I felt I had to tell Donna or go crazy.

"Because ... I don't know ... he is just ... well, he's an engineer, OK? And I don't think I need to say anything more than that. You get the drift. I couldn't tell my kids, or my tennis teammates. There was only Eileen."

I started to laugh as I remembered my own reaction years ago. "What was Eileen's reaction?"

"Well, she couldn't come over immediately because she was getting ready to move from one house to another. So I loaded it in the van and drove right over. Eileen was blown away. We took the picture outside and photographed it. Eileen called the local newspaper with the story. She had just opened an angel shop, and had me bring the painting to the shop for the newspaper interview. Right in the middle of the interview, some lady walks by the shop and freezes in front of the painting, gazing at it through the window. She then hustles herself into the shop and plants herself right in front of the painting, with the strangest expression on her face, as if she had seen God. And then starts weeping. I can't describe what this did to me as I stood there stupefied, my mouth hanging open watching tears roll down her face. She looks over at us and asks, 'Is this for sale?' The reporter stops the interview as I stammer, 'I, literally, just finished this.' And all of a sudden, my friend, Eileen, who was standing behind the counter, blurts out, 'It's $3,000.' Then the daughter of this woman walks into the store and stares at the painting. 'Mom,' she says, 'I've got to have this.' And the mother whips out this Gold Card, and it's a done deal. After the reporter left, I yelled at Eileen, 'I can't believe you did that!' I wanted

to kill her. I didn't want to argue in front of the reporter. He was quite amused by the whole thing."

"So did you say anything to the lady afterwards?"

"Well, I found out her name was Mary, and she was going through a horrible divorce. She told me if I ever wanted to visit the painting, I could. After seeing how much comfort the painting brought her, I said, 'Judging by your reaction, Mary, it's meant to be yours, especially because the voice told me it was healing art.' And I released my attachment to it."

"What was the title of the painting?"

"Oh, I called it 'Guardian Angel.' "

It was time for us to leave. Either that or we would have to pay rent and take up residence in the booth. As we drove on over to my house, the conversation continued. What I had already heard was a story in itself. But what continued floored me even more. Joanne had spent more time with Mary telling her how the voice, who Joanne now called Gladyss, had guided Joanne to create 'Guardian Angel.' At hearing this, Mary started crying again, confessing to that her sister's name had been Gladyss. From that point on, Joanne knew the painting was meant for Mary.

Joanne wasn't sure where to go with her painting after that. Then one day, while on her way to visit Eileen at the angel shop, a car driven by an elderly man careened out of a parking plaza and smashed into Joanne's car — the driver's side — crushing her hand against the dashboard. The pain stabbed her like a thousand needles, enveloping her in horror as she realized she might never play tennis or paint again. As the medical staff examined her in the hospital, the doctor delivered the bad news. Ligaments were torn, several bones broken, the hand crumpled, requiring rehabilitation. Numbness filled her as she stared at the ceiling. This couldn't be happening. Joanne's stomach turned sick from the shock.

The auto crash was not the first time Joanne had been hit by a car. In 1980, while living in Chicago, a drunk driver had rammed into her, traveling at 100 miles per hour. The injuries had damaged all the discs from her neck down to her lumbar region. The doctors had warned her she might later suffer arthritis or back problems from the trauma. And now this. How could she cope?

"How on earth did you deal with this?" I asked her, trying to keep my attention on the road. Her story hit me like no other I had heard.

"Ya know, while I sat there in the hospital, I kept looking at all the loss: all my work with miniature paintings behind me, the car totaled from the crash, all the practicing tennis five hours a day. And then it hit me — just hit me like a ton of bricks. It was time to do my God work. Heaven was showing me it was time to put the tennis racket down and to pick up twigs and pigment tubes to do this new work. Those five hours of practice a day were nothing more than whittling away at life. You can't believe the emotion that flooded me. It was like an epiphany, a waking from a long sleep.

"As soon as I got settled again at home, I sold off my tennis equipment, all of it, and said that's it. My teammates thought I was out of my mind, that I had had a nervous breakdown, that I had lost it. The car crash had sent me over the edge. They kept trying to talk me into returning to the team, telling me, 'Joannee, you can heal, you're going to heal, you can overcome this, you can learn a new backhand.' And I'm going, 'Nope, I'm done with tennis.' I felt so bad for them. Because at that level of play, you have to know what your partner is thinking, when she is breathing, and vice versa. Your minds have to be connected to one another; you have to be in sync. And I had worked that hard to get to that point — and walked away from it all. They just thought I went off the deep end. I couldn't tell them about the angel. They knew I wasn't religious, knew I stopped going to church. But I had to do this work. I had to paint these angels."

Our conversation drifted to the more mundane things, how the gathering of the next seven would take place, who the other people were, what we could look forward to. A sense of appreciation filled me as we drove up to my house. Donna and the dogs came out to welcome our early guest. It was like the coming together of family. Joanne continued the amazing string of tales that had brought her to this point, sitting across the table from me and Donna. The more I listened, the more I knew this artistic woman was ready to claim the role of a master soul with the teachings of the angels. What a force she was to be reckoned with.

Over dessert, Joannee described how the angels had given her the next painting to do, which she called "Nature Angel." In the creation of the painting, she felt the forces of nature teaching her how mankind abuses nature, how we tear down the forests, how every tree we rip out should be replaced by another, how we are meant to be stewards of

nature, not exploiters. Part of the angel had been painted using plant roots, with the wings of the angel detailed by a fern stem. After "Nature Angel," came one of her most famous paintings, "World Peace Angel." I could have listened to her all night long. The constant occurrence of miracle moments that had taken both the painting and Joannee to new heights inspired me in carrying on the work I had been given.

When "World Peace Angel" appeared in a national magazine, orders flooded in. And after the orders came the healing stories. Listening to Joannee told me she loved to tell the healing stories most of all. "I started hearing from people all over the United States. One lady called from her hospital bed burdened with cancer, telling me she had been praying to God for an angel to help her. And the nurse walked in and said, 'Here, honey, you want a magazine to read?' She opened it up and ... boom ... this full-page angel is staring her right in the face. She said she had to call me and tell me her experience.

"Another lady from Indiana called and said, 'Joanne, my teen-age son insisted I get this painting of yours. He rarely gets into any religious related stuff. He's into motorcycles. But he insisted I order your painting.' The funny thing is, that on that particular painting I decided to autograph it with the phrase, 'An angel to watch over you.' So when she continued her story and told me the weekend after the painting arrived that her son had been killed in an auto accident, I almost cried right there on the phone. She told me that the angel had helped her keep her sanity. It was as if her son knew what was going to happen. Because of that story, I now sign all my prints with 'An angel to watch over you.'

"The most touching story came from the rep of the magazine. She helped get the film ready for the angel to appear in the magazine. This was in Orlando, Florida, where *Early American Life* magazine was published. When the rep received my film of the angel print, she had just been diagnosed as having a questionable lump on her breast. It scared her to death. After the mammogram revealed the lump, she had been scheduled for a biopsy. While spending the morning before her visit working on the color proofs of "World Peace Angel," she said she just kept getting this really peaceful feeling. Every time she would pick up the proof and do more work in getting it ready to print, the peace would flood her again. By the time she arrived at the doctor's office at 10:30 a.m., she said she could feel the angel there with her. When she went in for the

biopsy, they had to cancel surgery because they couldn't find the lump. She was sobbing on the phone as she told me the story. It was then that I began to realize that what the angels had told me was coming true."

Joannee told me how "World Peace Angel" did more than heal people. It also brought healing among nations. Prints of the angel hung in the United Nations, in the office of the United States Secretary of State, Madelyn Albright, then ambassador to the UN, and in homes and bunkers throughout Bosnia and Kosovo. World Citizens Diplomats, headed by Louise Nicoli, took the painting on a World Peace Tour throughout Europe, handing out prints to dignitaries, diplomats, and mayors. The tour then continued throughout Canada. What a testimonial to the power of art. And such art is a testimony to what can happen when each of us lives in our giftedness.

After cleaning the dinner table and washing dishes, Joannee and I resumed our conversation. I asked her what happened after the "World Peace Angel" had been portrayed around the globe. A gleam sparkled in her eye as she looked off into empty space. I could tell she was trying to paint with words once again. "One day, Gladyss, my angel guide, asked me to paint this seven-foot angel. She gave me specific measurements, as if the mathematics of the painting were a key part of the painting. The days I spent creating this vision on canvas were days of wonder for me. The colors, the slivers of mica rock, the objects from nature used to bring forth this incredible image filled me with awe. When I finished the last touches, I stood back and knew immediately it was to be called 'Light of the Universe.' Because it was so personal to me, I called it L.O.U. or Lou. It's not often that I get so caught up in something I have helped create. But this painting so moved me, I sat in front of it and began to pray a prayer of thanksgiving. After prayer, I centered myself and moved into a meditative state. Almost immediately, I heard that I was to go to my computer and log on to AOL and sign into a chat room. You can imagine my curiosity over this. I had no idea what to expect. After logging on, I went into one of the spiritual chat rooms and chatted with a lady I hadn't spoken to in three years. In the same room was a man from Texas who just kind of hung out, not typing any messages. After a while, he sent me a message saying he needed to talk to me at home. And, of course, you don't do that sort of thing. You don't give out your phone number. But the voice in my mind said, 'Do it.' He called me a few minutes after I logged off the computer. In his Texas accent, he introduced himself and said,

'When I watched you tell your friend the story of the seven-foot angel you just painted, I knew you were the one I am supposed to help.' Now I was really getting suspicious. He asked me how much it would cost to make lithographs of Lou by Christmas, and I told him around $3,000. 'Good,' he replied, 'I'll overnight the money to you.' Immediately, I started laughing, thinking this guy was going to hit on me, or something. This was one of his lines, or something like that. It was Halloween day, so I asked, 'This is a joke, right? Like trick or treat?' And he assured me it was no joke. The next day, the money arrived along with a book on *How to Speak to Your Angels*. A letter was attached. In the letter, this man told me I was his daughter in a past life. He told me that whenever I might stumble along my path, he was here to assist me, to help me. He was to pick me up, brush me off, and get me back on my path again. The guy's been like a father to me ever since."

"So, this $3,000 is different than what you needed for the magazine?" I asked.

"Yes. This was to make lithographs of Lou. When I received the check, I was totally blown away. There was also a request along with the check. He said, 'I don't want this money back, Joannee. You're an inspiration to this world. Thank you for listening to the message. Could you please send some of your angel prints to this little girl.' It was a kid living in Louisiana, dying from some disease I never heard of. Some kind of leukemia, a blood disease. Apparently, she was very poor. Well, I thought the least I could do for this patron would be to send this child some angel prints. Her name was Audrianna."

These kinds of stories always grab me, so I pumped Joannee for more information. "Did you ever hear back from her?"

"Not from her, but a month later, I heard from the Texas fellow, and asked him how she was doing, whether she was alive or not. He told me how she had gone in for the blood work-ups, and the doctors could find no trace of the disease. They called her their miracle patient. I was just flabbergasted. The Texas guy told me that I should continue sending my work out to the world. He also requested that I never give out his name. I can only refer to him as my Texas angel. And I have always honored that."

As the evening wore on, Joannee and I swapped more stories about healings the two of us had seen or been involved in that could not be explained. It only convinced me more than I already was convinced that

the messages from the angelic realm were manifesting before our very eyes. We truly are entering the days of wonder.

The next day, the rest of the seven showed up for the gathering. And like the first gathering in California, all experienced profound realization on a spiritual and emotional level as they entered into the Formation of the Sevens and the Formation of Giving and Receiving. On the third day of the gathering, all of us discussed how we were to live out our giftedness and how we were to use this new information from the angelic realm in assisting others to heal themselves. Later that evening, after taking most of the others back to the airport, Joannee took me aside and said, "You know, I have helped others with their healing, but I, myself am in need of healing."

"What's the problem, Joannee?" She sounded serious.

"I've been involved in two serious car crashes. The first accident damaged all the vertebrae from my neck down to my lumbar region. The doctors told me I might suffer severe back problems and arthritis later on. Well, a couple of months ago, at the Whole Life Expo in Chicago, I was lifting boxes in my booth space and wrenched my back. The pain shot from my neck down to the small of my back. Quite painful. As the Expo progressed, the pain got worse. I found it almost impossible to concentrate on sales of my art. A woman from France gave me some sacred oil to apply, and some Reiki masters did some work on me right there in the booth, but nothing helped. The day after the Expo, I made an appointment with my doctor for an exam. After examining me, he immediately scheduled an appointment at the hospital for an MRI of the spine. The results showed the right central disc had herniated. Plus, there were protuberances from osteophyte formation at the C5 and C6 vertebrae. In other words, I am a mess. I didn't want any surgery done, even though the doctor said the pain is only going to get worse. I'm getting numbing in parts of my body now, and have experienced reduced movement in my arms. I'm afraid it will move into my hands where I won't be able to paint anymore. I know I'm asking a lot, Joe, but would you be willing to work on me?"

It's at moments like this, facing a dear friend, when you want either to stand in complete awe of their trust or run screaming to the nearest cave, hiding from the great responsibility before you. It is with the most sincere hope in your heart that you want healing to sweep through them,

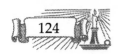

but right next to that hope lurks a dreaded fear that you might fail them, or for that matter, make things worse by dashing their hopes and yours. Truly, Michael knew what he was doing when he gave the teachings the way he did. For it is at moments like these when I replay what he said to me: **"You have heard it said, 'No one has ever healed anyone,' and this is true. Even Jesus said that he never healed anyone. What he did say was 'Your faith has healed you, for I have done nothing.' What he did was create a space for healing to take place. All the energy in the world cannot cause healing."**

Carefully, I reviewed with Joannee what Michael had taught me about healing. We discussed the three conditions for healing Michael had spoken of. Included in our discussion was what might be going on her life to manifest her back problems: the guilt she had carried in abandoning her teammates, the responsibilities she carried for peoples and even nations in bringing her paintings to the world, and the sufferings of others she had taken upon herself in hopes that those less fortunate than she might find healing. It is quite revealing when we look at ourselves in terms of being more than one body, more than just a physical body. We also have an emotional body, a mental body, and a spiritual body. If there is disharmony or discord or trauma or injury to any of these bodies, it can eventually manifest into the physical body, if not addressed. Joannee realized that her painting was a gift to be shared with the world, not a responsibility to be loaded upon her back. Sure she was concerned about being an independent woman and bringing in enough income to justify the tremendous amount of time and effort she spent with others and for others. But was it not more important to see the beauty she created rather than the responsibilities she felt in wanting to help others? Everything about being a seven stems from embracing our gifts.

After our discussion, I said to her, "Joannee, if you are open to it, I'd like to take you out to the Gate of Grace and place you in the middle, the place for receiving."

"But of course, Joe. That would be fine. Shall we go out there now?" By this time, night had descended. So, while Joannee searched for her coat, I grabbed a lantern from my work shed and hung it in the tree. Luckily, it was late enough that none of the neighbors would be watching. The two of us took off our shoes. The ground still radiated modest warmth from the sunny day. Joannee stood in the middle while I stood in

the place of the servant. The night air hung on us with a chill. "Do I have your permission to scan you?" I asked.

"Absolutely," she responded in a confident and strong voice, gazing at the ground. She was ready for this. I lifted my right hand and began my scanning by trying to see her body through the back of my hand. Right away I picked up a red dot in her neck — where she had said the C5 and C6 vertebrae had been injured — a yellow dot in the area between her shoulder blades, and an orange dot in the lumbar region. When I brought my hand down, I could see Joannee was in a meditative state. Not wanting to disturb her, I waited silently until she opened her eyes. "My angels are talking to me, Joe. They said I would find healing through the grace of God and three oils."

"What kind of oils?" I asked. This was new to me. As she stated what the three oils were, I remembered that Donna had a set of essential oils she distributed as a sideline. "Wait right there. I'll be back in a flash." I knew it was too cold for scorpions, and ran back barefooted to the house. I asked Donna if she had the three oils Joannee said needed to be used. Donna had all but one. However, she had a blended oil which contained the third oil. Good enough for me. Thanking her profusely, I shuffled back to the Gate of Grace where Joannee still stood. The two of us reviewed what she had heard as to where each of the oils was to be placed. After applying each oil, I then sent grace into that area as well as the three areas I had seen the glowing dots, until the dots turned white or disappeared. "How do you feel?"

"A bit spacey. Whoa. Kind of like getting off a merry-go-round."

I grinned. "Well, let's call it a night." The chill had crept into my bones, plus I was desperately in need of a smoke. After wishing Joannee sweet dreams, I donned a jacket and quietly stood out under the stars. A part of me wanted to beg Michael to bring healing to Joannee, but I knew better. Joanne was the healer, not Michael, not me, not anyone. Had we created a space for healing to occur? Yeah, it felt as though we had. With Joannee's openness, she had heard her angels and allowed me to send grace to the areas where I had seen the dots. It was up to her to use that grace to her highest good. And something in me told me she had.

The next morning, as I was downing my typical tankard of java to wash away the sleep, I heard Joannee rustling around in her guestroom. The door flung open, and like a swan landing on a lake of glass, she

coasted into the kitchen. "Joe. It's happened," she said, her voice fighting for control. The look on her face was that of some ugly duckling who'd been rudely surprised at discovering swanhood.

"What's happened?" I asked, swigging a gulp of coffee. Not knowing whether she was going to kiss me or dowse me with my own coffee, I patiently waited as she tried to form the words.

"The pain. It's completely gone. I'm healed. Look, I've got full motion in my arms." There she stood in the kitchen flapping her arms like a swan ready to fly into the heavens. Trying to hide my emotions, I took another swig of coffee but couldn't swallow it. I stood there like a chipmunk with pouched cheeks who'd found too many acorns. Tears trickled down Joannee's face. I reached out to hug her, struggling not to unleash my mouthful of wake-me-up. Gentle sobs told me how grateful she felt for my helping her to come to this point.

Later that morning, I ushered Joannee to the airport where she would return to Chicago a changed human being. The next morning she had an appointment with her orthopedic surgeon. A fresh MRI still showed anomalies in the backbone, but could not explain the fact that Joanne was pain-free. The doctor repeatedly had her lift her arms at different angles, testing for range of motion. He could only shake his head. "I'm sorry, Joanne, but according to the MRI, there is no way you should be able to do this. The nerves around the bulged disc should be giving you more than tolerable pain. I'm having a hard time believing what you are telling me. You are experiencing no pain whatsoever?"

"None," she had said. To illustrate the point further, Joannee e-mailed me a copy of what the doctor's report said: "Normal motor strength in the upper and lower extremity groups. Provocative testing of the brachial plexus and peripheral nerves, likewise, was unrevealing." What was showing up on the MRI and what was happening in Joannee's body were two different realities. As I reread the full letter Joannee had e-mailed, once again I thought about what Michael had told me about different dimensions. It was as if two parallel realities co-existed. The doctor saw what he understood from his own reality, while Joannee existed in a reality which was totally unexplainable. To this day, she is pain-free, active like never before, giving seminars, workshops, and lectures all around the world. Like the angels she paints, she is a living mystery, an inspiration to me and others — a walking symbol of the art of healing.

Part II

THE HEALING GIFTS OF HEAVEN

THE MIRACLE OF MANIFESTING

*I*t has been said that time doesn't exist for the angelic realm. Their actions sometimes indicate otherwise. Perhaps time doesn't exist for them, but timing does. For there has been and continues to be information which Michael has asked me not to reveal until a later time or a later event. Such was the case with one of the most dynamic teachings he asked me to give to the sevens.

Joanne Macko had graciously put together a conference in Chicago and asked me to speak on the information around healing. But what she didn't know was that Michael had presented me with three teachings that I would reveal to no one until that conference. To add to the event, Joannee had also captivated twenty-one interested people to attend three simultaneous gatherings that same weekend. Before I knew it, a triple gathering had been put into place to dovetail with the conference. Joannee would be servant for one of the gatherings, I would serve the second gathering, while the only missing church yet to gather (Pergamum), would serve the third gathering. All colors except yellow had been servants for a gathering. Thus the last of the seven colors would finally complete the first ring of the Tree of Life. We knew from past teachings that this would have an impact in the angelic realm. The

rumble in the jungle spread quickly — something special loomed around this conference. And before I knew it, the first Seven had decided to come together again (a rare occurrence, as it turns out) for this triple gathering and the presentation of the new teachings. Even more significantly, the other masters who were the first of a color or church to gather would be there as well, four of that group coming from the first seven masters. Thoughts of a bonanza event flashed in the minds of the sevens. They knew something was up. Like elephants smelling water in the distance, a near stampede headed toward the October 1999 event.

The Friday night of the weekend conference, those who would participate in the triple gathering convened at Joannee's house. It was there that I decided to let the group know that I would present them the three teachings Michael had asked me to keep quiet until this event. There was no exaggeration in my telling them the information would knock their socks off. Before the conference would begin the next morning, word spread at the speed of gossip across the Internet. All the sevens wanted to know what was up.

A cloud of buzzing voices hit me as I walked into the large ballroom at the Holiday Inn where the conference had been scheduled. I spotted Gary off in one corner and decided to have a word with him. We work well together, and I had decided to ask if he wouldn't mind serving back-up in adding technical detail on some of the information I would address. Gary holds information like a keg holds beer. If you want to have a fun time, just tap it. He agreed to help me out. As we finished talking, he told me that one of the first seven had not been able to make the weekend, which was a disappointment for him and the others. These first seven masters love being in each other's company. Nonetheless, those attending the conference treated the six original masters as celebrities. It's amazing what happens when your name ends up in a book.

Joannee and I led the audience through elementary information during the morning session; many had not been exposed to all the earlier teachings from the angelic realm. A lunch buffet had been spread at the noon break with a special table set aside for the first seven-minus-one masters, plus the other three masters of the First Ring, as they decided to call themselves. A joy filled my soul to see how far the sevens phenomenon had come in such a short time since that night when Michael

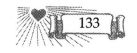

had first appeared to me. We chattered away, oblivious to anything around us.

The first of the three delayed teachings followed shortly after the opening of the afternoon session. Unlike the other two teachings to follow, the first teaching would tease the mind in a modest way. Michael had shown me that certain sounds could be created with the body, and that these sounds could be used to break up spots of pain or spasms. The particular sound he asked me to create involved the snapping of fingers. The snapping sound from our fingers unleashes a sonic vibration capable breaking up physical problems we foster by not keeping ourselves in balance either physically, emotionally, mentally, or even spiritually. These imbalances often manifest as painful spots or muscular spasms which do not want to release. The way to send the sound to a particular affected area, either on oneself or another, is to take the left hand and rest the second and third knuckles against blocked area. Then place the first knuckle of the middle finger of the right hand and press it against the first knuckle of the left hand. Then simply begin snapping the fingers of the right hand while leaning the hands into the problem spot.

Naturally, the crowd loved this information, filling the ballroom with the sounds of castanets as neighbor experimented on neighbor. For some reason, the sound evoked laughter in almost everyone. Who knows, maybe the laughter works as a key component. Many in the room raised their eyebrows in surprise that such a simple technique could prove so effective.

The time had arrived for the second teaching, also related to sound. Michael had shown me that we have the capacity to block our chakras, or to scramble them with negativity, in the same way we create problems in our bodies. Not only that, but my angelic friend had also surprised me with the information that humans possess twelve chakras instead of the customary seven. Chakras are like openings or gateways in our bodies. Some traditions describe them as spinning wheels of energy, with each chakra holding a different kind of energy or power. Normally, the seven chakras are described from the tailbone up to top of the head like so:

1st chakra	root chakra	tailbone	red light
2nd chakra	sacral chakra	small of back	orange light
3rd chakra	solar plexus	below sternum	yellow light
4th chakra	heart chakra	heart/mid-sternum	green light

5th chakra	throat chakra	larynx	blue light
6th chakra	third eye	mid-brow	indigo light
7th chakra	crown chakra	top of head	violet light

But Michael described the twelve chakras in a different fashion. He began with the heart chakra. The color associated with that chakra was still green, however there was a tone associated with the chakra, which was F. One of the ways to create this tone was with a tuning fork. For the conference, I had brought a complete set of tuning forks made up of the seven primary notes of the musical scale. However, these tones were not based upon typical piano sounds, which are equal interval tones. These tuning forks had been specially made to match the Pythagorean tones, sometimes called the diatonic scale. Michael had shown me that the true openings to the chakras were not on the body but in front of and behind the body, like two cones, one pointing inward toward the heart, the other pointing inward from to the back in the heart region. He had instructed me to strike the tuning fork and point the vibrating tine toward the body. With several efforts at practicing, he showed me how to find the chakras with my hands. And I spent time with the audience trying to show them how to find these chakras by asking for a volunteer to come up and lie down on a massage table.

Each of the chakras required a different tuning fork. The next chakra to be worked on was the solar plexus chakra, and after that the throat chakra, bouncing back and forth like a tennis match with the heart being the net in the center. Here is a list of the chakras and the tones:

CHAKRA	TONE(S)	BODY AREA (THE PERSON LYING DOWN)
1. Heart chakra	F	about 8 inches above the chest
2. Solar plexus	E	about 1 inch below the sternum, 8 inches high
3. Throat chakra	G	larynx area, about 8 inches high
4. Sacral chakra	D	about 1 inch below the bellybutton, 8 inches high
5. Third eye	A	above the brow
6. Root chakra	C	above the pelvic area where the tailbone sits
7. Crown chakra	B	above the top of the head

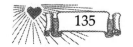

8.	Omega chakra	C/E	between the hips and knees, centered high by about 8 inches
9.	Alpha chakra	B/G	between 12 and 18 inches above the head, about 8 inches high
10.	Terra chakra	C/D	between the mid-calf and ankles, centered high by about 8 inches
11.	Angelic chakra	A/B	between 24 and 36 inches above the head, about 8 inches high.
12.	Divine chakra	grace	place the right hand on the heart chakra (optional), and say, "As a child of God, I bless your heart," while sending in grace.

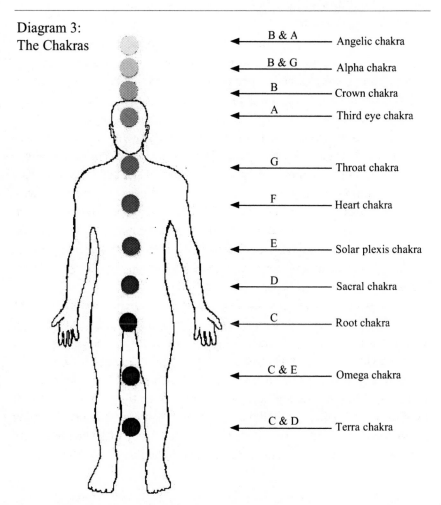

Diagram 3:
The Chakras

B & A — Angelic chakra
B & G — Alpha chakra
B — Crown chakra
A — Third eye chakra
G — Throat chakra
F — Heart chakra
E — Solar plexis chakra
D — Sacral chakra
C — Root chakra
C & E — Omega chakra
C & D — Terra chakra

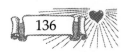

After demonstrating how to detect the openings to the chakras, I asked the first six masters to come up and collectively detect the chakras and use the tuning forks. The crowd murmured with delight, the volunteer on the table jokingly objecting, "I don't know if I'm prepared for this or not. I don't want to get fried." The ease and familiarity shown by everyone changed the typical officious workshop setting to a picnic-like environment. After the six masters detected the chakras opening and used the tuning forks on all eleven of the tunable chakras, they were then asked to place their hands on the heart of the volunteer and bless her heart. Tears came to her eyes as the exercise was finished. When asked how she felt, she responded, "I feel like my whole body has woken up. I've been a bit sluggish for a while but now feel quite vibrant. I feel great." Little did any of us know how important tuning of the chakras would later prove to be.

But now had come the moment I wasn't sure of. Michael had asked me to talk to people about the water we drank and the food we ate. Our water systems are pumped under pressure to our faucets through metal pipes. Chemicals of one kind or another are often added to prevent disease. But in the process of assuring an unhealthy environment for disease we have also lost the life force of natural flowing water. So what's the big deal? Water is water, isn't it? Well, not exactly. With the changes now affecting our bodies, we once again need water for more than just hydrating our body, we now also need that life force. The same thing with food. Food has become so processed that our foods have lost the life force found in natural foods. Some food is even radiated, some altered genetically, some sprayed with chemicals to create a hostile environment for fungus or bacteria or pests. But have we thrown the proverbial baby out with the bath water? I was about to find out.

Volunteers rolled in several cases of freshly purchased bottled water from a local store. At my instruction, each person attending the workshop was given two bottles of water. I kept an eye on Gary, seeing whether he'd even take the water. He was notorious about drinking Chicago water. He considered the water so unpalatable that anytime he ventured into Chicago, he'd seek out a grocery store and buy distilled water. That's all he'd drink. If he were invited out to dinner at someone's house, he'd lug his gallon of distilled water with him. If he ate out at a Chicago restaurant, the water glass stood orphaned. Being born in the Pacific Northwest most

likely spoiled him with good water. Come to think of it, when he'd visit me in Texas, he'd shun the water there as well. So a smile snuck across my face as I watched Gary accept the two half-pint bottles of water like a new father taking a dirty diaper. I found out later that he assumed the water had been imported from the mountains. It hadn't.

"OK," I said to everyone, still wondering what Michael had gotten me into. "Randomly pick two bottles of water, and then pick one of the two bottles to place below your chair." The audience buzzed like a hive of bees as bottles were stored under chairs. All eyes focused on me. A secret prayer went out to Michael. *I sure hope this works, Michael. You gotta help with this, cuz I'm not sure what I'm doing.* After taking a deep breath, I said, "Now take the bottle of water you kept and place it in your hands like so." A half-pint bottle rested in my left hand with my right hand on top of it. Lifting the clasped bottle in the air so all could see, I continued, "Now, I want you to put grace into the water. That's right, grace. Those of you who have stood in the middle of the Gate of Grace know what that feels like. Those of you who don't know what grace is, just think of it as the divine essence of God's love. So think of yourselves as taking love from all around you and moving that love down through the top of your head and through your arms and into the water. Focus only on the love, the grace. Take your time and trust your intuition. You'll know when the grace is through moving into the water." Walking down the aisle, I examined everyone's hands to make sure they held their bottle just like Michael had instructed me. "Now, here is what I want you to say as you move the grace into the water: 'As a child of God, I bless this water that it may nourish my soul and enrich my body.' " A few people tried to write down the blessing and then raised their hands, which told me they hadn't really gotten the message. Two more times I repeated the blessing. The entire ballroom went silent. Would this work? I sure hoped so. My eyes involuntarily strayed over to Gary to see how he was doing with the blessing. He was like a monk in prayer.

About half a minute had passed with a few heads popping up from the blessing of the water. Others took more than a minute. The air itself seemed to have changed texture. An electricity of expectation emanated from the crowd. "What I'd like you to do is to take the bottle of blessed water and take a few drinks from it." Everyone unscrewed the sealed water and began to drink. Everyone, including Gary, seemed pleasant,

enjoying the water, wondering what all the fuss was about. "Now take the bottle from underneath your chair and open it up and drink from it. These bottles of water should taste exactly the same. They all came from the same store, from the same cases."

If anyone would detect a difference, it would be Gary. So I watched out of the corner of my eye as he took a swig from the unblessed bottle. I thought he was going to vomit, as he almost spit out the water from his second bottle. Without explanation, he got up and left the room. Returning my focus to the audience, I asked, "How many taste a difference in the water?" All but about four hands reached for the air. Some faces mimicked Gary's, others displayed tongues sticking out as if having tasted rancid water from the second bottle. "Can anyone describe the difference?"

There was no shortage of volunteers as descriptions came forth saying how the unblessed water tasted like plastic from the bottle. Others described how the chemicals were quite evident in the unblessed water while not present in the blessed water. Still others described how smooth and springlike the blessed water tasted. Many stated that the blessed water actually tasted sweet while the unblessed water tasted flat or dead. Well, once again Michael had proven to be right. "The angelic realm wants us to bless everything that goes into our bodies. Our bodies need it."

That evening, I had to laugh watching all the attendees blessing their food and drinks in the restaurant. It's not that it looked all that strange, it just made me feel good. Not wanting to make a spectacle of myself, I moved one of my hands under the table with the other hand next to my plate, blessing the food and drinks. It worked, and no one would have suspected a thing. Dinner was delicious. Just as I was about to leave, I spied Gary coming in to dine. I had to find out what had happened, and waved him down. "What happened to you during class? You left in kind of a hurry."

"Joe, I had to find out if this blessing thing was for real. You know how I am about all this information we get. A little skepticism goes a long way. The taste in the second bottle of water was sooooo bad, I almost gagged. You know how I am about drinking Chicago water. I couldn't believe the blessing had made that much a difference. I thought it had to be from the power of suggestion. This couldn't be real. So I dashed up to my room, where I had most of a gallon of distilled water sitting. I sat down on my bed and grabbed the jug of distilled water. You know how

distilled water tastes. It doesn't. It's like drinking melted snow. So I held the whole jug in my hands and blessed it, thinking that if this phenomenon were real, a near-full jug would tell the tale. I snagged an empty cup off my nightstand, and filled it with the blessed distilled water. To my amazement, it was like drinking spring-fresh water. I was flabbergasted. After waiting an hour, I decided to try it again. It was even sweeter and fresher tasting. In fact, the longer you wait, the better the water gets. At least to a point. Anyway, the shock of what I was seeing filled me with awe. I've spent the last couple of hours just pondering what this means. This just isn't that much different than Jesus turning water into wine, Joe. In fact, I have a sneaky suspicion that the only reason the water doesn't turn into wine is because it doesn't need to."

Gary and I spoke for a long while about the powers of manifestation that the angels wanted us to reacquaint ourselves with. Hadn't Michael pointed out in one of his appearances that a day would come when we could bring healing with a glance? Well, if we can change the property of water in less than a minute, how long before we change the state of our health with similar ease? How long are we, as inherently divine beings, going to hang onto our limitations? Only we know the answer.

The final day of the conference included all the new sevens from the triple gathering. The ballroom buzzed with enthusiasm because of all the new information and new experiences everyone had discovered. But all good things must come to an end, and the conference was no different. As a closing thought, I wanted people to understand that these gifts given to us by the angels were only half the equation to solving the problems of pain, struggle, and disease. The other half depended on us. Can we forgive ourselves for our self-judgment or for our mistakes so that we can then, in turn, forgive others? Can we allow ourselves to be seen as worthy of these gifts we have been given? Sometimes we find it hard because we feel the need to hold on to our pain, or our anger, or our disappointments. So, I asked the combined group of people to quiet themselves for a few minutes and to focus on how many times life had brought them injury, or deep sadness, or hurt. After waiting for the hush to sink in, I began to speak.

"I want to tell you I am sorry. Not because I did something to you. Nor am I trying to get off the hook for something. I am sorry that as a child your innocence was used against you. I am sorry for all the times you wanted to share your words of wisdom, and you were told to shut up.

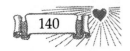

I am sorry for the genius you possessed in the ideas you gave, and you were told that you were stupid. I am sorry for the times you did your very best, and you were told it wasn't good enough. I am sorry for the times you were made fun of because you were different in some way. I am also sorry that your feelings were hurt and no one was there to comfort you. I am sorry for the tears you cried from pain and no one was there to wipe them. I am sorry that you gave your heart like a precious present, and it was refused. I am sorry for the times you were laid a hand to, whether justly or unjustly, and for the times you were alone and afraid, with no one there for you. I am sorry for all promises made to you that were broken. I am sorry for the wishes you made that were not fulfilled, and hope-filled dreams that were shattered. I am sorry for the times you were helpless and at the mercy of others, finding none to stand by your side. I am sorry for the times in your life you felt like you didn't matter. I am truly sorry for the times you felt unworthy even of God's love. Someone owes you an apology just for who you are — I am so, so sorry.

"You are a child of God who is perfect, whole and complete. You are a magnificent human being and deserving of love and happiness. Your happiness is not mine to give. If it were, I would gladly give it. Love for you, on the other hand, is easy to give. I love you just the way you are. I bless your heart and ask that you teach only love."

Soft weeping echoed across the ballroom. Hankies appeared like butterflies from cocoons. Nothing more needed to be said. I exited the ballroom in silence. Before reaching the door, handclapping turned into thunderous applause. It would be too easy to think they were applauding me. In all truth, they applauded what the weekend had given them — themselves. This information, these teachings presented to us through the angelic realm, is given for no other reason than for us once again to embrace the fullness of what it means to be human.

GABRIEL'S GIFT

*I*s it not enough that my life has become a living Twilight Zone? *Am I now to face even the possible end of my marriage?* I anguished. Michael informed me that, like everyone else, I was facing the process of working out my sums. But Donna could no longer endure those "sums," and we separated for the time being. If I had known my life would have come to that, I'm not so sure I would have answered the angel when it called out my name that night in the bedroom. Surely, like everyone else, I have learned and grown from these times of difficulty and confusion. At least, I hope so.

Donna asked me to come and take care of the dogs while she was out of town. Besides feeling like a stranger in what used to be my home, there seemed to be weirdness in the air. I drove to the store for dog food and TV dinners, and on my return noticed that the security gate was open. It closes automatically after driving out. What was it doing open? After I drove through, I stopped to inspect the gate. It was fine. After pushing the remote button and watching the gate swing shut, I scratched my head and chalked it up to quirky electronics. Maybe somebody's cell phone triggered it, or sunspots activated it. Technology is wonderful but sometimes can be as much a mystery as the appearance of angels.

As I entered the house, the hall light turned on all by itself. The dogs started barking. As I plopped the bags on the kitchen counter, I mused to myself, "There must be angels afoot." That's what Gary says all the time when something strange is going on. Just to make sure it wasn't anything other than angels, I searched the house for signs of intrusion — which is unlikely with four mastiffs standing guard. Nothing lurked under the beds nor hid in closets, so I assumed the only thing left was to lay back and observe. A kind of silent nervousness wrapped around me as I fed the dogs and microwaved a spaghetti dinner with chicken-fried steak. TV dinners had become a staple for me these last several weeks, and I made a game out of looking forward to the yummy dessert as the perfect ending to a culinary masterpiece. This time I had pulled out all the stops by buying a whole cheesecake just for myself.

After dinner, I stretched out on the couch to zone out on HBO. My eyes began to droop as I nuzzled my head against my arm. As I closed my eyes, I felt what was like an index finger brushing across my brow. My first thought was of Ebbie's tail. The new mastiff had many of the same habits that Annie used to have. Which didn't surprise me, since Annie didn't show up along with Michael anymore, when he appeared. As I reached over to catch her wagging tail, my hand found only empty space. My eyes popped open. She wasn't there. I bolted up to see if one of the other dogs had drifted by. Poppy was sleeping in the hallway and Bogie was snoring in front of the chair across the room. With my head turning like a searchlight, I spotted Ebbie sleeping yonder in the living room. Baron was not to be found, so I roused myself and walked to the bedroom, and sure enough, he was dozing in his favorite spot where Donna usually slept. The bedroom was as close as he could get to her while she was away. I knew I had felt something brush my brow. But what could it have been? As I snuggled back on the couch, all my senses were on alert for anymore strangeness. As I began to nod off, I told myself that I must have imagined the caressing touch.

The second night, the sensation happened again as I once again folded into the couch with my head laid back looking up to the ceiling — the same warm touch again lovingly brushing my forehead. *Hmm. This is now getting interesting*, I thought. This time with my eyes closed, I just sat still and let it happen again. An invisible hand brushed my forehead three times and then stopped. When I opened my eyes, no one was there.

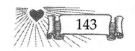

"OK," I said in a loud voice, "Whoever you are and whatever you want, let's get it over with." There was no answer. The next day, while checking my e-mail in the office, a hand tenderly covered the top of my head. It was a big hand with long fingers. I reached up and placed my hand on top of whoever's hand was there but all I felt was the top of my head.

As the days continued, I found myself being touched on the shoulders, arms, the back of my legs and even my feet being rubbed. Whoever or whatever it was did it in a loving, tender way. At one point, I wondered if a ghost might be responsible, but it didn't strike me as a ghost. I don't know why but it just didn't.

On the final day of my stay at the house, I decided to clean up before leaving for the airport to pick up Donna. Part of the reason for changing into Mr. Clean stemmed from my promise to Donna that I would cart the recyclables over to the recycling center in town. After backing the truck up to the opened garage door, I grabbed a fresh plastic bag to throw empty dog food cans into. Donna already had quite a pile of bags stuffed with recyclable material, nicely spray painted with red R's on them. A smile crossed my face, knowing this was her way of telling me, Don't forget. As I started tossing the bags into the back of the pickup truck, the phone rang. It might be Donna, so I abandoned my task and ran into the kitchen to catch the call. A phone telemarketer chewed on my ear about some prize I might get for buying property. Rather than tell the guy to quit bothering me, I turned the whole thing into a joke, hung up, and headed back to the garage. As I closed the door behind me, I froze in my tracks. The hairs on the back of my neck bristled. Moving only my eyeballs, I searched the garage for some mysterious stranger. For right there in front me, stacked as neatly as a linen closet, lay all the trash bags in the bed of the pickup. Every single bag. As I stared at all the red R's, they reminded me of Rudolph, who had obviously kidnapped a squadron of Santa's elves.

Rather than spook myself out over the unexplainable, I chuckled, *This could come in handy*. It's not my way to analyze what can't be analyzed, so I raised my hand and uttered, "Thanks ... uhhh ... whoever you are. Really." While driving to the recycling center, I mulled over all the strangeness of the past days, wondering what else was in store for me. If Gary had been here, he'd have proclaimed, "Angels are afoot, and they do nothing without a reason." But what if it weren't angels?

The recycling center people are always nice, but this time they were implementing a new program, and the guy in charge asked if I could separate out everything, which I was glad to do. He thanked me as he gave me my receipt. Plenty of time to get back to the house, clean the filter system in the pond and go get Donna. As I drove up to the driveway entrance, once again I noticed the security gate was gaping open. And once again I could find nothing wrong with it. I knew I hadn't left it open because I'm always concerned the dogs might wander if they get out of the house while I am gone. After watching the gate close from my rearview mirror, I drove on ahead only to find myself blinking in wonder as to why the garage door was now closed. I knew I had left it open because I was coming right back and didn't want to have to open it again to get into the house. Perhaps Donna had caught an early flight back and taken a taxi home. A search of the house proved no one was home. What was going on?

As I undressed to climb into my swimming trunks to clean the pond filter, I kept shaking my head as to all this strangeness these last several days. Either I was losing my mind or Gary's adage was going to come true. At this point, I wasn't sure what was going to happen. Ebbie followed me out to the pond, plopping herself in a pile of flesh after lapping up a drink of water. After taking the filter system apart, cleaning it up, and putting it back together, I had a great idea. All the beautiful water lilies in the pond bloomed with the seven colors of the rainbow, or actually, all the colors of the seven churches. Water lilies are a great love of mine. But instead of leaving them randomly spread across the ten-foot diameter of pond, my brainstorm was to place them in the same geometric formation as the stones in the Gate of Grace. Rather than put mud on the bottom of my homemade pond, and plant the roots permanently, I had potted all the water lilies in separate containers so they could be cared for more easily. I'd learned this trick with the small pond I had at the place Donna and I lived in California. So, moving them around wasn't a real big deal. The pond was only about hip deep with the each potting container about the size of a large punch bowl.

Like a hippo in a pool, I bent down to lift the orange water lily over to the position of the church of Ephesus, grunting the whole way. Ebbie eyed my every move, probably wondering if I would disappear below the surface of the water. One after the other, I lugged all the different colored water lilies to their respective places. "There," I said, standing in the water with all the little fishes nipping at the hairs on my legs, "All are where they should be." But as I looked around, something seemed out of place. *Let's see,* I said to myself. *Red is where it should be, and the purple is, and the violet, and the orange, and the blue. The blue? The blue is in the east, which is correct. But there needs to be blue in the west as well. And I don't have another blue water lily. Well, it was a good idea, anyway.* After further inspection, I realized I had two yellow water lilies. If I moved the blue water lily over the west, that would put the yellow water lily in the place of the servant. In the back of my mind, I remembered Donna arguing that any color or church could act as the servant. *Of course That's the solution.* Yellow is the color of the church of Pergamum and the color of Gabriel. Surely Gabriel won't mind also occupying the place of the servant.

After playing water hippo again with the yellow water lily, I picked up the pot of the blue water lily just enough off the bottom so as to keep the whole plant immersed in water as much as possible. Waddling slowly through the water, with the pads and blossom trailing behind me, I reached the position in the west and slowly lowered the pot to the bottom. Once the lily was in place, I stood to check it out, and realized something very strange, indeed. More than one shadow of the blossom was cast on the surface of the water — as if there were two lights. One of the shadows lay to my right side, caused by the sun. The source of the other shadow shone from behind me. The length and darkness of the shadow betrayed a very bright source close to the ground. It had to be Michael.

As I turned slowly to greet the face of the angel I have come to know so well, I could plainly see this was not Michael. Before me stood one of the nine angels who I had seen in the Gate — the one with the appearance of an Arab. So I did what I thought was the best thing to do. I blurted, "As-salaam Alaikum."

"Wa Alaikum salaam," came a voice as beautiful as Michael's. **"It is time for you to learn from me."** Just by looking at the magnificence of this angel, I could tell he held great truths. *If this angel holds true to form with his placement in the Matrix, he would have to be Gabriel,* I thought to myself, *Could this be the angel that visited Mohammed?*

"May I ask who you are?" As with Michael, there came the sound vibrating my soul, with colors springing forth in my mind's eye, lending

pictures of who he was. Emotions welled up almost to the point of tears at the peace I felt, just like with Michael. Such an experience everyone should have at least once in their life: to hear with your body and soul the name of an angel, to feel the emotions similar to what I felt at the birth of a puppy when my mastiff brought forth her first litter. This angel affected me differently than Michael had. I couldn't call it a feeling because I didn't feel it. It was more like an awareness, an opening of the mind to a pleasure, if the mind can feel such a thing. If I were to describe it in human terms, I'd call it the opposite of having a headache. There was a moment when I thought I knew the secrets of the universe had unfolded within me. When Shakespeare asked what was in a name, I know he had never heard the name of an angel, otherwise he would not have asked.

"You may call me whatever you like, if it helps you to know me."

My thoughts returned to Michael telling me the same thing and all the trouble it caused me, before finding out he was the one that was referred to as the Archangel Michael. I had joked about if I had it to do all over again I would have called Michael, "Bob." So I said to this angel, "I will call you Bob."

"As you wish," was all he said, but I knew full well who he was.

"Unless I am mistaken, you are the one known as Gabriel. You are the one that gave the world Islam."

"I have served God as this one before." This so similar to what Michael had said when I had asked him if he were the Archangel Michael.

"OK. I will call you Gabriel, too. I am just happy your English name is easier to say than some of the other angels' names are."

"Your humor is more delightful, as I stand with you, than it is as I watch and am told by Michael."

Hmm, I thought to myself, *the great Joe Crane: Comedian to the Angels*. What a hoot. However, I could see I was avoiding the reason for this visit, as I have done with Michael. Not knowing why an angel is standing in front of me makes me nervous. You never know what they have up their robe.

"Our time is short and there is much to be set in motion, that your understanding will be great. You must be able to know the things we will give to you."

"I see you have a box in your hands. Does it have something to do with the gifts Michael told me would come?"

"Yes."

The box in his hands sparkled with gold and jewels. I noticed a keyhole, which implied there must be a key. The top had no seam, indicating no lid to open. But I knew there had to be a lid. What use is a gift that can't be opened? As his long dark fingers held the box in his grasp, I could see his fingernails were like rays of light rather than the hard substance ours are made of. My eyes traced his fingers back to his hands and then back to his wrists. His hands were powerful looking but his wrists were truly amazing. They were thick and big around, appearing to be of someone who had done a great deal of manual labor. His skin was what attracted my eyes the most, for he had the best tan I have ever seen. The richness of the color and the skin tones almost pulled me into gazing at its lush light forever. As my eyes followed the arm to the robe he wore, I was astounded by the many colors of yellow woven in it. Gold and silver trimmed all the edges of the garment, if that's what it was covering his immense body. I looked up into his face and eyes again. The blackishness of his eyes shone as the light off a black pearl with a strong light on it. His hair was black, also, with what looked like rays of light where the highlights should have been. I was totally taken in by all of this as I stood in the presence of the angel Gabriel.

"So, given you are the angel in the yellow spot, representing the church of Pergamum, you must be here to get my mind right."

"That is a way of saying what I am to teach you."

Something puzzled me. When I had last seen Gabriel with the other angels, he usually stood in the south position with the church of Sardis. Yet here he was standing in the church of Pergamum. Normally, the angel standing in the place of Pergamum is Raphael, who I call the Green Angel of the Indian/Pakistani race. So why was Gabriel not standing in the south as the helping angel to the church of Sardis? He asked me if I wanted a hint, and of course I did. His explanation still left me confused as he asked me what I thought. "Well, in different situations with different people, you guys seem to move around in different ways. All I can come up with is that the races you display are there to show a correlation between us humans and you angels."

"There is your answer."

"What is my answer?" No further words came from him as he reached out to me with his left hand, palm up.

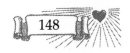

"Look."

I did as I was told. In his palm, I could see there a yellow liquid, which looked like a bead of sweat or maybe a tear. "What is it?" I asked.

"This is the anointing oil of Pergamum I give to you."

It was so small, only a drop, if that much. I was honored to be getting anything but I would have rather he gave me the gold box resting in his other hand. As I reached out to try and retrieve the small drop of oil, he closed his fingers as if he were protecting the droplet of oil, leaving only his index finger extended.

"Show me your hand."

I thought he wanted to see if my hand was clean, so I showed him my palm and then the back of my hand with my fingers spread wide apart. He took his index finger and pointed to the middle finger on my right hand.

"Gather the oil with this one."

Closing the rest of my fingers with only my middle finger sticking out, I wondered if he was aware of how inappropriate this seemed to me. Here is this wonderful gift the angel is trying to give to me, and I'm receiving it in a fashion I sometimes greet idiot drivers on the freeway. His left hand opened again as I moved my finger to do as he suggested. Ever so gently, I eased my finger closer and closer to the drop of the oil. It reminded me of someone trying to pluck a drop of dew from a leaf. He rotated his hand to let the droplet fall onto the tip my finger. I examined it, noting the yellowness was not like the yellow it had been in his hand. Staring up at him, I waited to see if he was going to instruct me further. He said nothing as I wondered if it had a smell. After bringing the drop close to my nose, I blurted out, "Bananas!" Damned if it didn't smell like bananas.

"More than that is of this oil. Place the oil on the softness below your breastbone."

Lifting up my t-shirt with my left hand, I placed my finger with the oil in the area known as the solar plexus, rubbing in the oil with small circles.

"That which is left place on your forehead."

I moved my hand up to the place where my third eye should be and rubbed in the last of the oil. "And this is for?" I asked.

"This is to open the mind of your kind that you may see. The anointing oil is to heal the mind that it may be one with spirit. Your

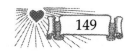

kind has come to believe that the mental is separated from spiritual, and that which is must be understood through logic. Everything must make sense to you or it is not to be trusted. As the mind and the spirit work as one, you will know the love God is. This oil will help you to know that which comes from God, and which the mind makes up to reason away what it cannot yet grasp." Gabriel stopped talking as if to hear what I was going to say next. I didn't disappoint him. I did know something about how some essential oils worked and what they were for.

"Gabriel, I think I know what is going on here with the oil. I know that oils have a vibration, as do all things, and when an oil is used, the human body has its vibrations raised. Each oil has a frequency of its own, as do the different parts of the human body. The simplest way of putting it is to say it is like being a musical instrument. When it is in tune it will sound beautiful but when it gets out of tune it sounds awful and is not working as it should. Once it is brought back into tune, the sound vibrations are pleasant to the ears."

"You do have an understanding of oils. Go on with that you are saying." I smiled to think I did know something of what I was talking about with this angel.

"So, Gabriel, is this why you are giving me this oil? To raise the vibrations of the mind so we are open to greater concepts? Is this oil's frequency as powerful as rose oil's is, given rose is the highest?"

"This which I give you is fourfold the power that comes from a rose."

"That must make it about a thousand megahertz or better. I can see someone using it, and they start buzzing all over the place."

"Reason would tell you this, yet it is not so. Your kind, as you say, has grown to believe that more is better. What I have given is more powerful than rose for the purpose it is to be used. Would you use a mighty ship to catch one guppy?"

"Well no. I would use the best tool for the job. I do hear what you are saying about how we have gotten into overkill. I know what you are saying by more powerful than rose, for the job it does. Maybe the oil you gave doesn't have me buzzing like oil with a higher frequency would. As a matter of fact, I don't feel any smarter than when we started."

"Would you like to test what you just said?"

"Sure, this should be fun. How do we do that?"

"I said there is your answer, and you said, 'What is my answer?' **Yes?"**

"We were talking about the places where the angels stand and why the races are where they are."

"What do you know?"

" 'Stand' is a clue to the answer, isn't it? It is more than just where you are standing; it has to do with what you are standing for. Each of you has something about your being the people you look like. We have been looking at only the gifts each church has and not the races you are. I know as a people, each race has a gift, too. There is something about where each lives and comes from. I got it! I got it! There are seven churches, seven colors, seven notes to a scale, and seven masters with gifts. I also know it takes these seven to have everything work. It takes the gifts of seven masters to have a business be successful or a community work. I now see there are these seven different types of humans here on earth to have an earth that works. Each race has gifts that are not so readily available to the others — just like the churches. I guess bottom line in all of this is, we need each other if we are ever to have the kind of world we want."

"You are doing well."

"I knew that without the oil."

"You did in the mind and in the spirit, yet they were separate from each other. Tell me more of what you know."

"I know that you angels stand where you are for a reason, too. Not just in the Matrix but in your coming to us now. In a way, you need us, too, as we need you. Your kind changes places with one another to have what could be the gifts of the angel you changed places with. Also, you bring your gift to the other angel's spot and to the place that one of the seven masters stands. It is almost like you are a helper angel to us and to each other.

"I just had a thought about something. I would bet that we are coming together as angels and humans for a bigger picture. You angels commune with us so we can commune with others because we can't do it on our own. Now for the big kicker in this: You need us, too, and I can even tell you why. Angels are of the same oneness but have different gifts, much like we do. Angels draw from one another all the time. And by changing places, you gave me the hint I need to figure it out. Let me use a metaphor to help explain this so everyone else might understand. If we look at it like breathing, one angel is the breath in and the other angel is the breath

out. This works fine in our understanding but something is missing in this. We can understand the motion but what we have missed is the lungs. The breath you angels are doesn't have lungs to complete the flow. The breath is there and has always been, but unless there is the physical, it cannot be used. Angel and the helper angel, so to speak, are one with each other, and only lack the space for creation to take place. What else I know is that creation can only take place in what we call the third dimension. This is where we come into the equation. We cannot create on the level we are capable of because we separated ourselves from the divine nature, thus, the Fall of Man."

"The wisdom you speak is abounding."

"When we separated ourselves from each other, we did the same with your kind. The only thing we really had left was the oneness with the love of God, and we even forgot that in time. Now you and others like you are here to help us to become the oneness we all are again."

"Do you see the oil is opening you to a greater understanding? Or are you just smart?"

"Oh my God. You have a sense of humor, too. Yes, I do see I know some things on a deeper level and don't have the words to explain it. Will the oil help me to do this, too?"

"You and others."

"Cool. How much oil can I have?"

"It is for you to make."

"How do I do that?"

"You can find what you need in your world. Gather the oil of a banana, glycerin and frankincense. Mix them as I tell you and place them where I tell you to for seven days. They will rest there through the evening and morning of the seven days. When the time is done you will remove them that they may be used by your kind. As you are visited, you will be given oils by the others to heal that which is, as you say, out of balance. The other angels will tell you how to make their oils."

"Let me see if I have this. I am to make oils and see that others get them. Just where do I get the money to do this? The stuff needed is going to cost me, and so will postage. In case you haven't noticed, I am not Mr. Big Bucks. I don't know how much to make or how much oil to package."

"Donna has small bottles."

"You mean the five-milliliter bottles she gets oil in?"

"Yes. Fill them with the oil and place them where I tell you. Tell no one where that is, for others will come to take them before it is time. You may gather three quarters of twenty for your labor and that which you need to hold the oil."

"What does that mean? If it is twenty cents, it won't even pay for the bottles, so that can't be it. You must mean dollars. Is that right?"

"That is a fair exchange."

"Cool. Then that it is." Gabriel told me where to place them, and it was a pretty good spot, come to think of it. He told me how to mix the oils as far as to what part of which to use with which part of the other oil. "I do have one question about how the oil works."

"Ask it."

"Does this oil from you raise the frequency to a higher level?"

"You have used it. What do you say it does?"

"My hit on it is that the oil sets the frequency to the level it needs to be at. Like the brain operates at a certain level and the oil brings the brain to that frequency. Once the brain is at that level we become open to receive."

"Joe, what you say is true, yet there is more to it. The oil helps to link the thinking to the spirit until a time you can do it on your own."

"Can you tell me when that will be?"

"Yes, yet there is more to this than one oil bringing the mind into spirit and being as one. All will be made clear in time. Do as I have asked of you and we will speak when the oil is made whole. Our time is done for now. Be at peace and teach only love."

Gabriel folded back into the light as Michael does when he leaves. I didn't feel any wiser nor did I think I was any smarter than before Gabriel showed up. One thing for sure: I knew I had better get out of the water before my toes looked like white prunes. After cleaning up, I wondered where I would get all the stuff I needed to make this mixture of oils. Donna would know. And it was time to pick her up at the airport.

RAPHAEL'S GIFT

*M*ixing the oils Gabriel had instructed me to use in the making of the Oil of Pergamum was not as easy as I had thought it would be. Finding banana oil was like finding gold. Hunting down a supplier for the other oils proved nearly as difficult. Hours of driving time and numerous phone calls produced only seven small bottles in which to place the mixed oils. I said to myself, *This must be some kind of a sign.* But then I always say that when something strikes me as odd. There are seven masters, seven colors, seven churches, and now only seven bottles. Sitting down and mixing the oils filled me with excitement. With the carefulness of a surgeon laying out his instruments, I set each group of bottles in specific locations. Just to make sure none of the seven bottles accidentally got filled twice with the same round of oil filling, I'd pick one up, add the new oil and then set it safely over in my do-not-fill area. After completing a round of one oil, I'd move the seven bottles back over to the to-be-filled area and start all over. The whole process sped by, adding to mybuilding excitement. Lifting a fully-mixed bottle to my nose, I took a whiff, drawing the aroma in ever so lightly. The oil blend yielded quite a pleasant aroma, teasing me to take another whiff. "Hey," I said to empty air, "this ain't bad at all. As a matter of fact, it's good. It's

very good." Packing all the seven bottles into a bag, I headed out to the secret place where they would rest for seven days. The drive took about an hour and a half. According to Gabriel, the oils had to be placed after sunset of the first day, and would rest until the morning of the seventh day.

Darkness had descended by the time I left for the secret place. As I climbed into the car, I thought how nice that the oils would be ready by the time I would teach my seminar next week. This would be my first occasion to let people know of this wonderful gift given to us by Heaven. Dodging deer and a skunk or two along the way, I began laughing at myself for the crazy things I had gotten myself into over the last year. Now I was sneaking out at night to a secret place where the angels would assist in changing the oil, readying it for humanity. All the things I've done just because an angel asked me to. *What next?* I asked myself. Well, that was the wrong question to ask, because right then and there a light started to form on the passenger's side of the car. *Here we go again. I guess these angels must love riding in cars and trucks.* A greenish light grew brighter to the point of brilliance. Driving and wanting to witness what would emerge from the green light was not a good combination. I could imagine the traffic citation in my mind: "Driving while under the influence of an angel." The body began materializing fully. *The angel of Sardis?* I questioned. *Green is the color of the church Sardis.*

When the angel fully materialized, it appeared just like Raphael on the night all seven angels had been introduced by Michael. The beautiful green light emitted a peace that radiated deep into my heart. As before, he reminded me of an ascetic holy man from India or Pakistan similar to what I've seen on videos. In his hand rested a gold box, much like the one Gabriel had brought. "You must be Raphael," I finally commented, still trying to keep the car on the road and at the same time take in all the beauty radiating next to me.

"I have ..." and I chimed in, **"served our God as such."** He looked at me with kind eyes, knowing I was joking with him. "**I bring you the second anointing oil.**"

"Your timing is just great," I told him. "Here I am on my way to place the first oil where I was told, and you show up. It's like a guy can't get one thing done before you guys show up with something else to do. OK, so lay it on me what the next one is."

"Take the oil of the olive, the purest you find. Mix with it the oil of the lemon grass — you know where to find this. Mix with these the oil of myrrh and add the cutting of a lime skin for the oil of the lime. Olive oil brings peace to the heart. Lemon grass oil is for the healing of the heart. The oil of the lime skin brings joy. Myrrh gives foundation and balance to the human heart. Place this anointing oil with the other one for six days. Give me your hand."

It was time to pull over. After giving him my hand, palm up, he pointed to my index finger and told me to take the droplet he held. As I started to dab at the drop of oil, Raphael stopped me saying I was using the incorrect finger. Strange that a finger would be so important. He then let me know that I also had used the wrong finger with the Oil of Pergamum after blending it. So much to remember.

"You took the oil with your ring finger and it was the long [middle] finger you were to take that oil with."

"So why is it I wasn't told then?"

"It was not for him to say to you."

Him? I guessed "him" meant Gabriel. "But, you can? Oh yeah, I get it. If something is out of whack, it is the green (of the church of Sardis) who will tell you first. All things must add up, and if there were right and wrong, a green lets you know straight away which is which."

"You are wise. Such is the gift of Sardis."

"Gift, my eye. I think it is more like a trap for them." I was trying to be funny but Raphael, obviously, was not impressed.

"Don't give up this work you do."

I started to laugh, thinking of the old saying he was trying to refer to, about not giving up your day job. "You have a sense of humor, too."

"We all do. Humor is the light in the darkness. It lights the soul and spirit when nothing will. God has given this to all. It is God. Your kind is too serious, for even a turtle has a smile."

I had to think about what he was saying, and damn if he isn't right.

"You do have a way of stopping what the angels have to say to you."

"OK, go on with what you were saying about my fingers being mixed up. How should it be?"

"Each oil has a finger to be used. The Oil of Pergamum is the long finger. The Oil of Sardis is the index finger. Place this oil on the heart and on the third eye."

Gently taking the drop of oil, I placed it on my chest and on my third eye. A little of a tingle swept through my heart, filling it with warmth, if that makes sense. The warmth left me with a joy or happiness within.

"Our time is done. Teach only love."

With that, he was gone, back into the light from where he came. While continuing to drive to the secret place, I said a little prayer to myself: *God I hope you know what you are doing, because I sure don't.* After arriving at the secret spot and placing the Oil of Pergamum where I had been told, I looked around and thought, *This must be some kind of special location,* for Raphael had asked me to place the Oil of Sardis at the same site after I blended it. Returning to the car, I started up the engine and drove back to where I was staying, half expecting another angel to materialize and give me another oil.

The next day was taken up with getting things done for the coming seminar that following weekend. Knowing people would want to build their own Gates of Grace after hearing these wonderful teachings from the angelic realm, I had found a good source for the seven stones and was packaging together sets of stones with printed booklets of instructions. To make the stones more uniform, I purchased a lapidary blade to cut them to size. The day zipped by, and soon it was time to leave town for Austin where the seminar would be held. The pickup had been packed with everything I'd need for the weekend. I've always liked driving, and this trip filled me with even greater joy, knowing what I was about to bring to humanity for the first time. A sack lunch sat on the floorboard next to me, and a mug of coffee danced back on forth on the dashboard. Couldn't be more perfect. And then it started.

A red glow filled the cab of the truck — and then glowings of blue, purple, orange, and finally violet. *How in the name of all that is sacred are five angels going to fit in the cab of my pick-up along with me?* Once again, I had to divide my attention between driving and ogling angels. My mind fought to understand what was happening in the cab of my truck. All five angels materialized as if one into the other, a kind of optical illusion almost making me cross-eyed. Whichever angel I focused on moved into full materialization and then faded again once my focus changed to one of the other angels. Four of the angels were visible at any one time but did not take up space while the remaining angel would

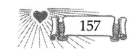

materialize, gaining substance. It was the strangest thing I had seen yet, as they seemed to lose or gain mass depending on which one I looked at.

"You have much to do and our time is short with you."

Something within had told me the remaining angels were going to come and give me the rest of the oils, but I didn't think it would be like this. "You guys must really like truck rides," I said to them. But it went on deaf ears. They had their own agenda in mind and didn't say anything back. The angel with the red hair started the show, and it struck me as odd to see her with a violet light surrounding her. If memory served me correctly, she was of church of Smyrna, probably the reason she was speaking first. I mused, *So much like a red to want to go first, but if you are violet you should go last. Oh well. What do I know about how these angels work?* Every time I think I know what they are going to do, they change everything. Khamael is the name of the angel of Smyrna; her long red hair and green eyes make her a real looker, if you can say that about an angel. Her soft voice had great power in it as she started to speak.

"I give you the anointing oil of Smyrna. Mix the oil of the honeysuckle, frankincense, and rose, as I tell you, with that of grapeseed oil, that it may bring courage to the faint heart to manifest that which has not been. The honeysuckle gives the sweetness of determination — that once started is almost impossible to stop. Mixed with rose, it draws power for what others would see as a hopeless battle. Frankincense brings spiritual balance to them both and will heal the body. The grapeseed oil adds wisdom to the works of this church. Place the oil on the third eye, base of the spine, and on the instep in front of the heels of both feet."

I started to ask a question when the next angel took on mass — or came to the forefront might be a better way of putting it. A Native American woman, as young as a maiden and as wise as an old woman, started to speak. Her dark eyes shone with love, pouring forth like two waterfalls with the compassion of God.

"I come to give you the anointing oil of Laodicea. Take the oil of lavender, nutmeg and cinnamon. Mix these as I tell you in grapeseed oil. Take this oil to the place where the others lay in rest until they are born anew as the anointing oil of Laodicea. This oil soothes the burning heart and brings the gentleness of spiritual love. It will bind the physical to the spiritual with mercy and forgiveness. Place it on

the third eye, the top of the head, and also on the bottom of the great toe of the right foot. Do this with the little finger of the left hand."

Tzadqiel was the name of this angel who gave the Oil of Laodicea. My attention was drawn away from the angels, as I looked out the truck window. The scenery passed by in a very strange way. Normally, when you look out the window you watch an even flow of the landscape zip by. I looked out the window to see it strobe as if it were a movie flashing by me frame by frame as the truck continued down the highway. Was I in another dimension or was reality being altered to accommodate these heavenly beings? Could I be caught in some kind of time warp and really be going through it frame by frame? My attention was quickly brought back to the angels in the truck as the next angel started to speak. This one was Tzaphqiel, the Polynesian-looking angel.

"I give you the anointing oil of Ephesus to be mixed as I tell you. Take the oil of the orange, tangerine, and carrot to be mixed with that of the apricot. The brightness of the orange mixed with the darkness of the tangerine skin balances the emotions. The sweetness is encased in bitterness to keep it in balance. The oil of carrot serves to ground the emotions and the tartness of the apricot binds the oils together. Place this oil on the third eye, sacral, navel, and on the instep of the left foot."

Before I could ask which finger to place the oil on, the angel was replaced with the next angel.

"I bring you the anointing Oil of Thyatira."

This angel had a purple glow about him, surrounding him with the character of an Asian master of great power and knowledge. The box he carried exhibited more ornateness than any of the boxes I had seen so far. Its surface glittered of gold, and fashioned as if a great deal of work went into the making of it. This box functioned as more than the repository of a gift; it also served as a display of divine art. I wondered what mysteries of the East it held.

"Take the oil of myrrh (for grounding the creative spirit), the oil of raspberry leaf (for making abundant one's visions), the oil of anise (for binding the spiritual emotion with the human emotion, flavoring one's works with love), and mix them with glycerin to make clean that which is not clean. Place the anointing oil on the top of the head and on the third eye. Place it on the sides of the great toes."

This angel had to be Haniel, if they were running true to form. Before this one faded away, I said, "I need to ask about which finger to apply the oil." I shot out my question, "Which finger do you use for anointing?"

"The African will tell you how to use them."

No sooner had he said that, and he was gone. As the purple light faded, the blue light grew brighter, and this tall Zulu looking warrior sat next to me. Michael had introduced this angel to me before as Ratziel. Power exuded from his every pore. All the angels exuded a different kind of power. The Zulu carried a kind of power one would feel in the presence of a great wise being. All of these angels could intimidate or lavish love. They were like living mixtures of oil and water, frightening power mixed with absolute tenderness and love that could bring a tear to your eye. I said "Jambo," which I remembered, from a TV show I had seen, was supposed to be a greeting.

He smiled and said, "Good afternoon," in the most proper English. I had to chuckle to myself because he did sound like James Earl Jones. I also thought to myself, *If this angel had been Darth Vader, the Federation would have won.*

"I bring you the anointing oil of Philadelphia and more. Take the oil of hyssop that binds all things with God and cleans that which interferes with that union. Take the oil of juniper berry as a solvent to clean that which is made in the body and mind. Take the oil of sandalwood to open the lungs, this to help you speak only love. Take the petal of a blue water lily for the gentle love God is. Mix these with the oil of the grapeseed to bind them. Place this anointing oil on the third eye, throat, and on the underside of the great toes.

"Joe, you have questions as to how the anointing oils are to be applied."

I started to ask something, but was cut off.

"Show me your right hand."

I did as he asked, holding out my hand with the fingers spread apart. He touched my little finger and said, **"With this finger, place the anointing oil of Smyrna where you have been told. This is to bring health to the physical and to make you strong in that which you do. The next finger on the right hand** [ring finger] **is used to place the anointing oil of Ephesus. With this finger take this oil and place it where you have been told, for it gives the balance to the emotions.**

When the emotions of this church are under control great works will they do."

He moved on to the next finger, middle finger, and said, **"With this finger, place the anointing oil of Pergamum, where you have been told. This oil opens the mind for greater spiritual concepts and brings balance to the mental and the spiritual. With the index finger take the anointing oil of Sardis and place it where you have been told. This oil aligns the human heart together with the divine heart. It brings peace, compassion, and love, which are needed by a healer."** Ratziel then reminded me that the Oil of Pergamum is also to be applied to the bottom of the left big toe, while the Oil of Sardis additionally should be applied to the sole of the left foot, three fingers down from the middle toe.

"Show me your left hand." Dropping my right, I quickly raised the left as he asked. He reached down and touched the little finger of the left hand.

"With this finger, place the anointing oil of Laodicea where you have been told. This oil soothes the passion that burns in the heart and brings the gentleness of spirit for forgiveness and mercy, binding the spiritual and the physical together." He moved on to the left ring finger and said, **"This is the finger to place the anointing oil of Thyatira. Place the anointing oil where you have been told. This oil grounds the creative spirit and cleans the path to the mind's eye for divine knowledge. This oil also binds the human emotion with the spiritual emotion for creativity with love. The great finger** [middle finger] **of the left hand is for the placing of the anointing oil of Philadelphia. Place this oil where you have been told. This oil cleans the path to the divine mind and opens your lungs to teach only love. It calms the human mind that you may hear the divine thoughts."**

"I have one finger left on my left hand. Does that mean I have another oil coming or are there three oils coming, if you consider the thumbs?"

"Michael will tell you what you have yet to learn. For now, place these anointing oils with the others for four days that they may rest and be life [come alive].

"You have been teaching of a stone that stores energy from the Gate."

"OOPS. Have I been doing something wrong in how I teach about it?"

"**No. What you speak of is true. Yet, I would give you a way so that you would not have to find this stone.**"

"Well, please do. The people who mine it have a patent, and they make it hard to get it for the healing work." What I will say about this stone is that it was shown to me by one of the seven, who had noticed its capacity to hold grace. When I first tried the stone, I noticed it changed color after being used. I had wanted to purchase a few for others but they were just too expensive.

"**Joe, when you cut the stones for Gate sets, that which falls to the bottom of the water may be used to serve as the stone.**"

"Too cool, and the sediment is all I need in replacing these healing stones?" Because so many people were finding it too expensive to buy all the stones needed to create a Gate of Grace, I discovered I could buy them in larger sizes and in quantity, and then cut them to smaller sizes. This allowed me to make several packages at an affordable price for others.

"**No. Go to where you place the oils, for the ground is holy.**" He pointed to my windshield and I saw some dirt there. "**This is where you may gather the sacred earth to add to the sediment. Use this much earth and this much sediment.**" He showed me, and told me to place the combined sacred earth and residue from cut Gate stones in a small bag, about the size of an old tobacco pouch. "**When the bag is charged in the Gate of the person using it, the bag will do as well as the stones,**" he said. "**The earth will allow for the energy of the stone sediment to become stable for the gathering of Grace essence**". That made perfect sense to me. Because the stones in the Gate of Grace normally had to sit for an hour before the grace essence built to its optimum.

"Tell me something. Can people take some dirt, put it in their Gates, and get it to do the same thing?"

"**No. Joe, the holy ground you are to use cannot be made. Make it as I have told you, for too little will not hold the grace and too much will do what you call 'short out.'**"

"That means like blow a fuse doesn't it?"

"**You can say it that way. Our time is done for now. Teach only love.**"

And with that, all five angels folded into the glowing light and faded from view. The scenery along the highway returned to normal, blurring by like before. Not a soul would have known that an angel convention had taken place in the cab of my pickup truck. My mind whirred at all that occurred. Mental notes competed with a thousand questions as to how this phenomenon had transpired. Usually, when my memory is not as fine-tuned as I would like when I write down all that has happened, I can sense the angels assisting me with my memory. Nevertheless, I make every effort to remember everything myself. Gary even asked me to start carrying around a hand-held tape recorder. He's such a stickler for detail. It was nice that Ratziel had reminded me of some of the instructions from Gabriel and Raphael that I hadn't written down. More and more I'm beginning to realize that angels are similar to humans: We are all here to help one other. Especially when we need to work out our sums.

THE OILS OF I AM

*W*hen the sevens heard about the seven oils, and what they were supposed to bring to those who anointed themselves, I couldn't make sets of oils fast enough. For those who wanted all the oils, and right away, Michael had recommended that the seven oils should be applied on seven different days during the anointing process. And once all oils had been used, a second round of anointing should not be repeated within forty days. He had also said that no more than three different oils should be used at any one time. No explanation as to why. I assumed there must be such a thing as oil overdose.

Some of the sevens reacted like the proverbial joke about taking smart'nin' pills. They didn't feel any smarter after applying the Oil of Pergamum, or any wiser from applying the Oil of Philadelphia. But of course, the whole point of the smart'nin' pills joke is that the pills are actually rabbit droppings. The moral of the joke is that anyone who is dumb enough to take rabbit turds to get smarter, learns by taking the first 'pill' that he's gotten rapidly smarter in a way he didn't expect. And so it was with the oils. You don't anoint yourself to get smarter or wiser. It's not like taking a pill to make yourself feel better. The whole point of the anointing is to open oneself to the forces within us and about us. Wisdom

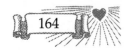

and understanding come about by the living of life, opening to life. And sometimes we either don't want to be open or we don't want to see what is already before us or within us. An anointing is an act of acknowledging. To acknowledge that true wisdom and true understanding are more than what originates in one's head leaves one open to the very forces which foster these gifts. In one of the books of Wisdom, found in the Bible, it says, If you wish to be wise then visit the company of wise men. Such a statement is an acknowledgment that wisdom is beyond purchasing or inheriting. Wisdom embraces us if we allow it, if we create space for it, if we move into an environment that acknowledges who we are and what we do, in tandem with others who also have acquired different experiences. Space is created in the visiting of wise men or wise women. The anointing of the oils works similarly in that it opens us to these gifts, whether they be wisdom or love or mercy. These gifts don't infect us like some virus; they open us so we find ourselves standing in the presence of, the space of, giftedness.

But as the weeks passed, I began to wonder if there weren't more to these oils than just anointing. Something Shekinah had said haunted me: **"Your kind has suffered for too long. You will be given gifts to bring you all into the light of love. Wholeness will be with all. We will be with you and others to bring this to pass.... Tell them** [the sevens] **to make ready our coming. I am to come to make things new."** The seven angels had been particular in telling me they were giving me these oils as gifts for humanity. So, were these gifts actually the same gifts Shekinah had promised for the ending of suffering? If so, how would these oils be used to bring about the cessation of suffering? I would have to wait to find that out.

Gary called. He, too, had questions. I can't count the number of times he has told me that everything about and around angels is a combination of perfect order within chaos. Like some angel detective, he had analyzed the components of the seven oils. His findings revealed some interesting coincidences (something he doesn't believe in). The seven oils were made from twelve different trees: boswellia (from which frankincense is derived), commifora (from which myrrh is derived), sandalwood, olive, apricot, orange, tangerine, lime, banana, nutmeg, and cinnamon. And likewise, the Oils of I Am also are made from twelve different trees. He then reminded me of a passage from the *Revelation* codex found in *On*

the Wings of Heaven, which states, "**Each of the twelve trees bears a different fruit and so does each month. The leaves of the trees heal all the nations, and nothing accursed will be found there.**" [Rev 22: 2] Gary asked me if these oils might be somehow linked to a day when all the nations would be healed. As much as I hoped such a link existed, I had no way of knowing — for now. Gary also pointed out that in addition to the twelve trees, nine plants were used in the making of the church oils as well as the Oils of I Am, making a total of twenty-one (7+7+7) species. Was it mere coincidence that twenty-one feet was the primary component making up the dimensions in the Gate of Grace? Not according to my discerning friend. Like I said, one of his favorite sayings is, "There are no coincidences."

All of this played in my mind as the weeks passed. Returning from placing a new batch of oils in the sacred place, I was thinking how this whole oil thing was getting to be a real chore. Sure seemed like more than a one-man job to me. As my truck rumbled on down the road, a light started to form on the passenger side. *Which angel will it be this time,* I wondered. You can imagine my happiness when Michael's form began to materialize. It had been a while since I had spent time just with him. His platinum hair sparkled with light that waved much like water on the ocean. His skin was soft, and I could see the muscles that formed underneath. The light color of his skin didn't look like someone in bad need of a tan because you could say he radiated with perfect health. That is, of course, if you can label an angel as "healthy." He turned and pierced me with those magnificent blue eyes that always melted my heart no matter how I felt.

"**I told you it would work,**" were the first words out of his mouth.

"What would work, Michael?"

"**That which you call 'water to wine.'** "

"Oh, you mean the changing of the water. So now you are into 'I told you so'?" It had been some time since the Chicago workshop. With all these angels showing up, it nearly slipped my mind.

"**No. Yet, your faith was not as strong as it could have been.**"

"Well, you did tell me not to do it before the Chicago workshop? I didn't know if it would work. Not for sure anyway. You must have known I did have faith in what you said about it. I must have known it would work on some level or I would not have done it. So if I trusted you enough to do it, I must have had faith."

"You do split hairs well, Joe. The class went well, as did the gatherings." After coming back home and having had time to rest, I had almost forgotten what a rip tide of a weekend that had been having the workshop with three simultaneous gatherings — first one direction, then another and back again.

"It all did go well, Michael, but it took a lot out of me. I was really beat after the whole thing was over."

"Yet now the root of the tree is set. It will surprise you how quickly it will grow."

"I hope you are right. I was thinking about the other angels and about the oils being made, and how much is involved in making them."

"You have done well. This is why I come to you at this time."

"Oh crap, not again. What is it this time? I know all too well, when you start off with congratulations, that you are about to give me something else to do. When does a guy get a break here?"

"You are about to get a break. For I give you that which you and others will do."

"Each time you say 'others,' you also give me something to do, and the others usually do as they please. Which means, most of the time, I end up doing the doing."

"Not this time. There are four oils to be made."

"So now I get to make these and get the word out to the other sevens?"

"Not so. You will make my oil, and the others I tell you of will make the oils of the other three."

"OK. What does this look like?"

"I will give you the oils to be made. You will give them [the ingredients of the other three oils] **to the ones who will make them. You will make mine and the others will make the holy oils of the three aspects of I Am."**

I wondered what he meant by the three aspects of I Am, making a mental note to ask Gary about this later. It seemed Michael was not to be sidelined. "Well this should be fun. I bet I can guess some of what is involved with these four oils."

"Guess? You do not know?"

"Well, Michael, if I am saying something that rings true, then I know. But if not, I am just guessing."

"**Fair enough, as you would say.**"

"OK. Here goes. I know there is but one finger left in the anointing oil process — the left index finger — and that must be yours. I think this is your oil that I will make."

"**This is the oil you will make.**"

"There is just one thing out with this — at least as I see it."

"**Speak that which you see.**"

"All the oils, so far, go in a place where a chakra is, or so it is said to be. These are energy fields, so to speak, in the body. And I teach of twelve chakras as you have taught me. Most people only know of seven. But I have no idea, yet, as to how to place oil on the other five chakras which are not in or on the body."

"**These oils are and are not of this of which you speak.**"

"Well, OK, let's get to it. What is the rest of the information?"

"**You will make my oil as I say, and place it with the other oils for three days to rest.**"

"Got it."

"**Take the oil of spikenard, niaouli, honey, sandalwood, and goldwater.**"

"Michael, you have no idea what I am thinking about the last thing you gave me."

"**Yes, I do, and it is not as you think. This is what you call colloidal gold made in water.**"

"Oh. Like the silver, only gold."

"**Mix them as I tell you but tell no one.**"

He told me how and I wrote it down.

"**This oil is to be placed on all the spots that were given for the other oils, with the finger that is left. My oil will bring all of these into balance. As I have come to you, and the others like me are come to the other seven, I balance the Well of Souls.**"

"Can your oil be used with any of the other oils, or does the same rule of only three at a time go with this one, too?"

"**My oil may be used at any time. Yet I tell you truly that the other three oils [of I Am] may be used only with mine or by themselves.**"

"Pretty powerful stuff, huh?"

"**This is rightfully so.**"

"Who else gets to make the other oils?"

"There is another man and two women."

"I am just dying to know."

"I give them to you as they are given to me. The first oil is given to Donna. This is the oil of what you could call "I Am," or the Metatron. It is made in this manner: Take the oil of ravensara, mix with myrrh, birch, and rosewood oil. She will take them to a place sacred to her, and let it rest from sundown on Saturday until sunrise on Sunday. She will bless the oil as one would the water, saying 'As a child of God I bless this oil with the great Love of God, the I Am.' She will place the oil in her spot and leave it until it is done. The right thumb is used to apply it.

"The next oil is made by Gary, and it is of the Christ or the Christ Consciousness. This oil is made of the mixing of galbanum, frankincense, petitgrain, and helichrysum. He will also take it to a spot he has chosen. He will bless the oil as the water, yet saying, 'As a child of God I bless this oil with the Christ-works and the love in the Christ-teachings.' When this is done he will place the oil in his spot from sundown on Friday to rest until sunrise on Sunday. The palms of the hands are used to apply it.

"The next oil is to be made by Robbie in this way, for it is the Oil of Shekinah. Take the oil of laurus nobilis, jasmine, elemi and clove. She will bless the oil as the water by saying, 'As a Child of God I bless this oil with the vessel of love that Shekinah is for all.' She will take it to her sacred place for seven days, where it shall rest. This oil is applied with the left thumb."

"OK. Michael that only leaves a few things unanswered. And what you did answer is a bit vague. I have a basic knowledge of the 'who' you are talking about because of what Gary has told me, but not all that much. How do these Oils of I Am fit in with the oils you and the other seven angels have given us? Like, what do they do? Where do they go?"

"What I tell you now you will hold until all the oils are made. They are given to you now to open and bind us [the realm of angels with the realm of humans] **together. When one of the seven has mastered the gifts and the traps they are, we will be in the Oneness, as it is meant to be. To use the oils, without mastering the gifts, will help one to reach mastery. Yet I say to you, when one has mastered their gifts, they will know the wonder God is."**

"This I got to see. I can only imagine what that would be like. So the new oils are only going to work out of the gifts we are."

"Joe, you need to listen. I say that the oils will help one to live in the gifts they are and will help those using it to rise above their petty traps your kind hold so dear."

"Boy, can I relate to that."

"Some say that they have mastered the traps and live out of their giftedness. Yet I say to you, there is but one who lives in the giftedness he is."

"Really? And which one of the Seven is it?"

"Not one of them. For they are struggling with being the gifts they are, yet not one has mastered their traps. Some are well on the way while others are only beginning."

"Yes, I can understand that, too, because some of the sevens have been with me for a long time now."

"Time has nothing to do with where they are in their giftedness. It is the willingness to be in one's trap and learn from it. Not to deny they are in the traps.

"The one that is now living in his giftedness is not gathered yet." My mind went into high speed trying to figure out who this might be. Michael would not be telling me this if I didn't have some contact or knowledge of this person.

"I am sure the sevens will be glad to hear this. They have been working really hard to be in their gifts."

"That which you call 'ego' is still in the way. Some will do the gifts of others, saying they know better the way it is to be. The one I speak of is living in the gift he is. It is not his ego that causes him to be who he is. His gift flows freely to all he is with. His judgments are none. This man is the only one the oils will bind us to, as he stands."

"OK. I think I know who you are talking about. The only one I can think of that hasn't been in the pattern of giving and receiving is me."

"It is not you. For you will not stand there."

"So does this mean I am like Moses, and don't get to go to the Promised Land?"

"No, it is that you are visited by us to give the message to the world."

"So what about my DNA? Isn't it going to be changed?" I had remembered an earlier statement Michael had made about the DNA of the sevens being changed in the Formation of Giving and Receiving. If I was never to be a receiver in this formation, then it stood to reason that I might not be allowed to undergo what the rest of the sevens had experienced.

"It has been changed. Do you not remember the time you found yourself on the bench?"

"You mean after the whiteout?" The whiteout of light had occurred after Gary had left Texas, right after we had created the first Gate of Grace with the seven stones.

"Yes."

"But that wasn't the first time something like that happened to me."

"I know. The first time was in Big Sur."

Michael was referring to the time right after the Vietnam War, when I lived the life of a road gypsy, even to the point of dwelling in the belly of a giant redwood. "I remember that was a time when I felt like everything was going to be OK with my life. Hey! That was years before you came to me. That was when my life started to change. Is what you are implying?"

"This is true."

"Now if that is true, then I got my DNA changed way back when it must have taken years. However, the sevens get theirs during the time they are in the pattern of Giving and Receiving?"

"This is true. Let us not speak of this now. The oils are for this time."

"OK, Michael, but will you tell me who the one person is that lives in his gifts?"

"I will tell you, yet take care in those you would tell. He is not to be interfered with, nor is the work he does."

Michael told me who it was and it was an automatic "Of course" for me. Of all the people I know, he is truly one living in his gifts.

"Now the oils."

"OK. Let's do it. Should we start with your oil?"

"The oils are to be made from the finest oils you can find. These oils are all but the last of the oils given to your kind. The oils I give you now are among the most precious of oils. Skimp not on their making, for they are the most sacred of the oils given. These oils are

not to be used by women with child. For the way of their work is being set in the womb and is being made ready to receive the soul.

"Spikenard, in olden times, was used only by kings, high priests, and high initiates. This was the oil used to anoint the feet of Jesus."

"Sandalwood I know. This one, Michael, is used for attaining deep sleep, for ailments of the skin, and for revitalizing the skin. It also stimulates the pineal gland, which is the third eye, in our way of speaking."

"This is true, as is niaouli used for healing. Honey is as the sweetness of God's love. Nothing harmful will flourish in it, as when the honey ages. For it becomes as a crystal solid like the love of God. Gold is that which is used by man as the highest of metals, given to honor someone. This goldwater you use is to honor yourselves as children of God."

"OK, Michael, how do we use it? I mean where does your oil go?"

"It may be placed on the areas where all the other oils are placed. This oil will bring them into balance."

"So you are telling me that I can use it with other oils?"

"Yes. Place my oil on the place you would use another oil. This makes ready the place to receive the other oil of the church you choose."

"Great. Kind of like cleaning before applying medicine on a cut."

"Not as I would have said, yet you understand its purpose. My oil makes way for all oils."

"So why didn't you give this oil before the other angels gave the oils of the churches?"

"Your kind was not ready." It was now beginning to make sense why he had placed the restriction earlier on the use of the seven oils. The seven different days of anointing with the seven different oils was a way of preparing those who were ready for what was coming now. Michael also relayed to me that the restriction of using no more than three oils would be lifted as long as the Michael Oil was used first.

"Now that I know where, tell me how."

He smiled and said, "With this oil, you will put a drop on the index finger of the left hand, placing it on the spots you wish to use. You will say, 'As a child of God, standing in God's love, I am open to receive the gifts of the angels.' This oil may be placed in a bath before using the oils of the other churches, or a drop [may be] placed in blessed water and drank. Listen to me in what I tell you now. The four oils are given to you

as they are to be used. In the order I give them to you. Will it hurt you if you use another one? No, yet you may miss some of what is given."

"Does this mean I have to use your oil all the time before I can use another oil?"

"No, Joe, it doesn't. It is, as you say, the best way of doing things."

"OK, I get it. We can use whatever oil we want, but to get the best result, do it in the order it was given."

"The oil of Metatron is made of the oil of the rosewood and birch. As with the Tree of Life, this oil sets the root in the earth for that which is heavenly. Myrrh is as the cleansing of the way of God's words to the soul. Ravensara is used to heal the way for bringing the voice of God to your mind. A drop of the Metatron Oil is to be placed on the ear lobes to clear the way for the voice of God. With this oil you will say, 'As a child of God, I open my ears that I may hear the love God has for me.' One drop of this oil may also be placed in a bath or in blessed water for drinking.

"The oil of the Christ, or the Christ Consciousness, is made with frankincense. Once given to Him, it is given to your kind, now. Of all oils, it is the one used most to raise the spirit and enrich the soul. Galbanum is one of the oils given to Jesus on a sponge to relieve his suffering. Helichrysum is an oil used to recall that which was given. The oil of petitgrain is to bring love to the heart, like the Christ's love for all. The Oil of the Christ is placed with the palms of the hands on the head and on the heart. You will say, 'As a child of God I open my mind and my heart to the Christ Consciousness, that I may live in the same light.' This oil may be used by placing a drop in a bath or in blessed water for drinking.

"The Oil of Shekinah is made of clove, jasmine, and laurus nobilis, for healing the body, mind, and emotions. Mixing these with the softness of elemi oil opens the soul as a vessel to be filled again. Place this oil with the thumb of the left hand to the temples and third eye. You will say, 'As a child of God, I stand before you to be created anew.' This oil may be placed in a bath or blessed water to drink."

"Well, Michael, this sounds like some powerful oils you have given this time. I know some of the past oils you said to use are expensive. The oils, this time, are made only from expensive oils without the adding of a

base oil. If we use the finest oils we can get, it will cost an arm and a leg just to make them."

"Your kind has a saying: 'You get what you pay for.' "

"I know that cheap is still cheap."

"When men would sacrifice to God animals, though it was unfitting, did they not give the finest of the flock? Would you take corrupted oils to do these blessings and to commune with God?"

"No, of course not. I was just asking if it was all right to do it to keep the price down so everyone could have it. If it is sold at the same price as the other oils, a person could go broke."

"Take the oils and split them by five as you sell them now."

"The price or the amount?"

"The oil is divided by five. There is more than enough to do its work."

"Does this mean to sell it at the same price as the oils of the seven churches, but less of it?" Previously, Michael had said to sell the oils of the churches for $15 for a 5 ml. bottle. So this meant that the four oils should be sold for $15 per milliliter.

"Yes. It is a fair amount for all."

"What if some choose to give it away? Is that all right to do, too?"

"Did not I tell you to sell the oils you made at three-fourths of twenty for each?"

"Yes, you did."

"Yet, you did not do this."

"I wanted to give people a deal if they got them all as a set."

"I tell you what is a fair price and you will do what you will. As the oils become more and more wanted by the children of God, so will your time be taken to make them. It is for you to say what is the price of your work.

"Now, I will tell you of our coming with gifts for your kind. Some will be visited by our kind and given that which is of the church they are."

"Yeah, I hear you have been pretty busy lately. I have been getting a lot of messages that you are visiting people."

"I have been with few, yet some say it is me, though it is not." Michael then gave me a way of telling in the future whether he or another is visiting others. He asked me to keep the information to myself.

"I take it, this is so they will not make stuff up just to make it sound like you."

"No, some being visited are being visited by others like me, yet it is not me. We are charged to be with some and not with others. Have you not been told that I did and said things that are unlike me to say and do?"

"Yes, I have."

"Yet, have not they said it was me?"

"That they have. So what you are telling me is that you visit only so many people. There are other angels like you with the same kind of energy, so to speak. This lets people think it is you. Then again you did say you served God as what we call the Archangel Michael before. So I guess other angels can do the same."

"This is true. Trouble yourselves not with which angel is come with gifts. Open your hearts to their coming. Is it not enough that one has been visited? Have the sevens fallen into the trap of the hierarchical order of angels? I will say this again. Angels are angels. Our time is done for now. Yet I say you will be visited in the new year with the last oil and with a great gift for all."

"What is it?"

"You will be told at that time. I will say it was given before to one of the twelve and was lost. The time for this is come again. Be at peace and teach only love."

After giving all the oils to the three other people, I waited for them to make their oils. In the meantime, I asked Gary for further information on what Michael had said about the three aspects of I Am. He told me that, according to the Jewish mystical tradition — known as the Kabbalah — Metatron was the masculine aspect of God, while Shekinah was the feminine. In the Tree of Life, Metatron and Shekinah were two sides of the same coin. The Christ was the child or the coming together of the masculine and the feminine — the Sacred Androgyne. In Christian tradition, the feminine aspect of God was also called the Holy Spirit, and that is why Michael says Shekinah comes from all. In Christianity, these three aspects of I Am are interpreted as the Holy Trinity: the Father, the Son, and the Holy Spirit. It amazes me how these different disciplines seem to cross-pollinate. In spite of all the differences, the basic truths aim at the same target.

And so it was with the three who were given the decision whether to make the three oils of I Am. Their reactions were as varied as different religions. One of the three came close to declining the making of their oil. Another needed a long period to meditate on the consequences. I had forgotten how burdened I once felt with parts of this incredible information I was to pass on to humanity. A great responsibility sets in when you realize the wonder appearing before us. Angels coming together with humans? Changes in our world and even our physical DNA? And had not Michael said something wonderful was about to happen, and hinted at it once again in this last visit? More gifts? I could hardly wait.

THE MASTERS OIL

*A*fter retrieving the Oil of Michael from the sacred place, I decided to pay Donna a visit. Our separation seemed to bring us closer on some days, and then not so close on other days. Enough time had elapsed that I needed to check in with her to see if she made the Oil of Metatron yet. She hadn't but would the next weekend. We chatted a while and I decided to give her a bottle of Michael's Oil in return for the Oil of Metatron when it was ready. We said good night, and I headed down the driveway toward the security gate. As the truck approached the gate, I reached up and pushed the button on the remote to swing the gate open. But it didn't work. *Could the battery have gone bad?* I thought. A year had passed since I last had changed it. Once again I pushed the button but no way would the gate open. After braking to a stop, I sat mulling over whether to search for batteries or whether to climb out of the truck and manually open the gate. As if cued by my thoughts, a ball of light began forming between the truck and the gate. Michael. "No wonder this gate won't open," I mumbled.

In the center of the ball of light, Michael's form began to solidify. Normally I would have worried about the neighbors but I remembered that no one sees him unless he wants them to. Wondering whether he

would say or motion something, I stayed put. There the two of us remained, like two teenagers on the first date, wondering who would speak first. Finally, I opened the door of the truck and got out. Walking toward him, I said, "I should have known you would show up just after I made the oil."

"I told you I would return after the first of your new year."

"I see you waited until your oil was done, too."

"I always return after that which I have given you has been done."

"Yes. I know — to give me something else to do, most likely. I take it this has to do with the last oil you hinted at before?"

"Yes, Joe, this is the last of the oils."

"Well, I hope it smells better then your oil does. To me it smelled like cleaning fluid when I first made it. However, after resting, it does smell better. Oh, by the way, I have been doing a painting of you."

"I have seen it. I helped you with it."

"Untrue, Michael, I am quite good on my own."

"You are very good, yet you would not have been finished with it if I hadn't inspired you."

"I thought it was me coming up with all the new ideas for it." Michael just smiled.

"You would have been content to have just the image of me. What I have led you to do with it brings more. The star and the colors of the seven are there for a reason. There is more in the painting than you see."

"Are you telling me that there is some kind of a hidden message in it, or it does something?"

"This is not why I have come. The time for Oil of the Masters has come."

"OK. Tell me how, and I will get started on it."

"This oil is to be made by the sevens."

"Great," I beamed with relief in my voice. "Tell me what I have to do."

"Tell the sevens to take the oils I give you and make them as a gift to themselves. They will take the oils, mixing them so."

"Can you give me the amounts in a way that's easy to understand?"

"Yes. Take two milliliters of frankincense with a drop of rose in it. Add one milliliter of each oil: nutmeg, hyssop, ginger, clove and lemongrass. Do this in the order the oils are given. Stray not from

this. As you add each oil to the frankincense and rose, you will say, 'As a child of God, I bless this anointing Oil of the Masters and make it holy.' When this is done, place it in a sacred spot to rest for twelve days. As you place the oil to rest say, 'I lay this oil in God's love with love, to give love and receive love.' Then let it be for the time that was given. Return at the end of the resting and say before you touch it, 'Blessed am I for the giving to I Am a child of God.' You will say this again when you use the oil."

Michael said no more and I waited for him to move on. When he remained silent, I knew it was my turn. "What in the world are you talking about? That doesn't make any sense to me at all."

"Joe, just say it. It will."

"OK. If you say so."

"I do."

"Tell me what this is supposed to do and where does it go?"

"Each will know where and how to place it. You will find it different for each one using it. Is this oil not a gift to you from you? Use it as you will."

"That still doesn't answer what it does. Is there a finger we should use to place the oil?"

"This oil has no one finger to use, for it is a bond to all. Take a drop of this oil and mix with a drop of the oil of your church. You will see the gift you have given to you. You may place this oil over the other three oils as well. That which I told you about a woman with child holds true with this oil most of all."

"Can you use this oil on someone else?"

"No. It is your oil. Do you not listen?"

"I just wanted to make sure."

"I tell you this. You may use this oil to awaken one who is unconscious. Two drops rubbed on the top of the head and they will awaken. This is the only time you may use it on someone other than yourself."

"Tell me something will you? Why are you giving us all this stuff now?"

"We have given you what some of the sevens are ready for. Others are not ready. This is why you were given the oils in the order they were given. You were given the oils of the seven churches to help clean

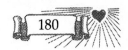

the path each is on. To make ready for the next step. I gave you then my oil and the three oils. Now I give you the Oil of the Masters. As some of you grow, there is a need to have what you call tools to help you. These tools we give you will help to clear the path."

"Cool. That means we will get whatever we are to get sooner."

"You will if you have done the work you need to do in the church you are. As with any tool, you must be ready to use the tool before it will help you."

"Well, in this case it looks like you have to be able to make the tool."

"There is truth in what you say."

"I thought so. I knew there was a catch in this. If you didn't do the groundwork in the beginning and follow the instructions as you went along, you won't get much out of it."

"Not true. You will be helped, yes. Yet it will be as nothing to those that have."

"Like paying your dues, as we say, will get you where you need to be. Otherwise you fake it until you make it. You have to learn something along the way until someday you get it."

"Again not as I would have said. Your understanding is near the truth."

"I do know what you mean— kind of like you have to learn to walk before you can run."

"Much closer to my words."

"I do have something to talk to you about."

"Speak. I will listen and give you counsel."

"It has to do with the things you have given me."

"Ah. You would speak of the selling of these things."

"Yes, I am, Michael. I have been told things like I shouldn't be selling what you have given me. Well, it is more like I shouldn't make any money on it. I have been told I shouldn't sell prints of the picture of you I painted. I think the exact words were, 'Michael should not be for sale.' "

"Did I not tell you that you would be taken care of? Does the grand order of the self-righteous ones dictate to me in what manner I will keep my promise to you?"

"Very funny, Michael." Sometimes it amazed me how he would try to use humor to diffuse a controversial situation. That seemed like such a human quality to me. But, truthfully, humor has incredible power to sway

without offending. I think that's why comedians are usually highly intelligent people. It takes an adept mind to know how to use a scalpel, whether that scalpel is made of steel or made of words.

"I knew you would think so. You will hear this from many. Let it bother you not. If there is any that would do the work I have given you for nothing in return, let them. They will be as the ones used by religions today. You shall receive a fair [value] for the work you do. I have given you that which you may collect for your labors. I have given you that which others may collect from their labors. Your kind has become lazy and wanting. Do they not see that receiving for nothing begets them little? Do they not see the damage they do in giving to those who will not give to themselves? I tell you one last time, and we shall not speak of it again. I say what it is you will and will not do, and sell and not sell. I have left it to you what is fair for your labor. Had I found fault in this, I would have told you."

"I am just getting sick of some of the sevens telling me what I should do. I love and respect them. I care about how they feel about the work. It really matters to me. I want to be on good terms with all of the sevens."

"You will not always please all the sevens. That is why you were chosen for the work. You will listen to the counsel of others and you will do that which you know is best. You will not bow down to the will of those who tell you they are right. You do not go against that which I have given. Your faith remains strong in the face of all else. You will find those who give you the most grief are the ones who have wanted out of the work or have left it. The work of the sevens is not easy. There is fear that holds them back. It is easier to walk away from the work than it is to do the work. It is easier to have the ego tell stories about it than it is to surrender to what needs to be done. Did I not tell you that many are chosen but few choose?"

"You mean like really choose to be the work. If the work you have given us is too hard, some will make up something to justifying their leaving."

"No one has to stay and do the work. All are free to go if they choose. Bless their hearts and let them go. They are the work or they are not. It is up to them to stay or leave. I warn you: Though you are not, you will be held to blame for some leaving."

"I know, some have already left."

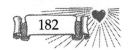

"Those who have left to go about changing the world in their own way, you may ask of them what have they done to make it better? Who is better off after the time they spent doing it their way? Who has been enlightened by being in their presence? What words of joy and love have they given to God's children? This is not said to punish them or to rebuff them. It is given to them to see they are a child of God and their personal responsibility is to teach only love."

"Wow. That is a little harsh isn't it?"

"Truth is at times. Change is hard for your kind. They will fight it, as it says in *Revelation*. Some will stay and some will leave. It is not for you to choose which ones do which. You are the child we have chosen to give the message, no better than any of the sevens, yet none of the sevens is better than you."

"You know, Michael, I see it as if sometimes people put turmoil into the mix and make that the important thing. Almost like starting all these little fires just so they can put them out, rather than to do the things that need to be done."

"Now you say it as I would. You have been told it would not be easy for you. I told you this from the start. Some think that *Revelation* is the story of the world, yet it holds true for each person. Read it, for it is the path your kind is on. Some think it is not about them. As you say, it is the microcosm of the macrocosm."

"I didn't think you knew that term. Pretty cool of you, Michael."

"Those that would read as if it [the *Revelation* codex] speaks of them will see it does. This is why the *Book of Bricks* was given. It will help one to pass through *Revelation*."

"I know it all ties in with the whole picture, and, at times, we focus only on a small part."

"Think of these two writings as hands. One is the right, the other is the left. When they work together the work is done."

"I think I know what you are saying. The writings are the hands and the oils are the tools."

"Now do you see why you were chosen? You know that which you are not told."

"It looks like we all have some homework to do. I think it would be a good time to break out the books."

"These are the charts for those lost at sea. The wind blows them, yet they have not set a course. For they know not where they are. The star of the Gate will guide them. The course that has been set in the book will bring them safely to port."

"Oh, Michael, what a beautiful way of putting it. I can see in my mind a picture of it now."

"Is your mind at rest? Have you come to understand what I have said?"

"Not with everything. But I know I can figure it out. What else do you have for me?"

"Our time is done for now. You prepare for the coming visit. This will change things as you know them. You will not be the same."

"When is this going to happen?"

"Soon. Be at peace and teach only love."

He stepped back into the light, and as the brightness began to fold in on itself, he faded from view. Slowly I walked back to the truck, my mind spinning with all he had to say to me. I wondered if I could remember it all and how some might take it. Then I remembered something else: *It ain't up to me.* All I do, and have done, is give the message I got. Write it down and send it out. That is what I said I would do. And after that, I am done. At least until the next time Michael shows up.

THE OILS AND HEALING

*F*rom the day of the very first gathering of the first seven until now, the angels have always left the sevens to figure out the details of the grand design created by their appearances and their gifts. As frustrating as it could be at times, the sevens grew to understand why so much of what was happening to all of us, what was changing all of us, grew out of the angels' hands-off approach in our personal lives. Many, if not most, at one time or another, wished Michael would appear to each, personally, in fully physical form and explain all our questions, our doubts, or our concerns. The notion that each of us recognized — or began to recognize — ourselves as master souls required that we give up any desire for angelic babysitting. Many of us realized sooner rather than later that we were changing. Comments from friends or family or perfect strangers brought us distinct awareness that we no longer functioned the same way we had before we decided to partake in a sevens gathering. And each of us knew the primary force behind these growing changes coming over us always pointed at the same source: ourselves, driven by our own free will. The angelic realm would have it no other way.

Slowly, with each successive gathering, I became less and less the center of attention. An online list server, dedicated to those who'd

participated in gatherings, fostered wild dialog between the sevens. This should have surprised no one. The seven gifts inherent in the seven archetypal churches predisposed us to having seven different views as to what we saw, felt, and understood. But rather than having factions develop, the gifts were supposed to show us how the whole is greater than the sum of the parts, that Oneness ultimately would prevail like the flowing together of seven separate rivers into one great lake. Some stepped back because of the spirited e-mail, wishing to seek answers to their own questions from within. Others walked away from the sevens phenomenon completely, feeling their own individuality threatened, or fearing other sevens had betrayed the messages of Michael and the other angels. Some even questioned Michael or questioned my own truthfulness in relaying his words. All of this chaos paralleled what Gary liked to call the birthing of perfect order out of perfect chaos. He insisted that the angelic realm operated out of mathematics even more than he did. Was not the Tree of Life a living fractal, he'd asked? And since we stood as the co-creators of the Tree of Life, were we not necessarily inheritors of this inevitable order rising out of perfect chaos? To be honest, half the time most of us couldn't understand Gary's theories, let alone his long-winded and complicated ideas. Like my relationship with my wife, my close friendship with Gary began to suffer. True, he had been blessed by heaven with the gift of wisdom, but wisdom does not equate to being a know-it-all. And in turn, he began to remind me that being blessed with leadership does not equate to being an arrogant S.O.B. How wrong we both would turn out to be. Many of us began to see the gifts and traps, spoken of by Michael, to be a dividing line: Gifts were "good," traps were "bad." But that is not what we had been taught. Our traps are simply another path to the eventual goal: becoming who we are. If we choose to live in our traps, then those traps will provide valuable experience leading to the eventual embracing of self-giftedness. Both Gary and I would learn this valuable lesson. And neither of us would realize it until an event that took place on March 24, 2000.

Driving through the hills on my way to work, I checked out the changing sky. The previous night, mare's tails had invaded a star-filled heaven, signaling a day of oncoming clouds. And sure enough, last night's wisps yielded to a thick blanket of white hiding the morning sky. Cooler temperatures hugged the ground as if trying to warn me of

impending rain. Who could complain? We desperately needed rain here in Texas. Deep thoughts crowded my mind as much as the clouds had crowded out the sun. What was to become of all these changes? Changes within me. Changes with the sevens. Even changes with the world. Gary had stated point blank that we were the co-creators in the fashioning of a new earth. And as the angels joined us, a new heaven paralleled every earthly change. "As above, so below. As below, so above," he loved to spout. And who could fault him? Who could deny all these changes?

A new gathering had just occurred the previous weekend. After the Chicago event, Michael had told me that the root in the Tree of Life had been set, and that great growth would occur. But instead, one of the first seven had decided to remove himself from the sevens. Once again, a hole existed in this "root" Michael had talked about. So, this last weekend produced no ordinary gathering. For it pieced together the last missing link in the Tree of Life, once again. Every color of the sevens, every church, now had a servant who had gathered seven more. Gary somehow knew this last gathering would serve as a launching pad. And I had every reason to believe him. Had not Michael said that when the last of the churches had gathered a group of seven, we would then understand the relationship of the sevens in the world? Well, the last church had now gathered. And each of us understood the full meaning of a gathering. Whenever a master gathered seven, the master became a servant. The balance of being both master and servant brought with it a gift of its own: The servant became a walking Gate of Grace. Which meant once a master had gathered seven others, the master/servant no longer required the use of stones in creating a Gateway. That person, de facto, became the Gateway, a living ball of grace. No one could take that away, unless the person willfully wished to harm another. Michael had told me earlier that anytime a negative intention entered a Gateway, the Gate of Grace immediately shut down. Those of us who stood as servants knew the impact of becoming a walking Gate of Grace. The realization stayed with you day and night. Love no longer existed as an ideal. Love cloaked you, and you wore it. And the cloak was not necessarily an invisible garment. Other people noticed it as well.

I couldn't get it out of my mind that all of us were in store for some awesome event. Not that anything that had happened previously had *not* been awesome. It's just that Michael's words haunted me. He had said we

would understand our place with the angels once a determining event like the previous weekend had occurred. Knowing how angels have no concept of time, I wasn't going to hold my breath until this understanding made itself known.

My truck climbed up the road through a pass cut into a limestone hillside. As I crested the hill and started down the other side, I spied something far down the road. At first I thought a motorcycle had broken down. And being one who loves to ride Harleys, I slowed down to see if I could be of assistance, thinking how fortunate that I was in the truck— just in case the rider needed me to haul him and his motorcycle to the nearest town for repairs.

Once I got closer, I realized the motorcycle was only a bike with saddlebags hung over the back fender, and that it had appeared bigger from a distance. Either that or my vision was getting worse than I thought. My experience as a biker had taught me that the only reason a rider stops on the downhill side is if there is a problem. So I coasted to a stop just a few truck lengths past the person with the bike. Looking in the rearview mirror, I could see the bike but couldn't see the person. *Strange*, I thought, and turned around. No one was there. The guy had disappeared. But where? There was nothing to hide behind, nowhere to go.

Slowly getting out of my truck, I scanned the whole area to assess what might be going on. *Nothing behind the truck.* "Are you OK?" I shouted. "Is anyone there?" As I walked toward the spot I had last seen the biker, I kept looking around me as if performing a pirouette. Nothing up the hill, nothing across the road. *What in hell is going on*, I thought. Then from behind me, I heard a woman's voice say, **"Blessed are you for aiding a traveler."** I knew in an instant who it was.

"Shekinah," I said, twirling around to find where she might be.

"I am come to speak with you."

"Why did I know you'd be showing up?"

"The base is set solid of the Tree."

"Well, that is good news." All I could see was her head. A white glow of light surrounded her beautiful face, red hair flowing down like living fire. The face was either in, or at least very near, a small cedar tree. *Wow, this is like the burning bush thing*, I thought to myself. *I don't see any of the others who make up the body of the Shekinah.* So I said, "This time it is just going to be ...," and was cut off.

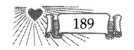

"**Shekinah. I am [here,] as is Michael.**"

"Where?" I said, not noticing Michael anywhere.

"**Michael holds you in his love, that you may speak to me.**"

For some reason, I decided to look above me. And there floated Michael, hovering over me with the most extraordinary display of what appeared to be wings. The brilliance of winglike rays of light spread around me like an umbrella of some kind, shielding me from an unseen force. The radiating light filled me with a sense of being protected with love. "There is some kind of lesson in this that I am about to learn."

"**Blessed are you for you know this without being told.**" Michael said.

"Oh yeah. I am getting very good at guessing what you are up to. I know when you show up in a new way there is something you have to teach. Where do we go from here?"

"**What is it you know so far?**" he asked.

"I know you are protecting me from something by the way you are above me. I bet it has something to do with the energy that comes from the Shekinah."

"**What more do you know?**"

"I am on my way to see a business acquaintance and work with her in healing a back problem she's struggling with. She also has a fever. I bet you are here to clue me in on something. I just happen to have my tuning forks and some oils I bought." After working with Joanee and using the oils she had been instructed to use, my interest in aromatherapy oils had blossomed.

"**Yet you have none of the oils we have given you.**"

"I know. I wanted to try these oils and a treatment I saw done a few times. It seemed to have some value in its ability to help in healing."

"**The oils do. Yet we are to give you a new way to use the oils of the seven churches.**"

"You guys are always coming up with something new. I just got done explaining to the sevens how the last set of oils worked, and here we go again. So what is it this time? No. Let me see if I can guess. There have been some sevens asking me if they can use the oils of the seven churches on other people. I have been telling them no because they are for anointing and bestowing the gifts of another church."

"**This is true. Yet there is more.**"

"Can we not play guessing games and just get on with it?"

"Joe," said the Shekinah, **"Michael comes between us that you will not be marked before [your] time. It is the same with the oils. They were given in the way they were for you to become accustomed to them. Each is a very gentle oil having gifts of its own. Each church's oil is mixed, as you were given, for a reason. The anointing is a process to build a path for the oils to flow. This is given for the sevens. For those who are not sevens, there is a way to receive the oils for healing."**

"You mean like do an anointing on someone else?"

"No. There is a way to apply the oils for healing."

"OK. I am game. Tell me how."

"How is it you set a Gate of Grace?"

"I thought we were talking about the use of oils, not the Gate."

"We are. It is done in the same way."

"Well, let me see. The way I do it is to start by finding out which way north is."

"With the body, north is the head. The feet are the south. The right arm is the east and the left arm is the west."

"That's easy to understand."

"They will lay face down. With the oils, you will build a Gate of Grace on the back."

"Wait a minute. I was told you could not use any more than three oils of the seven churches on any given day. So what has changed?"

"Two things. The first is you are not doing an anointing, you are doing a healing. The second is you now have the oil of Michael."

"I know his oil is to bring balance to the other oils. I do see some sense to this. It sounds to me that we can use all the oils of the seven if we use the Michael oil first."

"Only for this which I am giving you."

"Well then, go ahead and give it to me."

"You work with sounds," said Shekinah.

"Yes, first I do a chakra balancing and attuning of the twelve chakras. I also use tuning forks to send frequencies to a place that may need healing. Then, at other times, I muscle-check to see if sound or oils are needed. I also scan the body to find where something is out. Everything Michael has told me about, I use. Before, I found out that after having a

gathering I don't have to use the Gate set-up with the seven stones. Still, I like to use the stones whenever I can. It gives people a feeling of peace."

"You that have gathered [seven] will not need to use the Gate. You that have not gathered will set the Gate to do this work."

"OK," I said, "If I have gathered, or a seven has, we don't need to use the Gate to do this. And if they haven't they do."

"Yes. Yet I tell you truly, you will wash your hands thrice in the oil of the corn."

"I know I am going to be asked this, so I am asking you now. Is corn oil the only oil that can be used?"

"No. You may use the oil of the macadamia nut."

"We can use whichever of these two oils we want to?"

"Yes. Yet no others. You will then bless the oil by saying, 'As a child of God, I bless this oil that it may serve me in the work of healing I am about to do.'"

"After I wash my hands with the corn oil, I have the person needing work lie face down. Given I need to place oil on the skin I would imagine the back should be bare."

"Yes."

"Then I start with the finger for the oils as Michael gave them to me. I would start with the blue oil, that of Philadelphia, and work my way through the oils."

"No. You will start with the Oil of Michael. That is the reason for your receiving it. It matters not the fingers you use."

"Oh. OK. I get it. Michael's Oil is the oil to open the way for the other oils."

"You begin you see."

"Then I put the oil of the seven churches just like the energy would run if it were a Gate set with the stones."

"This is so," she confirmed.

"I would place the oil of Michael then Philadelphia, Pergamum, Ephesus, Thyatira, Smyrna, Sardis, Laodicea. Then what? Am I done?"

"You have done well with you have learned. Yet I say to you: Perform this healing work in this way. You may use your tuning forks to open the flow of Grace through the body.

"When you are to start, you will say, 'As a child of God I offer you the oil of Michael to prepare the way for the oils of the seven

churches.' They will say to you, 'As a child of God I accept the Oil of Michael.' When this is said, you will place the oil of Michael on the right side of the back. You will then say, 'As a child of God I offer the Oil of Philadelphia.' Again they will say, 'As a child of God I accept the Oil of Philadelphia.' Place the oil on the left side of the back across from the place of Michael's Oil. When this is done, you will say, 'As a child of God I offer the Oil of Pergamum.' They will say, 'I accept the Oil of Pergamum.' You will place this oil on the left side of the back where the place of Pergamum is in the Gate. Say, 'As a child of God I offer the Oil of Ephesus.' They repeat back, 'As a child of God I accept the Oil of Ephesus.' You will then move to the place of Thyatira saying, 'As a child of God I offer the Oil of Thyatira.' They will say, 'As a child of God I accept the Oil of Thyatira.' You will place the oil on their back as you would with the Gate. The next oil to be placed is Smyrna. Say, 'As a child of God I offer the Oil of Smyrna.' They will say, 'As a child of God I accept the Oil of Smyrna.' Place the oil on the back in the place of Smyrna.

"Move down to the spine to find the place of Sardis. Say, 'As a child of God I offer the Oil of Sardis.' In return they say, 'As a child of God I accept the Oil of Sardis.' After they have spoken, place the oil where the place of Sardis is in the gate. Before placing the last oil say, 'As a child of God I offer the Oil of Laodicea.' They say back to you, 'As a child of God I accept the Oil of Laodicea.' When they have answered, you will place the oil on the place of Laodicea in the Gate."

"I understand how it all works. I'm doing this healing by building a Gate with oils on the back. Which can happen now because I have the Michael Oil to balance out the seven oils of the churches."

"This is true, and there is more that you will do. Once you have built the Gate in oils on their back, you may use one of the oils of I Am."

"Really! How does this work?"

"Every oil has its purpose in a healing. You use the oil of Metatron for the mind if that's where the healing is needed. You use the oil of the Christ if the healing is of the emotions. The oil of the Shekinah is used to heal the physical body."

"So tell me something, like where do I put these oils?"

"Place the oil that is needed in the center of the Gate you have just made with the oils. Yet you must say, 'I, as a servant of God, offer

the oil the Shekinah for the healing of your body.' They say unto you, 'As servant of God I accept the oil of the Shekinah.' When this is done, place your right hand over the center of the Gate, touching the skin. Hold your hand there to seal the work you have done. You will then say, 'May the oil of Shekinah heal your body and bless your heart.' You will know when to remove your hand.

"Should you use the oil of Metatron, say, 'I, as a servant of God, offer the oil of Metatron for the healing of your mind.' In return they say, 'As a servant of God I accept the oil of Metatron.' When this is done, place your right hand over the center of the Gate, touching the skin. Hold your hand there to seal the work you have done. You will then say, 'May the oil of Metatron heal your mind and bless your heart.' You will know when to remove your hand.

"Should you use the oil of the Christ, say, 'I, as a servant of God, offer the oil of the Christ for the healing your emotions.' In return they say, 'As a servant of God I accept the oil of the Christ.' When this is done, place your right hand over the center of the Gate, touching the skin. Hold your hand there to seal the work you have done. You will then say, 'May the oil of the Christ heal your emotions and bless your heart.' You will know when to remove your hand."

"This will help a lot of the sevens to do their work. And you can count on my using it on my business client today."

"You will see the wonders of the healing she receives this day."

"This I have got to see. Thank you for this."

"It is given to the sevens to make their way in your world. My time is done for now. We will speak again."

She spoke again to me with a sound I hadn't heard in over five years. I knew it was Michael's name spoken in the language of the angels. God, I had almost forgotten the beauty of it. It was almost worth the visit just to hear it one more time.

"Michael shall speak with you more. Be at peace and teach only love."

The Shekinah moved back into the light surrounding her and was gone. Seeing the fire of light around her made me realize what it must have been like for Moses to see the burning bush on Mount Sinai. It is an awesome thing to behold. However, I wondered why Michael had to hold his wings around me. What did she mean by not 'marked' yet?

"Joe," the familiar voice said. I looked up to see Michael's face beaming down at me as I swiveled to face him, my head still looking up. Once I was facing him, I watched as his wings began to fold back behind him. I thought to myself, *He does look like the painting I did of him.* At least people will get some kind of an idea of how beautiful an angel really is. But it is nothing like standing in the presence of one.

"You have done well in the work you have been given. You have learned much. Yet I tell you now you are soon to receive the keys to the Kingdom of Heaven."

"Oh, really. I don't know if I want that honor. Because the last time someone had them he got nailed to a cross. Then the one he gave them to also got nailed to a cross, but upside down. Maybe I should just say, 'Thank you, but no thank you.' "

"Joe, your humor is wonderful. It will not happen to you."

"OK, Michael, what do these key things look like?"

"When Jesus was about to give Peter the keys, Peter asked Jesus, 'Where is the Kingdom?' Jesus said, 'It is within you and all around you.' It still is. Your kind has locked away what is theirs. What you will be given will open it again."

"There is something here I am not seeing."

"Exactly. Yet I tell you truly, you will, as will others."

I felt a soft touch of fur covering a powerful skull rise between my hand and leg. I knew it was Bogie, back with Michael. Bogie's death had not shocked me as much as Annie's death had. Mastiffs do not have long lives, and Bogie had not been a young dog when it was his time to go home. I looked down at my big son, as I had called him from the time I got him from the breeder. He paused for a moment to let me stroke his head and back. He walked to Michael and stood at his side.

Before leaving, Michael gave more information about the Masters Oil. There is a use for it other than making it for oneself. The Master's Oil can be used to raise the vibration on someone not involved in the work as a master. It is used to raise the vibration to promote healing and advance the consciousness to a higher understanding of the spiritual realm. We, as masters, were given the Masters Oil for our use, and were told not to use it except in the case of an emergency on someone other than a master. Now we have reached a new place in the consciousness level on the planet, and that makes ready the Masters Oil for others.

However, there is something that needs to be done to have this process work properly.

Let us consider why the oil is ready for others. If we look at it as a way of raising the vibration of others who have not had the benefits of a gathering, we can then see there is a way to help others that was not open to us before. We also know that not everyone is interested in becoming a sevens master. They do however have the same gifts and traps depending on the church archetype they align with. How is it we can help people to realize they are children of God and are at some level perfect, whole and complete? Everyone who has done the anointing process or has used their oil to help them in some way has come to see that the oils work rather well in assisting us on our path toward self-enlightenment. True, anointing oneself with the oil of another church does give a master some of the giftedness of that other church without the traps of that church. This is intended as a tool in our efforts to grow spiritually, so that we might be of greater assistance to ourselves and others.

When a person is in tune with the frequency of the church they are, they are able to receive spiritual enlightenment and the flow of healing grace for what is ailing them. So now we have a tool to assist those who have not gathered or have not aligned with the frequency of the church they are. By using the Masters Oil in a special way, the grace can go right to the place where healing is needed without having to try to tune the person to the church they are. This comes in handy for those who want to be gathered but haven't yet found someone that is holding a gathering for them to attend. We need to make it available to those who want it. With the oil, the person can start living in their giftedness well before the gathering ever takes place. Does this mean that the person won't have any of their traps of the church they are? Absolutely not. Each church has traps. Whether they surface now or later, they will come out.

Here is how you can help awaken or assist another in healing. First, you will have to determine which church that person aligns to. Once you know that, you will need to transform your Masters Oil to attune to that person you are helping. This requires three steps: (1) You will need your Masters Oil; (2) you will need a set of chakra-tuning forks; and (3) you will need to know the process and the blessing to be used.

Once you have everything in place, you need to cleanse the energy field of your body. This requires two tuning forks, one for the spiritual

tone of your church and the other for the physical tone of your church. If you are of Smyrna (or the red) you will need to take the C and the G tuning forks (which are also the same tuning forks for a blue, or Philadelphia). You would take the G tuning fork and hold it in your right hand and the C tuning fork in your left hand (a blue would hold the C tuning fork in the right hand). The right hand corresponds to the east side of the body (as we face north), east being the direction of the rising sun, or the spiritual side.

What follows is a list of the healing pairs for all the churches:

CHURCH	PHYSICAL TONE	SPIRITUAL TONE
Smyrna (red)	C	G (blue)
Ephesus (orange)	D	E (yellow)
Pergamum (yellow)	E	D (orange)
Sardis (green)	F	A (purple)
Philadelphia (blue)	G	C (red)
Thyatira (purple)	A	F (green)
Laodicea (violet)	B	B (violet)

Strike the two tuning forks at the same time, holding them by the stems. Next, raise them to the top of the head and slowly bring them down as if doing a long fanning motion. Go all the way down to your feet and back up to the top of your head. This is like a surgeon washing his hands before an operation. When this is done you are ready for step two. Now is the time for the oil. Whatever the amount you chose to use is fine, you may want to do a whole bottle or just a drop on a Q-tip. Take the oil and speak over it saying the person's name: "I bless this Masters Oil for (name), who is of the church of (name)."

Next, take the two tuning forks of the person's church for which you are to transform the oil. Again hold the church's tuning forks in the corresponding hands. Strike the forks and point them at the oil on either side, and say the following blessing: "As a child of God, I bless this Masters Oil that it may nourish their soul and enrich their body. As a servant of God, I transform this Masters Oil to assist him/her as the church of (name)."

When this is done you may now give the person you are helping the oil. There is nothing for them to say because their buying the oil is an

action of accepting it for their use. If you place the oil on the person you are working with, it is a different matter. You will need to say the following: "As a child of God, I offer the Oil of the Masters that is now of your church." And they will need to say, "I accept the oil."

Michael finished by saying, **"I have come to tell you of the coming of others who will teach you in the ways of the oils and herbs for healing. You will know of words left unspoken that will heal. Some will be placed in our 'Book of Healing.' Yet I tell you truly, the words you write will not be changed to suit the way of speaking of your kind. Our book will be written for an understanding of the soul, not the mind. Our time is done for now. Be at peace and teach only love."**

Michael, along with Bogie, folded back into the light and was gone. I looked around to see the sun beginning to come out from behind the clouds. Walking slowly back to my truck, I eased myself in behind the wheel. As I glanced down at my watch, I noticed it no longer agreed with the clock in the truck. Somehow, I had lost half an hour. *Wow,* I said to myself, *Shekinah's appearance must have completely warped time and space. No wonder Michael needed to protect me.* Shaking my head, I cranked the engine, put the truck into gear, and headed back on my way to town. Rather than go directly to my scheduled meeting, I stopped by my new office to pick up the oils I would need to perform the healing work. The drive to the client's office left me time to think about all that had transpired.

By the time I arrived at my destination, I had completely reviewed all the instructions provided me by the Shekinah. Upon entering the client's office, whose name was Adrienne, I saw that my friend Robbie had shown up as well. The two women were chatting away as I walked in. Adrienne looked up at me and said, "Fix me, please."

"Well, I have a bit of a surprise for you. But let's find a place where you can lie down."

Robbie interrupted, "You have had a visit haven't you?"

"Yes," I responded, "And I will need your help with this. I need to set the bottles of oil up while Adrienne gets a glass of water." Being the executive type, Adrienne had this bathroom bigger than some people's living rooms, plush carpet and all. It would have to do. There was something funny about performing the first angelic healing in a

bathroom. But I knew the angels wouldn't care. After arranging all the oils on the floor, I went out into the other room and asked Robbie if she could help Adrienne get ready. It's a touchy situation for a man to ask a woman client to bare her back for him. Robbie helped Adrienne remove her blouse and put it on backwards, kind of like a hospital smock. As I prepared my hands with the corn oil, I asked Robbie if she would lay Adrienne face down on the floor, and take the tuning forks to perform the clearing of the twelve chakras. Robbie was already a pro at using the tuning forks. She was a nurse by trade, and understood the human body much better than I. Working with the tuning forks came to her naturally.

The Shekinah had stated that the hands were to be coated three times with the corn oil, with time allowed for the hands to soak up the oil. By the time Robbie had finished clearing the twelve chakras, my hands were ready to create the Gate of Grace with the oils. As I placed each oil on Adrienne, I explained the blessing and the response she needed to say. After placing the last church oil on her back, I picked up the Oil of Shekinah. Again, I gave Adrienne the instructions given me, placed the oil in the center of the Gate on her back, and laid my hand in the middle of the Gate made of oil, saying, "May the Oil of the Shekinah heal your body and bless your heart." Adrienne jerked a little as I began pouring grace into her through my right hand. As instructed, I held my hand in place until I could feel no more grace flowing through.

After rolling over on her back, Adrienne asked, "Would you do me a favor and place your hands on my face and head as well?" Not seeing any reason to object, I did as she requested. The fever did not feel hot, but cool against the heat coming from my own hands.

"While your hand was on my back, I could feel something like electricity running through me," she said.

She wasn't the only one. After finishing up, a slight dizziness crept through me, leaving a kind of spaced-out sensation in my head. Not feeling in the mood to talk to anyone, I left Robbie with the task of helping Adrienne get redressed and comfortable. After returning to my office, I just sat there for a while staring into emptiness, trying to get a handle on what had just occurred, if anything. After about an hour of finishing up with paperwork, the phone rang. It was Robbie. "I don't know what you did for Adrienne, but she is feeling great. No aches, no back pains, and most importantly, no fever."

GABRIEL'S MESSAGE

*T*he first visits from Michael had hit me like a lightning bolt from the heavens. The messages washed through the first seven and myself like a river fed by warm springs. The awe left us giddy, even childlike with delight at realizing what incredible truths unfolded before us. But like young parents caught in reverie over a newborn child, the sevens slowly, inevitably, faced the growing obviousness: With gifts and giftedness there come responsibilities. This child has to be fed and raised. These days, awe had yielded to questions, doubts, expectations — even boredom. Of course, the human condition often issues forth the best in us when we are at our worst. Angels or not, that wasn't going to change.

Now, when Michael or the other angels appeared, my reaction no longer mimicked being hit by a lightning bolt. Now, it was more like guests had arrived, and here I am with a dirty living room and the beds unmade. The baby cries, wanting its diaper changed. Some of the sevens reacted to these visits by trying to clean up their collective living rooms or making their messy beds, all the while acknowledging the presence of these guests, all the while apologizing for the disorder, or squabbling with other members of the family as to why their rooms were in such disarray. Other sevens wanted to ask these guests to sit quietly while they changed

the baby's diaper. But when angels show up, they don't sit quietly. And thus there came a day in May of 2000 when one of the angelic guests caught most of us by surprise.

"Joe, go to the Gate of Grace," the voice said. The whine of the weed-whacker ceased as I looked around. Robbie's yard increasingly had taken on the guise of a jungle. Her Gateway stood in the corner of her back yard. I dropped the weed-whacker and headed to the fence surrounding the back section. As I opened the gate to the back-forty, I saw the Gateway lit up with color. Seven angels stood over the stones of the seven churches, with Michael waiting in the place of the servant. *Oh great,* I thought. *It's going to be one of those visits.*

As I approached the outer edge of the Gate of Grace, Michael spoke. **"Stop. For you have need to see what you are to be given."**

"OK," I said. The edge of the Gateway stood some fifteen feet from where I stood. *That ought to be a good enough vantage point.* As I looked up, the figure of a man formed in the middle of the Gate. The figure seemed composed of a clear, plastic-looking light. *Good,* I thought to myself, *It's going to be a healing session.*

"This is what you would call recovery, more so than healing. Witness and remember." Michael pointed to the figure standing in the center of the Gate. The figure faced north, so I moved to the northerly part of the yard to get a frontal view. As I stood there gazing at this sight, the glow from the two blue stones, resting in the east and west points of the Gate, began moving. The blue light from the east floated over to the right foot of the prototypal man and rested just above the ground, inside the arch of his foot. Then the blue light from the west moved to the same place in the left foot. When the light in the left foot was set, the lights from the other stones also moved to the body creating what looked like a mini-Gate of Grace in and outside of the body. The lights not inside the body rested so very close to the plastic skin that I couldn't judge their distance from the body. As each of the lights took its place in and around the feet, they gave off a tone corresponding to the notes we had been taught which are associated with each church, or color. The blue light gave off the tone of C, the yellow light D, the orange light E, the purple light F, the red light G, the green light A, and the violet light B — the last light in the helixlike pattern resting above the ankle.

"This is cool, " I said, as I watched additional small balls of light leave the stones (or they could have come from the angels standing in the place of the stones — I wasn't sure). Additional lights moved around the positions in the east and the west moving up the legs. In particular, I noticed another yellow light drift over and connect to the position of the first yellow light, but turned blue as it arrived. Once the other seven lights joined it to make yet another small Gate-like pattern, the blueness shifted back to its original yellow color. Then the rest of the seven colors arrived like the yellow light had, first showing blue and then returning to its original color. As each light took its place, its corresponding tone would sound, but stronger and more vibrant with each successive geometric connection. As these additional Gate-like patterns attached to one another, it was becoming obvious that a kind of Tree of Life was being constructed out of light and sound within and around the body of the man. Faster and faster the lights moved into place, and at each successive level of connecting Gate-like structures, the tones would sound an octave higher. As the web of Gates continued up the body, sets of lights seemed to helix like a DNA strand, until they stopped just above the head. "Michael?" I asked. "How come it stopped?"

"There is a limited number that rests in one of your kind."

"Are you going to tell me how many that is?"

"Seventy-two is the number."

"So each of us has seventy-two sets of Gates in us?"

"Joe, these are not Gates. These are what your kind would call meridians, yet are truly points of grace. Look again."

As I stared at the prototypal man, he began to tilt to a horizontal position as if resting on his back. I could see down through the top of his head. All the Gates of light had formed a geometric pattern leaving an empty tube down the center of the body, all the way down to the feet. *This must be a tube that allows the grace of God to flow through*, I said to myself. Why I knew this, I don't know. It just made sense.

"You are wise to know this in your thinking. There is more to see," Michael said as the body turned to give me a length-long view. At the heart chakra, I heard a tone as a ball of green light the size of two fists formed. Below that began to form another ball of light, this time yellow. Again a tone sounded. Then above the heart chakra, I saw a blue ball of light forming at the throat, followed by the sounding of a tone. This went

on until there were eleven balls of light at the eleven chakras, just like what had been taught at the Chicago conference.

"Do you know this, Joe?"

"Of course I do, Michael. this is what I do when I align the twelve chakras. So what does this have to do with the seven of you (actually eight, if you include Michael) coming today?" As I finished the question, the Arab-looking angel (Gabriel) stepped forward. Perhaps stepping forward isn't the right term; he just became more present than the other angels.

"You and others may know the number of the Tree of Life, that the Kingdom of Heaven is here on earth. There are seven keys to the Kingdom, of which the world holds to unlock it. The way of understanding this is in the language of mathematics for your kind. You will need much help to know this, for it is beyond your thinking. Yet we say unto you, the answer is there. You will not know the sums of what we give you. Give them to Gary, for it is in his understanding. We give to you this to understand. The number 144,000 holds more than meets the eye in a story [referring to the *Book of Revelation*]. **It is more than the song that is known. This number holds in it the way to the sums. Take the number and divide it by seven five times and once by eight. This will give you the seventh number. The sum of the first** [gathering] **gives you three numbers, which is the key to the other numbers. Yet I say, seventy-two is what holds the way to the Tree. The times of the keys to the Kingdom are set in this as well."**

"I hope Gary will know what you are saying. I don't have a clue how this works. I know, I know, you just give us a hint and we take it from there. By they way, I need to ask you something. Gary wanted to know if ..."

Like a mind reader, Michael interrupted, **"What Gary said is true. One may call the Gate of Grace into being, yet only those who do may use it for themselves. What was given for the oils holds true."** Michael was responding to Gary's discovery that anyone who had been part of a gathering could summon the energy of the Gate of Grace by simply centering oneself and remembering the seven masters who had been with that person at their gathering. After acknowledging each of the fellow masters with one's thoughts, the energy of the Gate of Grace would surround that person as if he were actually standing in the Formation of the Sevens with his fellow masters. However, this does not hold true

when one is using the oils for healing. One cannot summon or call the energy of the Gate into being for another. The stones must be used, unless the one assisting in the healing has been a servant, or as Michael had put it, "has gathered." One must have been a servant at a gathering for the energy of the Gate to stay with them always. For when one becomes a servant to a gathering, they become a living Gate of Grace. **"The other [question] you would ask is of the Gate. The diamonds of which you were to speak of add nothing to the grace of the Gate. The one who does this may feel it does add, yet it is only the way he focuses the grace. These are all tools for healing work, nothing more. Each may do with it as they will. The Gate of Grace is the Gate of Grace."** Why people insist in trying to add this or that to the Gate is beyond me. But one of the seven had tried to use a special stone as an experiment in the Gate, only to report an increase of energy. What Michael is saying is that no stone can be substituted in the Gate. And those who report increased energy are focusing the energy themselves with their own intention. The stone, in this case a kind of diamond, was merely a tool for this seven to focus with. It was his focus and intent that had increased the energy, not the stone.

When I looked back to the plastic man with all the mini-Gates in him, I saw something else, but was told not to tell what I saw. Gary would find the answer to it. Then all the angels said at the same time, **"Teach only love,"** and they were gone.

When I passed on the information Gabriel had presented me to Gary, he reacted like a miner who had discovered a vein of gold. It took him three months to decipher the mathematics. If you are like me with math, you will understand that I was almost more bewildered by what he had discovered than what Gabriel had told me. In the interest of brevity, if not sanity, only part of what he wrote is presented here. For those who wish the entire message Gary sent, you can write and ask for a copy. What follows is an extract of that message written by Gary.

"The Mathematics of the Tree of Life"

On the new moon of May 3, Michael showed up early in the morning. He simply said, "Anoint yourself with the Oil of Pergamum,"

and disappeared. That was it. Joe had sent me the message from Gabriel regarding the 144,000 a few days earlier. I assumed the anointing with the oil would assist me in discerning the mathematics given to us. It has taken me several weeks since then, using geometry, mathematics, and parallel sacred texts to fully appreciate what Gabriel has given us. I will discuss what I have learned in three sections: (1) quantum significance of the mathematics; (2) the meaning of the Tree of Life within the body and in the world; and (3) the spiritual consequences of how we are creating a new Earth in conjunction with Heaven.

So let's start with the "sum of the first gives you three numbers." At the first gathering, there were three women and four men, three gays and four straights. These seven were found by the one who answered the call and gathered them: Joe. The three numbers are 1, 3, 4. In two-dimensional space, the geometry of the Formation of the Sevens (also called the Gate of Grace when the eight stones are in place) is made up of three-sided and four-sided figures. There are four triads which make up the Formation. Also inherent in the geometry are two squares, the outer and the inner square. In three-dimensional space these squares are literally the bases of two intersecting square pyramids (four-sided pyramids) of energy. We know that the two pyramids are geometrical representations of the coming together of Heaven (upside-down pyramid) and Earth (the regular pyramid).

The first sum of numbers, 1, 3, 4 add up to what is known as a Fibonacci sequence. In other words, 1+3=4, 3+4=7. The numbered set of 1, 3, 4, 7 is also known as a quantum number (or cell), which is a very special number. But one of the things you do with a quantum number is multiply the root (which is 1, 3, 4) and you get 12. This will also play an important role as the mathematics unfolds. A Fibonacci sequence is found throughout nature and is known as the growth sequence (growth spiral), or the numbers used by nature when life blossoms. This tells us that the Tree of Life is a living entity, and that the sevens are the "cells" which make up this blossoming tree.

A quantum number is derived from what is known as Pythagorean arithmetic, now called quantum arithmetic. This mathematics uses what are called Pythagorean prime triangles as its system of calculation, configuration, and transformation. The number sequence (1, 3, 4, 7) forms one of these prime triangles whose sides are of unit length 7, 24, and 25 (the hypotenuse). The perimeter of this prime triangle is 56 (7 +

7x7). What I want to tell you is that the Gate of Grace is more than a pretty geometric figure. When the stones are in place, or the seven masters plus a servant are in place, they literally create a quantum event. The angels have given tones to go with the geometry. And guess what? These tones correspond to what is called quantum harmonics. When we open an angelic gateway, we are imposing a quantum event on our dimension, thus creating an actual opening into another quantum reality (what we are calling "the angelic realm"). When the angels tell us we are creating a new Earth, they are not kidding.

One of the other factors in creating a quantum number is to add up all the numbers in the cell. So when you add the 1, 3, 4 you get 8. This now gets us back to Gabriel's instructions. The seventh of the seven numbers derived from Gabriel's mathematics is 1, and the sixth number is 8 (see below). There were eight people in the first gathering: one who answered the call (Joe) as the servant, and the seven (3+4) who gathered with this servant to make 8. So now we begin to understand part of the puzzle around 144,000 by looking at the divisions Gabriel asked us to perform:

Take the number and divide it by seven five times and once by 8. This will give you the seventh number. The sum of the first [gathering] gives you three numbers.

In mathematics, this is known as converting from one number base to another. In mathematics, the number 144,000 is in base ten. But when you divide as Gabriel asked, you convert it to base seven (those who are mathematicians are asked to hold their objection about dividing by 8 in the final division). The new number (in base 7) is determined by the remainders, or mantissas (in reverse order), after you divide. Let's look at this:

ordinal or whole number		mantissa or divisor	remainder
1st number	144,000	7	3
2nd no.	20571	7	5
3rd no.	2938	7	5
4th no.	419	7	6
5th no.	59	7	3
6th no.	8	8	0
7th no.	1		1

The seven ordinal numbers reflect two aspects of quantum realities. What I am implying is that the ancient mystics knew all along about these two realities and how they were related. It is only now that we have the power to operate in and with both. The ancients told us, "As above, so below. As below, so above." This is also the essence of the Egyptian Duat. In similar fashion, when Jesus originally gave Peter the "keys to the Kingdom of Heaven," a similar edict was fashioned: "Whatsoever you shall hold bound on earth shall be held bound in Heaven. Whatsoever you shall hold loosed on earth shall be held loosed in Heaven." But the keys to the Kingdom were lost. I will try to explain in the third section as to why. But let me say that the statements by Gabriel tell us not only that the keys are being returned to humanity, as a consequence, but that the two quantum realities are being brought together as well. What I will try to explain is that the Tree of Life is activated within the body of anyone who gathers, and in turn, we, ourselves, create the world-changing Tree of Life made up of sevens, which will transform our reality. In other words, we are living fractals, transforming what we call ordinary reality. Just as much as any single human cell contains the genetic code to create a fully developed new human being, so do we contain the codes to the Tree of Life which will ultimately create a fully transformed Earth. We are living holographs.

Gabriel tells us that the timing of the keys being returned is determined in these seven ordinal numbers. There are two ways of looking at these numbers, just as there are two quantum realities engaged in the Gate of Grace. In other words, a tree can grow in two directions: in height as well as in breadth. There are seven levels of geometry which correspond to the seven numbers. The seven levels are like a tree growing in height while the seven ordinal numbers are the number of sevens who need to be gathered, which represents the breadth (or branchings) of a tree. I have created a geometric representation of what Joe saw in the previous teaching about the Tree of Life being constructed by the coming together of angels and sevens. I have carried that geometry to four levels. That's as far as I can go with the software I have. It gets quite complicated at the fourth level. The first level was completed when Joe said yes, and gathered the first seven. The second level is also complete since seven masters of seven different colors have now gathered seven others. We are now approaching the third level where those who have been gathered by

the second-level sevens are about to start gathering. What I'm trying to say is that the giving of each key will be determined by the growth of the Tree. As each level is reached, we become candidates to receive a key. This tells me that the first two keys to the Kingdom of Heaven are soon to be given back to us. But as we continue, the Tree of Life will most likely grow faster in height (reaching a new level) than it will in breadth (continued gatherings adding to the total number of sevens). In other words, at the time of this writing we are about to have enough gatherings to have initiated 59 sevens, which would be the completion of the third level.

I have to tell you how amazed I was by the geometry of the Tree as I constructed it on my computer. As each level is complete, the geometry forms a ring, just like the growth ring of a living tree. Once again using the adage, "As above, so below...," it stands to reason that there exist corresponding "rings" within the human body which affect the consciousness of the planet. And here is how. We tend to see our bodies as a single unit. But in reality we have seven bodies that make up our composite earthly body. Six of the seven bodies take the form of and surround our physical body. The seventh body is elliptical in shape, kind of like an egg that surrounds the other six bodies. This body is called the body of Christ Consciousness, which connects us to what has been described theologically as the Mystical Body of Christ.

In my bombardment of Joe with questions, I discovered that the Gates of light began diminishing in number above the heart chakra. In other words, the geometry starts working in reverse once above the heart chakra. We know from what was taught at the Chicago Conference, that we possess twelve chakras. As it turns out, Joe saw these Gate-like structures connecting at these chakra points. Eleven of the chakra points are located within and around the body. In the geometry, I discovered that the chakras pair off above and below the heart chakra. In other words, the geometric connection at the third eye chakra is the same as the geometric configuration at the sacral chakra. These two chakra connections form the top and bottom edge of a torus (donut tube) of energy. When Joe looked down the head of the prototypal man, he saw a hole going down the entire body. This hole is made up of six torus tubes of energy, or six donuts of energy. Each of these tubes, or donuts of energy, form the sheath or boundary of one of the six bodies each human carries. And within each

torus tube (which appears like a ring when viewed from above), there are twelve helixes of light strands, made up of the combinations of seven colors, three of which reflect the feminine, four of which reflect the masculine (3x4=12). The twelve strands found in the physical body are directly related to what is traditionally known as the Chinese meridians used in acupuncture. The twelve meridians are found in each of the six earthly-based bodies, which adds up to seventy-two meridians in total.

What are these six bodies? They are the physical body, the emotional body, the mental body, the spiritual-mental body (astral body), the spiritual-emotional body (the causal/karmic body), and the spiritual-physical body (or etheric body). Beyond the geometry, there is a seventh body, which surrounds the six bodies in an elliptic shell, or an egg, that is accessed through the heart chakra. This is known as the spiritual body of Christ Consciousness, or the body of Oneness, which is a special case. This is why we bless a person's heart whenever we assist them with healing work. By blessing the heart, we access the person's Christ Consciousness, or Oneness. It is also the reason why we construct the Gate of Grace with healing oils over the person's heart chakra on their back.

These seven bodies we carry correspond to the seven ordinal numbers, or seven levels shown us mathematically by Gabriel. The seven ordinal numbers reflect how we will affect the entire planet. As the number of sevens reaches a threshold (such as 419 at the fourth level) we will impact the world's consciousness in a 100th-monkey phenomenon in that "body" of consciousness. We will affect one aspect of the "body" of humankind. When 419 sevens have been gathered, we will affect the spiritual-mental consciousness of earth. We will have engaged the coming together of Heaven and Earth into that aspect of human consciousness. And when the number of sevens has reached 144,000, we will have affected the complete consciousness of this planet.

That now gets us into the meaning of the 144,000. First I'd like to reference the quote from the *Book of Revelation*, as stated in the Bible:

The *Book of Revelation*, Chapter 14, verses 1-4 —
"Then I looked, and there before me was the Lamb standing on Mount Zion, and with him 144,000 who had his name and his Fathers' name written on their foreheads. And I heard a sound from heaven like the roar of rushing waters and like a loud peal of thunder. The sound I heard

was like that of harpists playing their harps. And they sang a new song before the four living creatures and the elders. No one could learn the song except the 144,000 who had been redeemed from the earth. These are those who did not defile themselves with women, for they kept themselves pure ..."

Please note the references to harps (sound). This is the same kind of sound Joe heard as the Tree of Life was being constructed in the body of the prototypal man. In comparison, notice the version of this text we get from I Am in the Codex found in *On the Wings of Heaven*:

Then were those that had the Father's and the Son's name written on them. No one could learn the new song but these. And they were those men that did not lay with women or women that did not lay with men. They have been chosen as the first fruits and are the spiritual teachers. They are blameless and speak the truth of God's love.

And further on, I Am states:

Then the angel showed the loving will of God for all of mankind. He showed of a world without want, and nothing unloving can be found there. The sign of God will be on the foreheads of all. All that is written will be; blessed are those that can already know this.

To show you the importance of this message, I need to refer to one other writing — the *Gospel of Thomas*, found in what is known as the apocrypha, or the Nag Hammadi Library (which is a recently discovered set of scrolls, not unlike the Dead Sea Scrolls). Today, biblical scholars consider the *Gospel of Thomas* to be the most authentic of all the gospels, including the four Synoptic Gospels found in the Christian Bible. Now I am going to quote from the *Gospel of Thomas*, which says:

Gospel of Thomas, verse 22 —
Jesus saw some infants nursing. He said to his disciples, 'These nursing infants are like those who enter the Kingdom of Heaven.'

They said to him, 'Then shall we enter the Kingdom of Heaven as infants?'

Jesus said to them, 'When you make the two into one, and when you make the inner like the outer and the outer like the inner, and the upper like the lower, and when you make male and female into a single one, so that the male will not be male nor the female be female, when you make eyes in place of an eye, a hand in place of a hand, a foot in place of a foot, an image in place of an image, then you will enter the Kingdom of Heaven.'

Gospel of Thomas, verse 114 —
Simon Peter said to them, 'Make Mary leave us, for females don't deserve life.'

Peter was objecting to Mary's sitting with the men who were listening and being taught by Jesus. It was Jewish law that women were not allowed to participate in such gatherings where sacred Scripture was discussed.

Jesus said, 'Look, I will guide her to make her male, so that she too may become a living spirit resembling you males. For every female who makes herself male, [and every male who makes himself female,] will enter the Kingdom of Heaven.'

Jesus was speaking about what is called the "Divine Marriage," or "Divine Androgyny," where we do not separate ourselves but see the oneness in ourselves, see the coming together of the masculine and feminine. So when you look at what Michael told us about gay men and women — who are the 144,000 referenced in the *Book of Revelation* — you begin to see what the keys to the Kingdom of Heaven are about:

From *On the Wings of Heaven* —
Of all the things Michael had shown Joe, this was something he was not ready for. He burst into tears as he saw people he knew and had known standing with what looked like, what appeared to be, the Christ. He sobbed at the sight of his past gay friends who had died years ago. The joy was almost more than he could stand, knowing that they had made it. Heaven was theirs. Some of the people he saw were still alive today, and some were dead long ago. When he saw his old friend, Chico, who had died from AIDS, in the crowd, happy and healthy, he lost it. Joe's knees buckled under him, hitting the ground. Losing even his sense of

balance, he fell, his back thumping against the fence. His emotions poured out of him....

As Joe's mind cleared, he thought, *Given the people I have just seen, and the fact that they were gay, does it mean I am too?* 'No,' Michael said, knowing his thoughts. 'You knew that these people were gay when I first gave you what to write. You and many others know things that you are not aware of yet. Be not surprised when you do. The song they sing has been learned, and is being learned, by the male and female in the male and female. These are the "first fruits" spoken of in *Revelation*. They are in touch with the male and female natures in all things. These are the ones who chose, and were chosen, to live life this way. The religions of the world have cast them out as sinners and allowed them not the love of God. Blessed were they, for the love of God was all they had. They were set free to find the connection with that love. They feel the spiritual connection of both masculine and feminine.'

Am I trying to say that the 144,000 will be gay men and women who bring the seven keys back to humanity? Far from it. I am saying they hold the knowingness of how to do it with their innate capacity of embracing both masculine and feminine within themselves and in life. This is called "androgyny." It is not a physical condition, it is a spiritual condition which anyone can discover. It is in our capacity to embrace both the masculine and the feminine within ourselves.

When Gabriel said, **"The number 144,000 holds more than meets the eye in a story. It is more than the song that is known,"** he meant that Michael's message to Joe was complete: **"The song they sing has been learned, and is being learned, by the male and female in the male and female."** It is no longer just left to gay men and women to carry the message of Oneness forward. It is now up to all of us who are sevens. It is why I Am told us, **"The sign of God will be on the foreheads of all."**

At the first gathering, there were three women and four men, three gays and four straights. Oddly enough, in the first Formation of the Seven, all the male masters were on one side of the Formation while all the female masters were on the other side — separated, as it were. Of the four triads making up the Formation of the Seven, the men sat in the west and the south triads, while the women sat in the north and the east triads. These triads have twelve paths of connection (including the connection to the servant). And it is through our connectedness to one another that we move into Oneness. These twelve paths to one another in the Formation of the Seven, carried through the six levels of consciousness (the seventh level being the arrival into Christ Consciousness), creates the seventy-two (12x6) paths to the Tree of Life. It is no coincidence when Jesus said, "I am the vine and you are the branches." If we can move into eliminating our separateness as our consciousness grows through the six earthly bodies of consciousness, then we in turn change everything within us and outside us. Or as Gabriel put it:

> **Yet I say, seventy-two is what holds the way to the Tree. The times of the keys to the Kingdom are set in this as well.**

Gabriel is telling us that we are not only the way to the Tree of Life, but at the seventh level, all of us together with the angelic realm *are* the Tree of Life. Within each one of us rests the seventy-two paths. As our living bodies, holding the twelve chakras, the twelve gateways to Life, move through the six earthly bodies of consciousness, we will eventually bring ourselves and the world into the seventh body of consciousness — full awareness of Christ Consciousness. I exhort all of you to move to a place of ending separateness, embracing our Oneness so that we may find ourselves ready and worthy to receive once again these seven keys to the Kingdom of Heaven.

FILLED VESSELS

As with all of nature, there is a time of growing and a time of resting. Tremendous information had poured forth from the angelic realm in a way that made one wonder what could possibly be up ahead. If the next twelve months were anything like the last twelve months, I'm not sure I'd survive it. Or any of the sevens, for that matter. The e-mail flashing across the Internet only proved the point. As I pondered this, I remembered a legend from an ancient tradition. That story told of a time before humanity had taken on the physical body, where this primal body was a great vehicle for the transformation of chaos, or the void, into creation. The Divine Spark within these marvelous bodies possessed the capacity to move creation in any direction it wished through the gift of free will. And thus chaos was transmuted into order through these sparks of God we call humanity. It was through the human condition that God grew.

For a great period of time our world operated in harmony, beauty, and order. So much so, that humanity then became impatient. We had transmuted the negative forces of the void so well that we began to say to one another, If we can do this so well, then why don't we transmute even more negativity and chaos? Thus, the collective human consciousness

approached what were called the eighty Lords of Chaos (or the Lords of Arulu) and demanded that the eighty gates at the edge of chaos be opened wider so that even more of creation might manifest. From the cosmos poured in unparalleled chaos and negativity to the point that humanity almost succumbed to it. This is what is traditionally known as "the fall."

Humankind lost itself in the wall of darkness it had demanded. The only way to escape and transmute this darkness and chaos was to move into the material realms, which humanity did. The bodies we now possess took on substance with the assistance of the realms of angels and masters. And to this day we have struggled to overcome and transmute the chaos through the forces of duality. Our bodies separated into the masculine and the feminine, enabling us to manifest creation in yet a new and wonderful way. Some among us carried both masculine and feminine to remind us of what we had once been, so that some day we might return, but in a new way. That day has come, according to the angels.

So much change weighed upon the sevens. Who could argue that chaos raged in our lives like never before? Yet were we not able to transmute that chaos with our love? That's what I hoped for. My steps halted at the sight of a light over toward where the Gate of Grace stood. As I followed my curiosity, I could spot Michael in the distance. It had been a while. I almost trotted to where he stood.

"Blessed are you with the work you have done. The masters who have gathered are twelve in number. This brings the time of darkness to the light. Those that would shine have taken the light inward. This is what you would call a 'good thing.' "

"OK, Michael, just how do I see this as a good thing?"

"Simple, Joe. You are at the place where your classes are being canceled, are you not?"

"Yes. I have lost a few. I just took it as a sign that people weren't ready to hear what you have given me to teach."

"The twelve pillars have been set, as are the masters who have gathered. In the setting of these, they have become their own light. They have become as a vessel that is full. There is no room for light to enter them."

"And you are telling me this is a good thing?" In my mind, I mulled over who had served as servants at gatherings. And sure enough, twelve people were responsible for all the gatherings to this date.

"In your words, 'It is a very good thing.' Have you forgotten the story of the fishes and loaves? When the people were finished consuming what was given to them, there was enough left over to fill twelve baskets. It has taken almost 2,000 years to become empty again. That is the way it is now. They will only nibble at the food for the spirit we give you for them."

"I know you are not telling me it will take another 2,000 years before the sevens are empty again."

"You have gone about it, as you say, 'the wrong way.' You would be about taking what you teach out to the world. You become disheartened when a class is canceled. You feel a loss. Yet I say to you, who is it that is at loss? You, because you cannot teach? Or those who are not there to learn? When they hunger they will call to you to come teach."

"Well, there are others that can teach what I taught them. So the teachings get out."

"Yes. They do know what you gave them, yet little more. Each will add to what they teach from what they know. Yet I ask you, from what well do they drink?"

"Beats me."

"They have drunk from the well our kind has brought with the Water of Life. They do not thirst now. They drink what little you were allowed to teach, and think they are in a sea. The flow with which you have given the water has in itself become too much. It washes over them and falls to the desert's floor. When the teachings become as water to the one dying in the desert, they will be ready to drink again. Do you not see this?"

"No."

"You have been teaching as you were given, and they were not allowed to become empty. You gave, each time, something new and kept filling them. Look to the classes you were to do. Have you done them?"

"Nope."

"For now, I tell you to honor the teachings, which are set for you to teach. Finish the 'Book of Healing' with that which I have given you. You will teach no more of what we give you until you are told to. This happened because those who were to have it be [receive] are as vessels that are full. They can hold no more. You must give them time

to empty themselves. You must stop the flow. You must restrict and resist the flow so that the vessel may become empty again."

"So what do I do now? Just go into hiding and don't have any contact with anyone? What about the new business and Web page Robbie and I have started? Do we just give up on it?"

"No, Joe. You can talk to the sevens about all that has been given. People will still need to get the tools you would sell. It is fitting for the one you chose to do the work you need on your Web page, as you call it. Trust him, for he will be guided that you all prosper from his labor. You will give that which we say to give in the 'Angelic Book of Healing.' Yet you will not give much of that we will now give and teach you. It is time for you to stand on your own with us. Let the others make the way for the wonders we give you to teach. They have more than they are ready for now. They have not the opening to understand all that the oils can do. Nor are they ready to learn how to use the tuning forks and the Gate to take them to where they can heal at a glance."

"You are talking about instant healing aren't you?"

"Yes, and about that which you call 'acutuning.' For you have the basic understanding of it. You will learn which tuning fork to use and where to place it. You will learn which oil to keep it open that it may heal. When you have learned this, you will learn to do it with grace. By the time the book is done they may be ready for some of what is given in it."

"Does this mean what I put in the book is not to go out now?"

"Yes. I will tell you what is to go into this book."

"Well, I may have a problem with that. You see I have one person editing it, and then Gary is putting it together for a publisher."

"Speak to them and say, 'Do not give out that which is written, and do not do the things that are written."

"Well, duh. — why didn't I think of that?"

"You would have. You will be given that which we would have you do. Worry not of the vessels that are full for they will become empty soon enough. Did it not speak of this time in *Revelation*?"

"I am sure it does but I don't know where."

"It matters not. Walk with me, for I have need to teach you the first of that which is not to be given now."

I walked with Michael and listened to what he had to say and teach. He explained a few things to me and showed me a few more. Wow! is all I can say.

"It is not your job to find the student to teach. You are to teach when the student is ready to learn. Be at peace and teach only love."

HEALING AMONG THE SEVENS

*T*he reactions of the sevens being told they were full vessels reminded me of falling snowflakes. No two reactions were alike. Some sevens insisted they could handle more, not unlike a fireman proclaiming his thirst while trying to drink water from a fire hose. Others acknowledged to being overwhelmed, feeling they needed time, lots of time, to absorb all they had been given. Yet others proclaimed the teachings left holes which needed to be filled, resulting in some curious experiments. All I knew was that I was not to teach any new information. What began to unfold struck me as a miracle in itself.

Nothing had yet manifested the Halls of Healing and Enlightenment. What was a hall? And who would create it? The angels? The sevens? No one in particular? Messages started drifting in from Montana as Gary began working with sevens in the Bitterroot and Missoula Valleys. Was this one of the seven spiritual centers that Michael had shown me? The location seemed right. Rumors began circulating about the large number of Gates created by sevens in that area. Roughly twenty-one Gates of Grace had been erected in less than a month. What effect would this have on the people of that region? For that matter, what would such a concentration of Gates have on the planet? Reports filtered down how

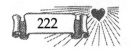

locals had heard for years that the region would be a hotbed of spiritual activity. The Native American prophecies had proclaimed that the Bitterroot Valley was a sacred land, a land of healing. The Whites had come in and ravaged the Native populations, creating a Trail of Tears not unlike what had happened to the Cherokee. The shamans had proclaimed that the Natives would return in the distant future and return the land to its sacredness, re-establishing it as a place of healing once again.

One afternoon, while Gary was visiting Miss S, who had set up a magnificent angelic Gateway on her rural property, an unexpected phenomenon surprised them both — Michael showed up. He presented a message to Gary that four people would be found — two men and two women — who would begin the first Hall of Healing. In Michael's aura, Gary could see the faces of two of the people who would establish this hall, one being Miss S and the other being Mr. H, a gentleman Gary had met at one of his speaking engagements in Hamilton, Montana, just south of Missoula. The other two people's images hazed in a blur of bright light. Gary took this to mean he would know the other two people later. Miss S detected Michael's presence as well, agreeing with Gary's assessment that a Hall of Healing should be attempted. But how? Miss S's skills as an organizer and people-person played no small part in creating a space for what was to unfold.

Over the next month, the third person came forward, a raven-haired man, Mr. W. He headed up a mountain retreat and healing center located just outside of Hamilton, Montana. Within a short time, Miss S, Mr. H, and Mr. W would join together in a sevens gathering, which would set the course of events for the spiritual development of what would eventually be called The Montana Hall of Healing. All three people met with Gary in an effort to try and understand what needed to happen for a Hall of Healing to operate. Should they operate on the concept "Build it and they will come"? Or should they simply be a loose-knit group adapting to situations as they appear? As it would turn out, this question would never be fully answered. When angels and humans come together in a common cause, just about anything can happen. And it did.

It was Gary who received the first request from a friend to have healing work done. Not only did his friend Shirley need some assistance but so did Shirley's best friend, Mrs. G, who had been diagnosed with lupus. Their conversation drifted into how a healing team had been

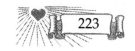

formed in Missoula, and would the two of them be interested in being the first two clients? Shirley had to talk to Mrs. G about all this, but in the end the two women flew into Missoula for what was to be a step into the unknown for all involved.

Over breakfast, Gary carefully reviewed the teachings the angels had given in how to assist others in their healing. Both Shirley and Mrs. G had to understand that the healing team was only there to assist them. The true healers were the women themselves. Mrs. G's lupus was far more advanced than Gary realized. Her condition was so severe that she hung on the edge of facing the rest of her days in a wheelchair. Severe pain troubled her knees and feet, making it almost impossible for her to get out of bed in the morning without an hour's worth of foot massage. Mrs. G simply dreaded the thought of becoming immobile.

Shirley's treatment would end up spanning more than one session. Her doctor would end up diagnosing her with having severe stomach ulcers, one of which would perforate to the point of severe bleeding. He warned her that perforation of the larger ulcer could result in her death. To exacerbate matters, Shirley was also troubled with a hiatal hernia. Both women were in their retirement years, facing the limits of modern medicine. The angels had made it clear that healing rested with each one of us. How we choose our method of healing is up to us. There is no separating of healing disciplines as right or wrong. Whatever it takes to bring a person back to health is all that matters. Modern medicine, even with its limits, is still important in the equation of assisting us in our healing. In other words, work with the angels, but also listen to your doctor. Some of us need to be touched as part of our therapy. Thus a chiropractor might be an essential part of one client's healing, while a nutritionist might better serve another. Certain clients may also need homeopathy as part of their journey back to health, while others may need massage therapy. Whatever it takes, the client's health stands as the main concern.

The two women arrived at Miss S's house for the healing session. Mr H and Gary would work together with Miss S this day. Mr. W couldn't get away from his duties but would later play a strong role in the eventual maturation of the Hall of Healing concept. Mrs. G volunteered to be the first to be worked on. Using techniques given by the angels — tuning forks, healing oils, and grace therapy — all contributed to the process.

Mr. H was an adept energy worker, and spent a great deal of time working on Mrs. G's blocks while Gary and Miss S worked on attuning chakras and releasing blocks in meridians. Miss S's experience as a Reiki master and chi gong practitioner only added to the effectiveness of the treatment. Midway in the process, Miss G began complaining how her knees felt like they were on fire. As the Gate of Grace was placed on her bare back using the sacred oils, tears began to flow freely. At the end of two hours, she was helped up from the massage table and asked to give herself time to adjust to the angelic oils. It is not uncommon for the oils to leave a person dizzy or disoriented, including the one administering the oils.

What everyone had just experienced was more than technique or application of knowledge. Gary had implied that, as we help heal others, we heal ourselves in the process. As Miss S hustled to prepare lunch for everyone, all began feeling an unexplainable joy. Who knew what would happen to Mrs. G? Results didn't matter one way or the other. The fact that human beings were endeavoring to foster unheard-of means to change their lives made an impact on all involved — an indescribable impact. Results would not change what all were experiencing at that moment. And never was that more pronounced than when everyone sat down to the sumptuous feast prepared by Miss S. Magnificent crab salad, delicious chowder, and a casserole to die for, lay before everyone — to say nothing of the awaiting dessert. All spread their hands as they blessed the food the way the angels had taught: "As children of God, we bless this food and drink, that it may nourish our souls and enrich our bodies." Anyone walking in would have sworn a picnic was in progress, not a healing session. As food passed among hands, details were swapped of what each person had experienced in the session. None could escape the feeling that the communal meal stood as a metaphor for the communal effort in bringing healing into each other's lives. What a world it would be if this glorious lunch were a hint of the upcoming feast being readied for all of humanity.

For the next two hours, Shirley entered into the healing process. Focused time was spent listening to what might be contributing to Shirley's conditions. Which of the bodies might be the source of the physical manifestation of the disease? Michael had been quite clear how all four bodies — the physical, the emotional, the mental, and the spiritual — had to be addressed. Unless a person was willing to bring healing into all of these bodies, they wasted everyone's time. So it was up to the team to discern

which bodies might be involved in manifesting the disease. In Shirley's case, the emotional body emerged as the primary culprit. Like Mrs. G, Shirley also experienced the results of releasing her troubles and pain. The smell of orange blossoms filled the air. Gary started laughing as the orange smell became overpowering at one point. "I guess Tzaphqiel is paying us a visit," he mused. Just to make sure, Gary opened the bottle containing the Oil of Ephesus given to humanity by Tzaphqiel. And Sure enough, the aroma wafting through the room smelled precisely the same as the Oil of Ephesus.

At the end of nearly five hours of work, everyone drank water as if they'd found an oasis in a desert. The water not only replenished fluids, it helped those involved in the sessions to ground themselves. The forces at play in working with the angels, causing movement in perceptions as well as physical changes in the body, places energetic and psychic demands on those involved. At one point, Gary broke into a sweat from a sudden release of pent-up emotional energy from Mrs. G. Mr. H had detected the blocked energy, Miss S had verified its need to be released. While she brought in Reiki techniques to assist, Mr. H used his dowsing abilities to blast the block loose. Gary had begun to use tuning forks to realign Mrs. G's twelve chakras before the Gate of Grace would be placed on her back with the healing oils. The unexpected release caught Gary by surprise, nearly knocking him to the floor. Everyone was learning from this session. And all were now drinking water to clear themselves of residual energy. Something surely had happened. The question now was, *What?*

The healing sessions had been demanding but amply rewarding for everyone. None of the team would know for days what would be the product of their combined work in assisting these dear women in their healing. Miss S spent careful time informing both women to take care in cleansing their bodies by drinking lots of water over the next couple of days. They were also told to watch out for what is called a "healing crisis." This is the body's attempt to get rid of toxins, which might result from the die-off of viruses or bacteria, or the release of chemical agents, which might need flushing from the system. Diarrhea might be a result of this.Sometimes an ailment will heal backwards, initally looking worse before it gets better. Both women understood what Miss S was trying to impart, thanking the team profusely for all the time and effort they had spent with the two friends. It was time for everyone to rest.

Gary agreed to meet with Shirley and Mrs. G the next morning to show them around Missoula, both women wanting to visit art galleries, especially the famous Monte Dolack Gallery. Gary spent the rest of the day recovering from the intensity of the sessions. The exhaustion was like nothing he had expected. The effort at focusing on the mental, emotional, physical, and spiritual bodies involved intense discussion, careful listening, and employing almost all the tools the angels had spoken of. Mrs. G's lupus had originated in her emotional body when she underwent an unspeakable trauma at the age of ten. To unearth this information required keen focus on the part of the three helpers. Miss S's experience in counseling, coupled with Mr H's adeptness with dowsing and Gary's abilities as a Gatekeeper pried open the ultimate combinations which had contributed to Mrs. G's disease. The dowsing proved fruitful in checking for imbalances in diet or chemicals in the body, as well as checking for energy imbalances in specific bodies. Dowsers not only have the capability of detecting energy signatures, they also have the ability of moving them, changing them, or transmuting them. Gatekeepers have the ability to move into other dimensions, allowing Gary to work with past loved ones in ferreting out family skeletons hidden in closets. One of the three conditions for healing is the creation of a space for healing to occur. Gatekeepers are blessed with the capacity for detecting dimensional changes, or dimensional space. Once the client (the true healer) creates healing space, Gatekeepers have the ability of sustaining the opening, not unlike a butler keeping a door open for an honored guest. The three facilitators had searched for the sources of Mrs. G's disease like detectives looking for clues to a robbery. Instead of possessions being stolen, Mrs. G had been robbed of her health. The natural state of the human body is to be healthy. Disease is the exception rather than the rule. If the sources of a disease can be discovered, then tools can be used to clear the troubles blocking the natural state of healthiness. Had Mrs. G's burning sensation in her knees been a telltale sign of important blocks being cleared? Had the buzzing sensation in her body and the heat enveloping her, near the end of the session, forecast the breaking up of a logjam that had prevented the flow of life forces (*chi*) needed to keep her body in balance? Only time would tell.

The next morning, Gary arrived at the motel where the two women were staying. As he tapped on door of their room, he could hear soft

weeping. Was everything OK? Shirley opened the door, an alarmed look in her eyes.

"What's wrong?" Gary asked, dreading the answer.

"C'mon in," she invited. "I'm not sure what's wrong. G's had diarrhea. Miss S gave her an herbal tea mixture to help in the cleansing. Could that have caused the diarrhea?"

"Nahhh. The stuff Miss S gave her was pretty plain. Let me talk to G."

Gary found Mrs. G sitting on the bed, applying a tissue to her eyes. The gentle lady wept softly, looking a bit upset.

"G, are you OK? What's happening?"

"Well, I don't know for sure. I've had diarrhea this morning. When I woke up ...." Gentle sobbing shook her for a moment. "Gary, it takes me over an hour just to get out of bed in the morning. My feet usually hurt so badly, that I have to massage them for a very long time before I can even put my feet on the floor. And even then, walking is very difficult for quite some time. But this morning, I just got right out of bed. I didn't have to massage my feet at all."

Silence hung in the air as Mrs. G continued dabbing her tears with the tissue. "And? What's the matter with that?" Gary asked, puzzled.

"Well, I'm afraid I'm making it all up. Is this really happening or am I pretending it? Am I making it up?"

"Oh, my dear," Gary cooed as he went over to give her a warm hug. Her sobbing erupted fully as the two embraced. "You're not making it up. This is yours. You allowed this to happen in your life. Go ahead and own it. You are doing great. Congratulate yourself for letting the healing begin so quickly."

"Gee, I don't know. I suppose you're right," she admitted as if embarrassed.

"And have you thought of the possibility that the diarrhea is a sign that the lupus virus is dying and your body is trying to dump the dead viral mass?"

"Hmm, I know Miss S talked about that, but this seems too quick. I thought maybe it might be the tea."

"No, I don't think so. Do you normally have difficulty drinking tea?"

"No, I drink it all the time."

"Well, let's keep an eye on things as we tour the art galleries. Are you going to be OK? I mean, are you going to need a toilet all the time?"

"It doesn't seem to be that bad. I'm sure I'll be fine."

Shirley had her hand cupped over her mouth watching all this. "G, I'm sure you'll be fine. Just between you and me, I think you've killed the lupus off. And I think Gary is right. You need to own it."

As the three prepared for the drive around town, plans were made for which of the galleries would be most interesting. Mrs. G could not walk for long before she had to rest. And too much walking in the past only heightened the pain in her knees and hips. Four galleries were picked, with plans for lunch afterwards. Shirley loved Monte Dolack's work, so a beeline was made for the middle of town. Mrs. G's walking seemed untroubled as they scooted from the parking garage to the gallery, but Gary didn't want to say anything just yet. Perhaps he might be the victim of wishful thinking. The last gallery of the morning nestled inside Fort Missoula, an old complex on the west of town. The art gallery attached itself to the historic museum inside what had been the old train depot. Unlike the rest of the gallery structures, the Fort Gallery stood on an elevated platform, a leftover of the olden days when people and cargo needed to be rolled into waiting cars. The sun shone brightly as Gary trotted up the steps to the entrance of the museum. Just as he was about to open the door he heard Mrs. G's voice. "Shirley!" A thought immediately pierced his mind. How inconsiderate had he been? He'd forgotten Mrs. G couldn't walk up stairs. She had described to him earlier how she had to physically lift one leg with her hands to the next step up and then grab on to the hand rail for dear life as she dragged the other leg behind, manually placing it next to the leading leg. This laborious process would continue with each single step until she reached the top. As he let go of the door to return to assist Mrs. G, he got the shock of his life.

Mrs. G was not only climbing the stairs by herself, she was climbing pain-free with the biggest grin on her face. Shirley opened her arms as the two friends embraced and wept buckets of sheer joy. The sobs of elation and wonder continued, Gary frozen like an ice sculpture. It was one thing to be told by the angels that such powers of healing are available and quite another to actually see it. In one short day, Mrs. G had gone from bemoaning her impending future in a wheelchair to climbing stairs like a normal healthy person. It had been seven years since last she was able to maneuver up stairs unaided. There on the steps of the Fort Missoula Museum, Gary witnessed his first miracle. Finally finding his feet, he eased

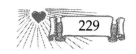

over to the two women now whooping like cheerleaders, and hugged them both. Mrs. G had not only changed her life, she had changed Gary's as well. Never again would he be able to look at disease in the same way.

Over lunch, the threesome could not stop talking about what had just transpired. Just before dessert, Mrs. G began to describe her concern as to what her doctor was going to think. She immediately wanted to drop all her medications, feeling they were no longer needed. Gary asked her to wait until she had seen her doctor. The doctor still was a member of her healing process. Give him the benefit of appraising what had happened. Then a look of shock swept across Mrs. G's face. "Oh dear. What am I going to tell my husband?" Not wanting to be dissuaded, Mrs. G had made up a story for her husband about the trip she and Shirley were about to take. She had not wanted him to know that she was traveling to Montana to place her life in the hands of the angels. Such craziness would not be acceptable to him. But now what? There was no way of hiding the fact that Mrs. G's lupus had left her, or at least was in the process of leaving her. What would she tell him?

Shirley acted as best friends do in such matters. "Tell him the truth. You have nothing to be ashamed of. You should be proud of yourself." Shirley convinced Mrs. G to spend the next three days with her in Idaho before Mrs. G returned home. That would give Mrs. G time to finish her healing process, as well as give her time to think of what she was going to tell her doctor. In the end, Mrs. G's doctor had no explanation for what had happened, taking Mrs. G off of all her lupus medication over a six-month course of time. The lupus was gone.

But Mrs. G's doctor wasn't the only one forced to face the unexplainable. Shirley's doctor had taken colored pictures of her ulcers, providing vivid evidence of the one ulcer, which had perforated, as well as the larger ulcer, which had the potential of killing her. He had prescribed acid blockers to assist her with her hiatal hernia as well as giving her stomach time to recover. But when he took a second set of pictures, a few days after her second healing session, he found no trace of either ulcer. What mystified him the most was that he couldn't even find scar tissue as evidence that the ulcers had ever existed. After pronouncing her "all healed," he asked her what she had done. All she would say was, "One of these days you're going to believe me when I tell you that these angels are here to help us."

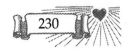

The Montana Hall of Healing continued to help many. As a model it took various forms, eventually becoming a resource center (without a building or office) and progenitor for other healing teams throughout the Northwest. What was perhaps most interesting were the discussions of how the angels had described not just a hall of healing but a hall of healing *and* enlightenment. Who, what, or how would the "enlightenment" half be supported? What evolved was the broadening of the charter of Mr. W's retreat center. His efforts at inviting established speakers, healers, entertainers, and workshop presenters from all schools of thought served Montana and surrounding states well. Would such a model serve the other six areas named by Michael? No one has an answer for that yet. The maturing process associated with the increasing number of gatherings and the input from sevens receiving additional information through their own intuitive discoveries was no different than the maturing of a living tree. The giant oak is nothing like the sapling, and the sapling nothing like the acorn. The evolvement and mutual growth of the sevens within the Tree of Life began to take on the same comparison as the various stages of the oak. Who knew how all this angelically inspired information would turn out?

It is one thing to be given information from Michael and the other angels, and quite another to witness these teachings being put into practice. Joanee and one of her seven, Mary Shipley, were beginning to explore the creation of a healing team in the Chicago area. Not to be stopped there, Joannee took the teachings from "The Book of Bricks" into a prison program for young offenders, only to find these hardened youth touched to the point of tears at being told they were perfect, whole, and complete, just the way they were. Don't think that wasn't a tough sell. Sevens in the Spokane, Washington, area incorporated the teachings into a hospice-type care program. Martha Granda, Jolene Delbridge, and Ronnie Mound, members of Compassion in Action (CIA), were opening the eyes of many as they devoted long and late hours of volunteer effort toward the dying. Mary Ellen and Atira Hatton used their gifts in the Seattle area, touching many thousands with their radio and television interviews, as well as workshops. Mary Ellen's work in bringing awareness to people about how angels work in our everyday lives took the form of an electronic good-news newsletter, reaching tens of thousands around the globe. Not be stopped there, she then wrote two

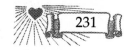

books based upon personal stories from her subscribers: *Expect Miracles*, and *A Christmas Full of Miracles*. More and more of the sevens were stepping forth in bringing healing and enlightenment to our world. But what about my own backyard?

In an effort to bring some kind of balance into my own life, I began to question whether I was more than just a human telephone the angels would network into. If I was to give forth no more teachings until the sevens digested what they'd already been given, then where was my focus to be? Should I go find work? Should I pursue presenting workshops of past material? A phone call with Gary prompted me to create reference materials for those wanting instruction material. I recorded several CDs and wrote *Teaching the Masters* as well as manuals explaining how to use tuning forks and healing oils in what I called "acu-tuning" — clearing of meridians by adapting Chinese acupuncture techniques without the needles. As I conducted workshops in the San Antonio area, people started telling about others in the area I should contact because of their work in healing. In my travels I often hear about others and their techniques. However, I understand that the healing information given to the sevens isn't necessarily for everyone. It serves neither me nor others to push these teachings on anyone. There are many healing modalities, and each is to be respected.

Synchronicity always brings a smile to my face. One afternoon, while checking e-mail on AOL, an instant message appeared on my computer screen:

```
Hi. You don't know me, but I have heard about you from
friends. My name is Julia Hanson. I live here in San
Antonio. I heard that your dog died, and wanted to offer
my condolences. I think her name was Annie? I lost my
favorite dog a short time ago. I sympathize with what you
must be going through. I've got a quick question I'd like
to ask you.
```

Nothing surprises me anymore. If I am often hearing about others, then it shouldn't surprise me that others hear about me. Half torn by curiosity, something in me knew this message came from no ordinary person. As fast as my hunt-and-peck fingers would type, I responded:

Hello Julia. Yes, Annie was like a child to me. I loved
her dearly. I've finally recovered from losing her. How
nice of you to think of me. What is it you would like to
ask me?

What I read next took me by surprise.

I was hoping to ask you regarding a situation in the
hospital. I've heard about your healing work with the
angels. My new dog's name is Baxter, and he is a special
one. Some dogs are used in hospitals to help people in their
recovery. You know, helping them to feel better. Baxter was
accepted into a program to assist hospitalized kids. These
dogs are called therapy dogs. There is this sweet kid in
the hospital who has had both her kidneys replaced. Baxter
has been spending time with her, but it looks like she is
rejecting both her new kidneys. I really would like to help
her and thought I might use prayer to assist her. I've heard
about the work you do with angels, and was wondering if
there is a prayer you could suggest that I might use with
this sweet child next time Baxter and I visit.

It's times like this when the logical mind wants to go hide — hit the
escape key and log off. How could I possibly help in a situation like this,
sending messages back and forth on the Internet? But one thing Michael
has taught me more than any other is to trust in my intuition. And my
intuition told me to do what I could to honor Julia's request.

I would suggest you hold your hands in the general area
of the kidneys and say this: "As a child of God, I ask
that you be made whole and your body healed. I do this to
nourish your soul and enrich your body." Then send grace
or love into her body and kidneys.

Julia typed back a message of thanks and started to sign off. But I
couldn't let this connection end there, so I asked her if it would be OK if
I called her to talk more about the work she did. She graciously gave me
permission and then sent her phone number across my screen. My
intention was to call Julia within a few days but time got away from me.
There was so much to do trying to get my life in order and fill orders for
various materials so that the sevens could have their oils and the work of

healing continue. About two weeks letter, an e-mail showed up on my screen from Julia.

> Wow! Joe, what you told me worked really well. I visited the little girl in the hospital and did the prayer thing you gave me. I also slipped an angel medallion into her hand afterwards. That's something I like to do for people. Well, she did a turnaround right away. She didn't reject her new kidneys after all, and is being released from the hospital today. It's only been a week and a half!!! Thank you so much.
>   Jewls

I had to find out more about this lady. Something inside me told me "Jewls" should be involved in forming a hall of healing in the San Antonio/Austin region. A week later, I finally decided to call this mystery woman. The conversation was like meeting a long-lost friend. Julia's enthusiasm for life came across strongly in her voice. There was no need to give her my background since she had already read *On the Wings of Heaven*. So I pursued my idea of having her and her close friend Cindy Shelton, who she normally worked with in healing environments, consider working with me and Robbie in a team environment, perhaps starting the San Antonio Hall of Healing. What I heard back pleasantly surprised me.

"Joe, I think that's a wonderful idea. I've been wanting to ask you if I could attend some of your classes or workshops on teaching people to heal themselves. I have close friends who have told me about you and the work you do. However, there's something I'd like taken care of first. I'm kinda of the mind that before I get involved in serious work in helping others, I really ought get my own house in order. You know what I mean? Kind of like 'Physician, heal thyself.' If you can't fix yourself, how can you help fix someone else?"

A broad smile spread across my face as I heard her use the very same words that Michael had used with me. It was then that I knew I had to meet this special woman. "Well, perhaps we could use whatever you need worked on as part of the class environment. What is it you'd like yourself to work on?"

"Throughout my life, I've had a history of back problems. These problems have just about crippled me. It first started when I was fifteen.

At the time, I was training at one of the big gymnastics camps, where I was slated as one of the lead gymnasts for the U.S. team. We were preparing for the World Games qualifying meet which was about two weeks off. Training was murderous. Our diets were strictly watched. And one night, after the dorm mother's birthday party, some friends and I decided to sneak out and steal a piece of carrot cake from the training camp kitchen because we hadn't been allowed to have any cake. Did I ever get into huge trouble! The next day, the coach made me run ten extra miles in the hot July sun, which thoroughly exhausted me. Just for having a piece of carrot cake. I was too tired to be working out that afternoon and suffered a fall, which broke my back. For a year and half I was in major traction. A knot the size of a grapefruit seized my back all this time. It was the worst. The pain was unbelievable. The doctors wantd to operate to correct the hairline fracture in the vertegra. They then told me I had a 50/50 chance of walking again after the operation. There was no way I was going to let them cut me. At that time there really wasn't much known about healing this kind of back injury, and I knew it. No one was going to experiment on me. There were many days when it was darn near impossible to get out of bed. My gymnastics career was over. And I had a good shot at the World Games. Devastated me. That was the first time I messed it up."

Joe wasn't sure he was hearing correctly. "You mean you broke your back more than once?"

"Oh, yeah. From the time I was fifteen years old I was always in pain. Later, I broke my back again and ruptured my stomach. My self-esteem was out the window. A chance meeting with an old man on an airplane changed all of that. I didn't know this guy from Adam, but he told me what a great person I was, how I deserved the best life had to give. Took me days to digest all he told me that day, but I ended up starting a new life."

"Are you able to walk now?" I needed to find out exactly how bad Julia's condition was if I was going to assist her in any way.

"Yes, I can walk now. I've learned to live with the pain. Some days are better than others, and I've been able to walk for exercise, lately. Over the years, a nerve has kind of slipped in and slipped out. When it's out, I don't exercise."

"What's been the latest diagnosis?" I asked.

"Well, I've seen a chiropractor here in the last six weeks. She took x-rays and said that I do not have the s-shape in my back like normal people. People with that kind of back are in constant pain, she tells me. Like I didn't already know that. Plus, she told me my vertebrae were pretty torqued."

"Was she able to help?"

"I've had two treatments. They've helped some, but I still have the chronic pain."

"Would you like me to work on you?"

"I think that would be terrific. When can we start?"

Jewls scheduled an appointment to attend one of my classes where she would be the person worked on. The beginning stages of the San Antonio Hall of Healing were emerging. The first part of the session involved scanning Jewls' body to spot where blockages existed. These showed up as spots of light in my visual field, using my third eye to see. I could see spots of blue and orange in areas along her backbone. In a few locations, red dots stood out. This told me that most of her back trouble existed in her emotional (orange) and spiritual-mental (blue) body. The actual physical problems flared in the areas of the red dots. Using the tuning forks and oils as Michael had taught me, I was able to start clearing most of the colored spots. Afterwards I placed my hand over the area and sent in grace.

"Oh, wow!" Julia blurted out. "I can feel this heat coming off your hand. This is incredible."

"If it gets too hot, let me know, and I'll stop," I informed her.

"It's OK, it's OK. My whole back is starting to tingle."

To clear a specific color like the orange dots, for instance, the orange tuning fork (the D tone) and the orange oil (Oil of Ephesus) are paired together. When grace is sent in, usually I see the color of the dot go clear. When this happens, I know the block in a meridian or a muscle or nerve has been released. Once all blocks had been removed, the next step was to attune all of Jewls' twelve chakras, also with the tuning forks. The final step was to create the Gate of Grace on her back using the seven oils and their blessings, along with Michael's Oil, and then finishing with the oils of I Am, as the Shekinah had instructed. When it was all over, I asked Jewls how she felt.

"Great!" was her immediate response. "I can't believe this. Like

wow! There's no pain at all." As the days went by, Julia kept telling friends and family, "I can't believe this." Eventually the pain returned, and so did Julia. And the main reason for it? Because she couldn't believe it. So when I worked on her for the second time I had an additional instruction to give her.

"Jewls, let me tell you something. You can believe in being pain-free; you can believe in healing yourself. Your body is the most powerful instrument you've got. Acknowledge that and use it to your benefit." After placing my hand on the affected area and sending in grace, Julia once again remarked how much heat was hitting her.

After ten minutes she reported, "It's gone again. The pain's gone! It went away immediately this time. Didn't take any time at all. Wow!" I loved her enthusiasm. Since that day, Jewls has taken up jogging over three miles a day. Her pain has not returned; her life has returned to normal. She sent me a thank you note after seeing her chiropractor.

Dear Joe,

I can't thank you enough for what you have brought into my life. Utter and complete joy has filled my life. There is an enlightenment within my spirit that is unbelievable. I feel I have jumped the final hurdle in my life, that I have been set free. All the horrible events of my past, I have now been able to let go of. It's like my life has started anew. I've discovered that when disease hits me or anyone else, it's got to start somewhere. So it starts in the etheric and then into the mental or emotional parts of ourselves, and finally gets to the physical.

All of your classes have taught me now to pay attention to this in others. If I can help people before these problems eventually show up in their physical bodies, it makes life much easier. I've discovered that love is the key. If you have love fully in your heart, there is no room for disease. I try to bring that kind of love to others and teach that to others.

Joe, I feel like my life has started over, that I've awakened to the powers of healing. I mean, people have started coming to my house, just showing up for the Hall of Healing. It's like I've been set free to do the work I

came here to do. Bless your heart for the role you've
played in helping me and others. What a time to be alive.
    Jewls

Jewls' chiropractor had found no sign of trouble in her back and wanted to know what had happened. Jewls provided all the details. Since then, her chiropractor has attended my classes as well. What is most heartwarming is that Jewls now gives to others what was given to her. She has become a dynamic force in the Hall of Healing here in Texas. Little did I know that Jewls would play an even more significant role as the angelic messages continued to come forth. But as I keep telling you, nothing surprises me anymore.

Gary sent me an e-mail asking what ever happened to the information on herbs that Michael had promised in one of his appearances. He has a way of asking for such information just before it is to be presented. And it happened again. Michael presented herb information to me that I was to give to Robbie. She in turn would flesh out the information, not unlike Gary had to in figuring out the message from Gabriel about the 144,000. And like Gary, she went crazy trying to figure out the role of the forty-nine herbs she was told of. The herbs parallel the ancient Chinese herb philosophies but work in a different manner. In Chinese medicine, the herbs are to balance the opposing forces within the body. Heat balances cold, feminine balances masculine, and yin balances yang. If one has too much of one, then other means must be brought in as a curative way of restoring balance. But Robbie discerned that the information given was to operate in a different manner. These herbs were to maintain a vibration within the body so that disease could not live. The angel had said that the herbs would be arranged in a manner similar to the Chinese version of the five elements. However, the herbs would be taken in cycles that matched the cycles of the moon. The elements of the earth were coupled with the moon's path in the heavens. Once again, the forces of heaven and earth were being brought together in an unusual way. Dreams flooded Robbie's thoughts as she struggled to figure out how all of this was to work. Michael showed up when any errors were made. And slowly but surely, Robbie was able to piece together a dazzling system by which the sevens, or anyone else, could use the plants of the earth to raise the vibrations of their bodies so that disease would no longer be a part of their lives. Seven categories of flora containing seven different species, aligned with seven

seasons, and plotted against the seven churches, created an array by which a complete change in dietary habits could be fostered. The information was so involved that Michael asked that it not be given to the sevens except in a workshop environment. Like other information that would be given, reading about it would not be enough. And Michael's request would be honored. As Robbie organized the information on the herbs — Michael called all flora "herbs" — she was then told that there would be forty-nine other herbs, called the helping herbs. That information would come later. There was no need to remind us that the sevens were still "full up." The amount of information presented to us by the angelic realm was becoming mind-boggling. However, the forces of change among the sevens were also starting to become mind-boggling. If this was a hint of what would face all of humanity, then Michael's early prediction of great changes in our world would be no exaggeration. Equally, his statement that "Something wonderful is going to happen, and there is nothing you can do about it," now stared many of us in the face.

The work of the sevens is no longer about any single individual; it's about all of us. As the number of gatherings increases, so does the connection to the angelic realm. The increase in numbers has bearing on the forthcoming keys to the Kingdom of Heaven. And the keys represent the unlocking of consciousness humanity once had in communion with the angelic realm eons ago. More and more it looks like that long-lost connection is moving back into place. And how shall that manifest? Certainly the Tree of Life is one allegory of the growth that is occurring in human consciousness as we begin to end our days of suffering, as promised by the Shekinah. But are there other allegories? Are the sevens the only ones being given information to foster the coming together of heaven and earth? Every evidence I have seen and have been shown says the sevens are only one aspect of this magnificent uncovering of ancient secrets and lost wisdom. There must be others. However, I can only address what I have been given by the forces of heaven to give to the people of the earth. Let us all rejoice in these gifts being given to us. The "Angelic Book of Healing" is only a beginning. Let us use the forthcoming keys to unlock the tremendous forces of love in our hearts, where we can honor our individual gifts, yet glorify in our Oneness with the realm of angels.

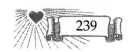

The End

EPILOGUE

As I reflect back on all the visits concerning healing and staying healthy, the words Michael shared with me ring in my mind. Below you will find a synopsis of visits on healing that will be in the next book. There is not enough space here to go into it all in depth. If you desire more information about any of these topics, I suggest my website at www.teachonlylove.com. Also found there are seminars for your area on these topics.

Michael:
I give you now the vibrations for healing. These frequencies will repair that which is out in the bodies of your kind. Use the tuning forks for that which you would balance the chakras. Place them on the points of light with a drop of the sacred oils, which I have shown you that your kind may heal.

Michael and other angels visited me many times past the span of this book, bringing with them new frequencies. I had tuning forks made that carry the frequencies they gave me for healing.

Michael:

You have been given the sacred oils and the oils of the I AM that your kind may raise their vibrations and heal themselves. You will be given more oils as you learn how to use the sacred oils.

The angels came again and again over the proceeding years and gave new sacred oils. All of the oils that the angels have given have done miraculous things when it comes to healing the body, mind, and emotions. I have seen pain disappear, nerves calmed, emotions come under control, joy replace despair — all in a moments time using these sacred oils.

Michael:

Again I say the herbs I give you hold the food for the seasons according to the church. For they will make ready the body to receive nourishment, raising the vibration for the spirit to become one with the body. This I give you now is for all in all seasons. That which Robbie has been given in herbs for helping is to be divided evenly among the churches according to the seasons.

Michael also taught about sacred herbs that we can take for us to stay healthy and raise our vibrations. Robbie took the herbs and made a calendar that tells when and how to use the herbs, based on the seven seasons (not four). These seasons are based on a calendar that contains thirteen months (not twelve). During these seasons, depending on what church a person belongs to, there are herbs one should take to maximize one's vibrations for health and spiritual growth. The people that have been taking the herbs according to the calendar have enjoyed better health and more energy in their daily lives. They have also experienced a greater spiritual awareness than they have ever had before.

Michael:

The time has come for you to call the masters together for the return of Eden. You will gather masters in the places of the Gate of Grace across your land to set the boundaries of Eden. I tell you truly when the masters gather in the numbers we

give you; their vibrations may heal the world on which you live.

Again the angels are giving us the information we need to get back what has been lost. Once a year the masters gather for what has come to be known as the Eden Event. We have the opportunity to bring Eden back to Earth and create a world that works for everyone. The angels have given us a way to change the consciousness of everyone on this planet. When our numbers reach critical mass we will through conscious, willful, spiritual intent alter the consciousness of our world and bring about Eden's return. If this is something you feel in your heart you are called to be a part of, go to my website (www.teachonlylove.com) for more information. We can heal ourselves and we can heal the planet.

This has been an incredible journey of healing over the years. I have been blessed to be the recipient of all this extraordinary healing information from the angels. I have traveled from coast to coast doing private sessions and teaching others how to help people heal. It's like I say when I begin a class: "I am not special nor more spiritual than anyone else — anyone can do this. I just know how to do things that work for helping people to heal. And when this class is over you will too." Bless your hearts, and teach only love.

TO CONTACT

G.W. HARDIN OR
DREAMSPEAKER CREATIONS

WEB SITE: www.gwhardin.com
E-MAIL: teachonlylove@yahoo.com

Direct all correspondence, scheduling of interviews or speaking engagements with G.W. Hardin to the following address:

DreamSpeaker Creations, Inc.
2911 Walnut St.
Denver - CO 80205

Hardin's interviews or speaking engagements can be chosen from the following topics:

- The writing of *The Messengers, On the Wings of Heaven, The Days of Wonder: Dawn of a Great Tomorrow, Indigo Rising*: *Awakening the Powers of the Children of the New Earth,* and *The Masters Return: The Angelic Book of Healing*
- Classes and workshops on "Radical Healing Techniques," "The Seven Gifts of Heaven for Humanity," "Powers of the Gatekeepers," "Hiking into the Quantum Worlds of Nature," "Sacred Geometry and the New Qaballah," and "The Angelic Merkaba"
- Gatekeepers and their roles in modern society
- Angelic prophecies of a new world
- Welcoming the Quantum Generation into their powers
- Indigenous societies and the sacredness of being gay

JOSEPH CRANE OR
ANGEL GATE CREATIONS

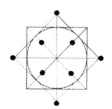

WEB SITE:	www.teachonlylove.com
E-MAIL:	info@teachonlylove.com
Orders :	(803) 751-2412

Direct all correspondence, scheduling of interviews or speaking engagements with Joseph Crane to the following address:

Angel Gate Creations
501 Joel Lane
Lakehills - TX 78063

Joseph Crane's seminars can cover any of the following topics:

- Teachings from the angelic realm
- The writing of *Blessings, Gifts, & Deeds*, *On the Wings of Heaven*, and *Teaching the Masters*
- *The Masters Return: The Angelic Book of Healing*
- Acu-tuning I and II
- " The Seven Sacred Herbs" with Robbie Nicolai-Crane
- The Sacred Solfeggio harmonics and the Tree of Life frequencies
- *The Book of Bricks* and how to build one's spiritual mansion
- Abundance and Prosperity from the angels
- The Gate of Grace
- Increasing your psychic abilities using frequencies
- Activating your bodies rejuvenation system

TEACH
ONLY
LOVE

CPSIA information can be obtained at www.ICGtesting.com
Printed in the USA
BVOW072235120713

325579BV00001B/3/A

9 780970 159311